Practical Microsoft
Visual Studio 2015

Peter Ritchie

Apress®

Practical Microsoft Visual Studio 2015

Peter Ritchie
Chandler, Arizona
USA

ISBN-13 (pbk): 978-1-4842-2312-3
DOI 10.1007/978-1-4842-2313-0

ISBN-13 (electronic): 978-1-4842-2313-0

Library of Congress Control Number: 2016959759

Managing Director: Welmoed Spahr
Lead Editor: James DeWolf
Technical Reviewer: Joseph Guadagno
Editorial Board: Steve Anglin, Pramila Balan, Laura Berendson, Aaron Black, Louise Corrigan,
    Jonathan Gennick, Robert Hutchinson, Celestin Suresh John, Nikhil Karkal, James Markham,
    Susan McDermott, Matthew Moodie, Natalie Pao, Gwenan Spearing
Coordinating Editor: Mark Powers
Copy Editor: Kezia Endsley
Compositor: SPi Global
Indexer: SPi Global
Artist: SPi Global

Distributed to the book trade worldwide by Springer Science+Business Media New York, 233 Spring Street, 6th Floor, New York, NY 10013. Phone 1-800-SPRINGER, fax (201) 348-4505, e-mail orders-ny@springer-sbm.com, or visit www.springeronline.com. Apress Media, LLC is a California LLC and the sole member (owner) is Springer Science + Business Media Finance Inc (SSBM Finance Inc). SSBM Finance Inc is a **Delaware** corporation.

For information on translations, please e-mail rights@apress.com, or visit www.apress.com.

Apress and friends of ED books may be purchased in bulk for academic, corporate, or promotional use. eBook versions and licenses are also available for most titles. For more information, reference our Special Bulk Sales–eBook Licensing web page at www.apress.com/bulk-sales.

Any source code or other supplementary materials referenced by the author in this text are available to readers at www.apress.com. For detailed information about how to locate your book's source code, go to www.apress.com/source-code/. Readers can also access source code at SpringerLink in the Supplementary Material section for each chapter.

Printed on acid-free paper

To my wife Sherry, thank you for everything you do.

Contents at a Glance

Contents

About the Author

Peter Ritchie is a software architect with Quicken Loans and has over 12 years of experience working with .NET applications in C#. Prior to focusing on C#, Peter worked primarily in C/C++, which accounts for the majority of his 26 years of programming and design experience. Peter has worked with a variety of applications and systems, including WinForms/WPF applications, client server applications, distributed applications, and web applications. Components include Windows services, TCP servers, TCP clients, HTTP servers, and HTTP clients. Peter has also worked with a variety of middleware products, including RabbitMQ and MSMQ.

Peter received the Microsoft MVP-Visual C# award (2006-2017) for his contributions to the online developer community.

About the Technical Reviewer

For 20 years or so, **Joseph Guadagno** has been in Software Development. During that time he has used many tools, languages, and technologies. He started out programming with a small book on QuickBASIC and later moved on to Visual Basic for DOS. Windows then came along and he started using Visual Basic for Windows, then migrated to Visual Basic .NET and eventually ended up using Visual C#. Guadagno works as a Team Leader at Quicken Loans, based in Detroit, MI. He is a public speaker and presents internationally on many different technology topics. A list of them is available at http://www.josephguadagno.net/presentations/. He has been recognized as a Microsoft MVP (jjg.me/MVPLink) in .NET (since 2009) and a Friends of Redgate program (jjg.me/Awyw83).

For more on Joseph Guadagno, visit http://jjg.me/aboutJJG.

CHAPTER 1

■ ■ ■

Introduction to Visual Studio 2015

Visual Studio 2015 is a major release of Visual Studio. It incorporated some major advancements that Microsoft has been working on, from Project Rosyln to .NET Core. It not only is the latest version of Visual Studio, but it also introduces some major new features, technologies, and abilities. Let's take a brief look at what's new in Visual Studio 2015.

Intro to IDEs

First, let's briefly go over what an Integrated Development Environment (IDE) means. IDEs provide a one-stop environment to do most of your development/testing tasks within one user experience. IDEs typically provide an environment to edit, refactor, and compile code; edit user interfaces; diagram logic; build applications; and perform some level of code analysis, testing, and source code control integration.

IDEs started when there were only console terminals, so they originally started as console-based applications. Early IDEs only performed editing, file management, compilation, and debugging/execution. These environments worked with console-based applications only and did not need to visually edit the user interface. Later, as graphical user interfaces became available, IDEs started to support editing user interfaces. Although every user interface is based on a specification that is textual in nature, it's rare that user interfaces are edited textually.

It wasn't until much later that features like code analysis, refactoring, testing, and diagramming were added to IDEs. Obviously refactoring wouldn't be added until after Martin Fowler's book, *Refactoring: Improving the Design of Existing Code* in 1999, and even then IDEs like Eclipse didn't get inherent refactoring until 2002 or 2003. (Visual Studio got it in Visual Studio 2005.)

Now we can't imagine an environment without refactoring, code analysis, UI editing, and debugging. Despite all these features inherent in Visual Studio, many prefer to use add-ons like ReSharper or CodeRush. With Visual Studio's rich plugin ecosystem, there's almost always some third-party extension to do what you need.

Visual Studio 2015 has several technologies related specifically to integrated development environments. For example, IntelliSense is the Visual Studio 2015 "autocomplete" component. It has several features such as Complete Word, Parameter Info, Quick Info, and List Members, that intelligently allow developers to complete what they are typing based on context. Complete Word provides options to complete the word you are typing, which could be the name of variable or command. Parameter Info provides information about the parameters you are typing, such as the parameters of a method call. It shows the documentation and name of each parameter. Quick Info is similar to Parameter Info, but provides the documentation information for any identifier in your code. List Members is autocomplete for member invocation while typing (after entering the .); it allows you to see the members that can be invoked for the given identifier and some quick documentation about each one.

© Peter Ritchie 2016
P. Ritchie, *Practical Microsoft Visual Studio 2015*, DOI 10.1007/978-1-4842-2313-0_1

Visual Studio 2015 has substantial debugging capabilities with features like IntelliTrace. IntelliTrace is a historical debugger for managed code that records events during execution within the debugger such as method calls, method parameters, exceptions, timings, memory usage, etc. This allows you to rewind code in the debugger should more information need be analyzed when a particular breakpoint is hit.

This book isn't specifically about working with an IDE. This information is provided to inform readers about the features of an IDE so that we can compare Visual Studio 2015 features.

Visual Studio 2015 Editions

Visual Studio 2015 continues the Editions idea of Visual Studio, providing multiple editions geared toward different segments of the market or toward different roles within organizations.

Difference from Version 2013

If you're familiar with Visual Studio 2013, it will be useful to look at what has changed in the Editions landscape. One of the biggest differences in 2015 from 2013 is the new Community Edition and the sunsetting of the Express Editions.

Prior to Visual Studio 2015 (Visual Studio 2013), Visual Studio had Express Editions. This wasn't merely one edition, it was really four—Visual Studio Express for Desktop, Visual Studio Express for Web, and Visual Studio Express for Windows. There was also a Team Foundation Server 2015 Express Edition.

Visual Studio Express for Desktop is an edition of Visual Studio 2013 that uses the familiar Visual Studio 2013 IDE that focuses on and facilitates development of desktop applications for Windows. This edition supports all the typical "native" platforms for windows: Windows Presentation Framework (WPF), Windows Forms, and Win32. Each platform generally has its own supported programming languages, but the Visual Studio Express for Desktop Edition supports C#, Visual Basic, and C++. While this edition allows you to create applications for Windows 7 and beyond, it isn't supported under Windows 10.

Visual Studio Express for Web is an edition of Visual Studio 2013 that uses the familiar Visual Studio 2013 IDE that facilitates development of web sites, web APIs, or ASP.NET. Visual Studio Express for Desktop edition supports C# and Visual Basic for ASP.NET and web APIs, and the typical web stack for web sites: JavaScript, HTML, CSS, etc. This edition also isn't supported under Windows 10.

Visual Studio Express for Windows is an edition of Visual Studio 2013 that uses the familiar Visual Studio 2013 IDE that facilitates development of Windows Store applications for Windows Phone and Windows 8.1+. Windows Store applications can be written in C#, Visual Basic, HTML5/JavaScript, and C++. While this edition allows you to create applications for Windows 8.1 and beyond, it isn't supported under Windows 10.

Express editions typically didn't support extensions (some versions supported Microsoft-only extensions). This changed with the 2013 Community Edition that allowed extensions. Using the Community Edition meant the ability to create application/web sites/etc. with Visual Studio for free but still use extensions (like TestDriven.NET, NUnit, etc.)

Visual Studio Team Foundation Server 2015 Express is an edition of Visual Studio for non-programmers and non-testers. These are team members who need to work with work items, bugs, tasks, etc. (Otherwise, for team members who need to work with developers and testers but didn't need to use any of the IDE features of Visual Studio, but just access TFS.) This edition became less and less important, as a web-based UI to TFS was created and has feature parity with Visual Studio Team Foundation Server 2015 Express (and in some cases, it's much more feature-rich).

In Visual Studio 2013 all the Express Editions and the Community Edition are replaced by the one Community Edition. Users download the plugins, extensions, packs, packages, etc. and then can develop for the platform or platforms of their choice.

The Visual Studio 2013 Ultimate and Premium Editions have not been carried forward to Visual Studio 2015. Instead there is an Enterprise Edition, which effectively has the features of the Visual Studio 2013 Premium and Visual Studio 2013 Ultimate Editions.

Community

As detailed, Microsoft has historically had Express Editions of Visual Studio that allow developers to create applications/web sites with Microsoft technologies at no cost. The Express Editions were criticized for not including all the basic tools that good software deployment needs. Things like unit testing and code analysis were lacking in some Express Editions, leaving the moniker "integrated" somewhat of a misnomer. There are literally thousands of extensions for Visual Studio and, while Express Editions might not have included all the tools for good software development, an extension could have been found to compensate. Alas, Express Editions did not support extensions.

After the Visual Studio 2013 Editions were released, Microsoft (or Microsoft Developer Division, DevDiv) started to move to a more componentized model with Visual Studio. Quickly Visual Studio proper was just a shell and the various things that made it an IDE were extensions, packs, add-ons, plugins, etc. The features could then be updated out-of-band (e.g., once a quarter as Microsoft also moved to a more iterative development cycle). It was clear with this extensible model that the lack of extensions would hurt more than it benefited. The Community Edition was introduced and it allowed developers to use Visual Studio for various platforms at no cost but still use extensions. This allowed the four Express Editions (and the costly management of different SKUs that went along with it) to be sunsetted while making the community as a whole happier.

For the most part, the Community Edition of Visual Studio 2015 is a slightly scaled back version of the Professional Edition. The Community Edition, like the Express Editions, does not support "enterprise" development (which means an organization with >250 PCs or >US$1 million annual revenue or more than five Visual Studio users writing software). The Community Edition provides no support over and above the support someone could get in the community: StackOverflow, MSDN Forums, etc.

The Community Edition provides features for debugging, unit testing, code editing and refactoring, UI design, viewing dependency graphs and code maps, code analysis, and team collaboration.

Professional

The Visual Studio 2015 Professional Edition is very similar to the Visual Studio 2015 Community Edition. Probably the most obvious difference is cost. The cost varies depending on the licensing/subscription model, quantity, and whether it includes MSDN. There are courses and much material on licensing with Microsoft, so we won't attempt to get into pricing here.

The important part of Visual Studio 2015 Professional is that the minimum requirement for use is "Enterprise Development" (five or more developers or an organization with >250 PCs, or an organization with >US$ 1 million in annual revenue).

Professional also includes *CodeLens*. CodeLens was introduced in Visual Studio 2013 (although only available in Ultimate) and allows developers to see what code references methods, how many unit tests there are, and how many are passing for a method, who was the last to edit the method, past and future edits to a method, and any work items associated with the method. Developers can see all this information without having to go out to the respective tools (TFS or GIT), therefore improving productivity.

In addition, Visual Studio 2015 Professional includes Team Foundation Server (TFS) features. It might seem a little strange that Visual Studio 2015 Professional is the lowest edition to support TFS since there is an Express (no-cost) edition of TFS, but this is mostly due to the fact that Visual Studio 2015 Professional includes a license for TFS, whereas Community does not. The Team Foundation Server "features" with Visual Studio 2015 Professional simply seem to be the Team Foundation Server features.

Enterprise

Visual Studio 2015 Enterprise Edition is the next level up from Visual Studio 2015 Professional. It's the first edition to include creation and editing of architectural and design diagrams (although lower editions can view them). Unfortunately it's also the lowest edition that supports architectural validation. Architectural validations perform validations based on design in diagrams. Diagrams like UML, Layer, etc. can be used to validate that the solution is abiding by the constraints of the diagrams. For the most part, this requires a lot of up-front design and isn't part of non-Enterprise users running of unit tests. In fact, it has to be run manually and separately from unit tests. Presumably someone would occasionally validate the architecture in this way, but this doesn't keep feedback close to when it was worked on, so this is problematic. It can, however, be set up on build in Team Foundation Server and be validated reasonably close to the work if gated check-ins are used. If you're using Git, however, this is a completely manual process.

Testing is greatly expanded in the Enterprise Edition. The Visual Studio 2015 Enterprise Edition includes lab management that manages the VMs you might want to use for your automated testing. This allows for load and performance testing, verifying code coverage, and performing coded UI tests, integration with manual and exploratory testing and managing test cases. Visual Studio 2015 Enterprise also includes IntelliTest and Fakes. If you're familiar with Pex/Moles, you know what IntelliTest and Fakes are. IntelliTest is the next evolution of Pex that gives you the ability to automatically generate unit tests for code—effectively automated white box testing. And Fakes (which has been around since Visual Studio 2012) is mole integration and it allows mocking out methods with a "fake" delegate for more thorough unit testing.

Code Clone is also included in the Enterprise Edition. Code Clone allows you to find the same or similar code in your solution and then employ the DRY principle and refactor your code so it's not duplicated. See Figure 1-1 for an example.

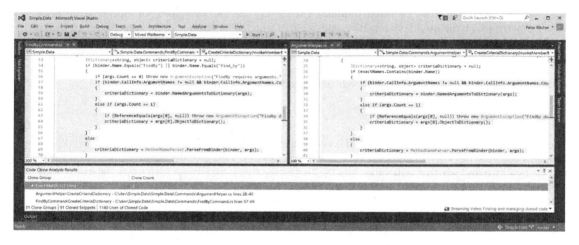

Figure 1-1. *Code Clone*

Test Professional

The "next" edition is Visual Studio 2015 Test Professional. Visual Studio 2015 Enterprise is really the top edition, so Visual Studio 2015 Test Professional isn't one up from Visual Studio 2015 Enterprise, it's really just off to the side. Visual Studio 2015 Test Professional is a scaled-down version of Visual Studio for testing professionals. It contains no IDE features like Code Lens, nor any debugging and diagnostic features, nor any architectural features. It just contains testing features.

Test Professional provides testing professional features like lab management, TFS features, manual and exploratory testing, as well as test case management. It also includes collaboration tools that are not related to code, like Storyboarding and Team Explorer.

This edition is intended solely for testing professionals to do testing and collaborate with the team.

What's New in Version 2015

Installer

The first new thing users will see is the installer. The look and feel of the installer has completely changed. It has taken on the "modern" look and feel. (Since Visual Studio was the first product released for Windows 8/10, it is assumed that the team had a mandate to promote the "modern" UI.) Figure 1-2 shows the installer as soon as it's executed.

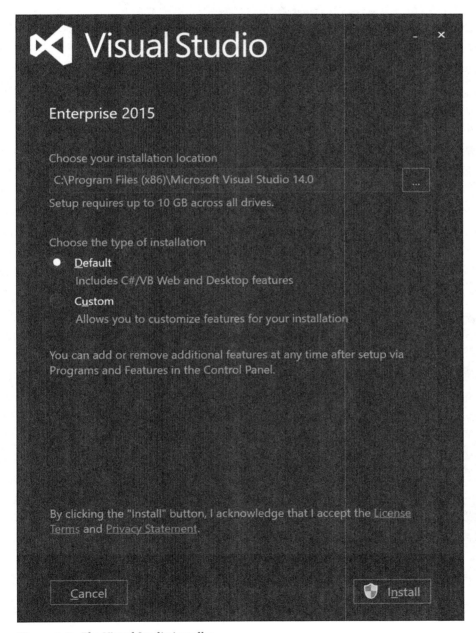

Figure 1-2. *The Visual Studio installer*

From the point of view of getting Visual Studio installed, not much has changed, obviously, but the process of installing has been streamlined from the typical Windows installer. The options are much more componentized so you can install "components" rather than selecting individual products. The installer figures out what "products" (if applicable) need to be installed, as shown in Figure 1-3.

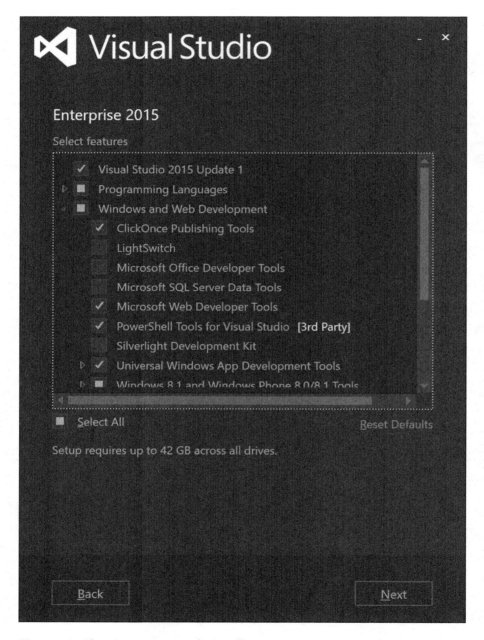

Figure 1-3. *Choosing components for installation*

Live Code Analysis

One of the biggest projects coming out of DevDiv in the last few years is Roslyn. Also called "compiler as a service," Roslyn decouples many of the things involved with compiling code into "services" that are available to developers (including Visual Studio IDE developers within Microsoft). One of the new features in Visual Studio 2015 takes advantage of compiler as a service to provide Live Code Analysis. Now, out of the box, Visual Studio 2015 includes a set of code analysis rules (very similar to FxCop or Static Code Analysis rules). What is exciting is the fact that this is extensible, which means any developer can add code analysis rules that can be checked as you type.

One of the more exciting features of Live Code analysis is that many of the rules include fixes. This means that not only will the analyzer warn you about issues in your code, but it will also provide a fix for the issue that you can optionally apply. An example is shown in Figure 1-4.

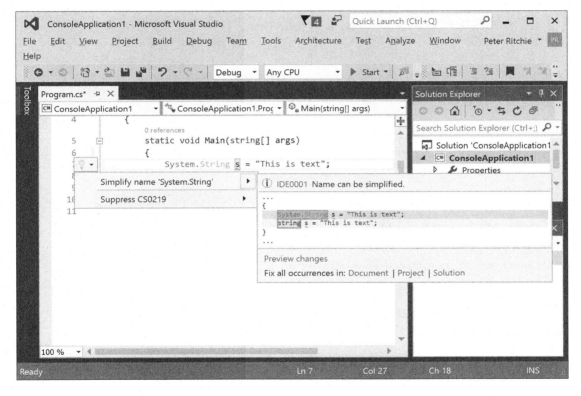

Figure 1-4. *Live Code Analysis with suggested fixes*

In fact, there are already a plethora of analyzers available, many aggregated in the .NET Analyzers project on GitHub (`http://lynk.at/dotNETa`).

Debugging

Many of the debugging features of past versions have been consolidated into one window, called the Diagnostics Tools Debugger window. This window allows you to see the diagnostic status of your application in one place, as shown in Figure 1-5.

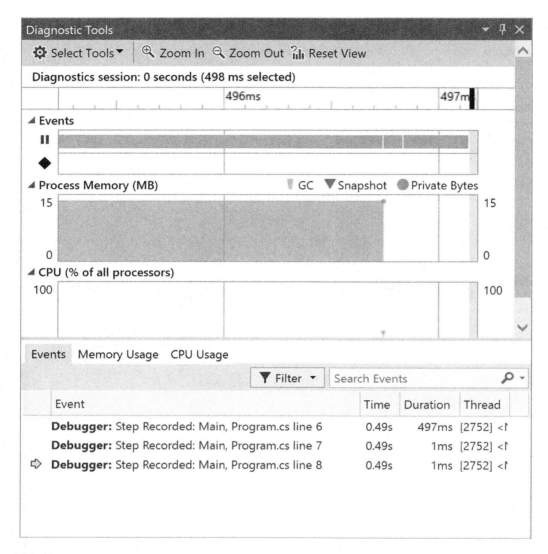

Figure 1-5. Diagnostics Tools Debugger window

Apache Cordova

Support for the Apache Cordova platform (formerly PhoneGap) was added to Visual Studio and included out of the box with Visual Studio 2015.

Apache Cordova enables application developers to develop applications for mobile devices with JavaScript, HTML5, and CSS3. Similar to HTML apps in Windows 8/10. Apache Cordova generally allows complete reuse of code across the supported platforms (iOS, Android, and Windows Phone).

New Platforms

Technically all the platforms listed here could be developed for in Visual Studio prior to Visual Studio 2015, but you had to track down the extensions/plugins/SDKs/packages/etc. to actually do it. Visual Studio 2015 now, out of the box, supports iOS, Android, and Universal Windows (over and above typical Windows applications).

iOS

Visual Studio 2015 enables using C# to develop applications for iOS. These applications are XAML-based and built with the Xamarin tools, extensions, and frameworks.

The Apache Cordova support also means that application developers can develop applications for iOS using HTML, JavaScript, and CSS.

Android

Visual Studio 2015 enables using C# to develop applications for Android. These applications are XAML-based and built with the Xamarin tools, extensions, and frameworks.

The Apache Cordova support also means that application developers can develop applications for Android using HTML, JavaScript, and CSS.

Universal Windows

Visual Studio 2015 is the first release of Visual Studio after the Universal Windows application frameworks were released. So, Visual Studio 2015 has support for Universal Windows applications out of the box. Writing a Universal Windows application means potentially supporting any Windows 10 device. This means supporting Windows Phone (or other phones supporting Windows 10), PCs, Xbox, Surface Hub, HoloLens, and Internet of Things (IoT) devices.

It's unlikely that you'd write one universal application to deploy on all these devices, but with class libraries and portable libraries, much of the code could be shared among the applications in cases where specialized universal application user experiences for a subset of Windows platforms is necessary.

New Bundled Third-Party Tools

Xamarin

One of the most exciting third-party tools that comes prepackaged with Visual Studio 2015 is the Xamarin suite of tools.

Xamarin allows you to build native apps for Windows Phone, Android, and IOS from a single shared code base. Each UI is 100% native to the platform and customized to each platform. This allows you to write one app and deploy it to multiple mobile platforms.

Git

Support for Git in Visual Studio started in one of the Visual Studio 2013 updates as a Git source code control provider. In Visual Studio 2015, Git support comes out of the box.

Visual Studio typically views source code control differently than Git. Git has the concept of your working directory, a staging area, and then the Git repository. Git assumes any modifications are in the working directory and are not automatically included during commit to the Git repo. The user must manually add modified files from the working directory to the staging area (and it's easy to add all modified files at once). Then the staging area can be committed to the Git repo. This is sort of an "opt-in" philosophy. This is different from the way Visual Studio works. Visual Studio assumes all modified files are, or need to be, "checked out" and will be included in a "check-in" unless otherwise excluded (Git works a bit that way too with .gitignore files, but that's for another time). So, in Git if you didn't want all your files committed, you wouldn't add them to the staging area before commit. With Visual Studio, you'd add those files to the excluded list before checking in. Visual Studio uses more of an opt-out philosophy.

Visual Studio is smart enough to know what type of source code control repository it is dealing with and use the appropriate terminology. So, if you have a Git repo you're working with, it does say "commit" in Team Explorer. You just have to use the opt-out-type workflow, click Commit to commit any modified files. It will add them to the staging area then commit them, as shown in Figure 1-6.

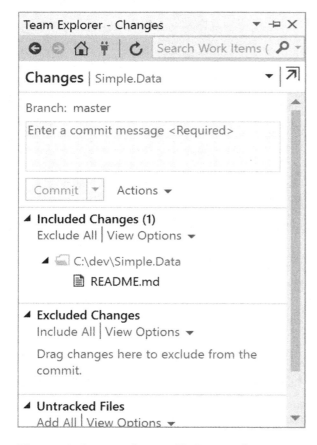

Figure 1-6. *Source code control in Team Explorer*

Visual Studio 2015 Solution Explorer also treats Git repositories as source code control repositories so it shows the current Git status of files. Modified files have a red checkmark and unmodified files have a padlock, as illustrated in Figure 1-7. This comes from the Visual Studio concept of checking-out files to modify them, which are otherwise locked until being checked out.

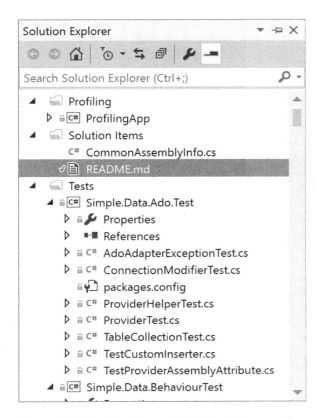

Figure 1-7. *Git status shown in Solution Explorer, with modified files marked with a red checkmark*

GitHub

The third-party GitHub add-on is much like the Git extensions, but is specific to GitHub. The GitHub extension, shown in Figure 1-8, allows you to connect to github.com or GitHub Enterprise and support two-factor authentication. You can clone GitHub repositories by mouse click as well as create GitHub repositories from Visual Studio 2015 Team Explorer.

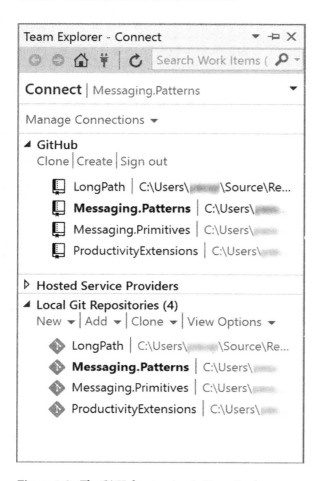

Figure 1-8. The GitHub extension in Team Explorer

It also provides all the Git-like integration that you'd expect in Visual Studio, including showing modified files (via a checkmark) and unmodified files (with a padlock), synchronizing (pushing and pulling) from a remote repo. Figure 1-9 illustrates this idea.

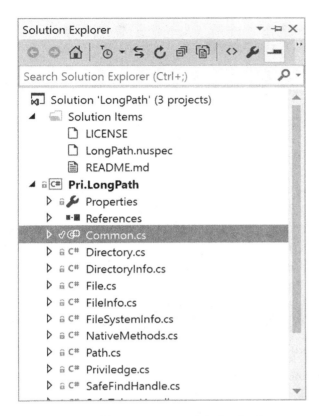

Figure 1-9. *Git-like integration in Solution Explorer*

Unity

The widely used platform for creating 2D and 3D games, Unity (not to be confused with Microsoft Unity, the dependency injection container included with Microsoft Enterprise Library) is still supported in Visual Studio 2015 via Unity Tools for Visual Studio 2.0. You can write games in C# to run natively on Android, iOS, Windows Phone, and many other platforms.

Unity support integrates with Unity to provide seamless game development in Visual Studio 2015, using Visual Studio 2015 features. Unity integration also includes support for the productivity features designed for Unity developers.

CodeLens

CodeLens is now available in Visual Studio Professional and it provides the ability to easily explore code changes, code history, and tests while you work in code. This includes C++, JavaScript, and SQL. CodeLens adds indicators above methods to detail things like the number of references, history, test and pass/fail, coding activity, and commits, as shown in Figure 1-10.

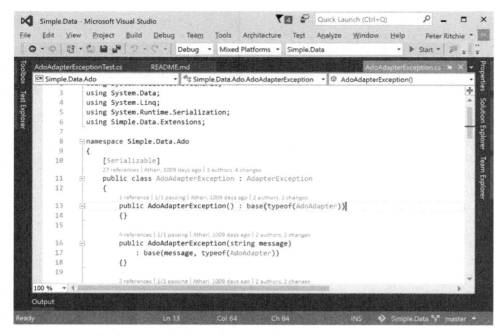

Figure 1-10. *Code changes and history detailed in CodeLens*

CodeLens shows you to view the code that references the member and provides links to jump to that code, as seen in Figure 1-11.

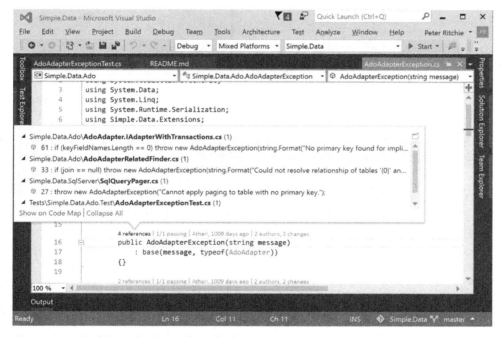

Figure 1-11. *CodeLens displaying the code that references the member and providing links to jump to that code*

CodeLens shows the tests run on this method in one way or another and provides a link to go to the tests, shown in Figure 1-12.

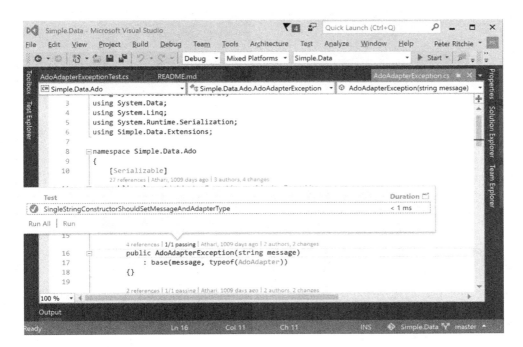

Figure 1-12. *CodeLens displaying the tests on a method and a link to go to that test*

Figure 1-13 illustrates how CodeLens lists the commits performed on a given method and provides links to view more details.

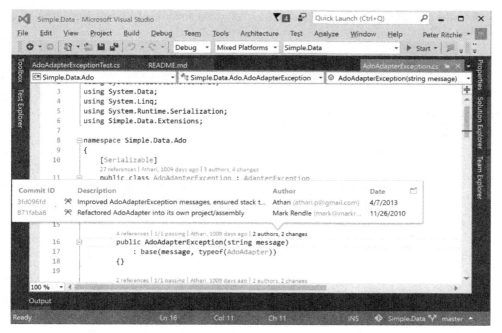

Figure 1-13. *CodeLens displaying the commits performed on a given method and a link to view more details*

CodeLens shows the team activity with the method, showing the quantity of changes over time. Figure 1-14 illustrates the team activity.

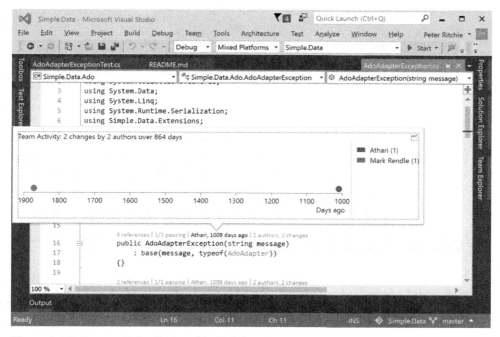

Figure 1-14. *Team activity displayed in CodeLens*

.NET 4.6

.NET 4.6 is the latest version of .NET. In fact, at the time of writing there was already a .NET 4.6.1 update. From one standpoint, it's just the next version of .NET. But there are some new exciting features. For one, there is a new 64-bit JIT compiler (the compiler that creates machine code from your assembly at runtime). This compiler has significant improvements over the old compiler, which was based on the 32-bit JIT compiler. This compiler will be used if your platform target is x64 or AnyCPU and is running on a 64-bit operating system. This is part of the runtime and you don't need to do anything special (other than use the correct target) for it to be used.

There are also a lot of new interesting APIs added to 4.6. Close to 150, so we won't detail them all here, but things like more `IReadOnlyCollection<T>` implementations like `Queue<T>` and `Stack<T>`, new `TryStartNoGCRegion` and `EndNoGCRegion` in the GC class to specify no garbage collection during critical code, and new SIMD-enabled types allowing operations on blocks of data instead of on individual values.

On a related note, by the time you read this, .NET 4.5.1 will no longer be supported. What does this mean? Well, it certainly doesn't mean your software will stop working (assuming it worked before). This means that standard support is ending, so if you have a problem related to .NET you will have to look into paid support options to get it fixed. This also means that security updates will no longer be issued, unless a fix is requested via paid support (and would be provided only to you as a hotfix). If you're working with Visual Studio 2013 (which supports up to 4.5.1 out of the box), does this mean you're forced to upgrade to Visual Studio 2015? No, it doesn't. In a prior version of Visual Studio they added the ability to work with future versions of .NET. There is a Developer Pack (`http://lynk.at/452DevPack`) that installs the necessary bits to be able to target .NET 4.5.2 in Visual Studio 2013.

.NET Core

.NET Core was created to be a subset of the .NET Framework. It was built to have parity with the .NET Framework (at least the applicable subset of it) while providing a core that was not coupled to a particular operating system. While it is technically an independent framework, the API it implements will be mirrored in the other .NET Frameworks, moving more away from a set of vertical frameworks to frameworks with a common core.

.NET Core is open source and will version quicker than .NET Framework (.NET Framework is typically once a year, whereas .NET Core is expected to version once a quarter. The .NET Core takes a different stance to delivery and will be delivered as NuGet packages. This means that the .NET Core is deployed locally per application. This facilitates XCOPY deployment because your application does not need ".NET Framework" installed to run, the "framework" is in the application directory. Another benefit of this is that your application is isolated from breaking changes. If a breaking change in the .NET Framework is introduced, it affects all applications using it because it's deployed on a machine-wide basis and not part of an application deployment. Applications may have no chance to see the breaking change or do anything about it until after the fact (when customers complain that your application stopped working). With .NET Core, you must accept updates via NuGet update and deploy them. Your customers won't see a new version of .NET Core until you've fully vetted it.

.NET Core is currently an option for ASP.NET 5 applications and console applications. In the future, it will likely be an option for Windows Store and Windows Phone. It's likely that .NET Framework will always be required for desktop applications like Windows Forms and WPF.

ASP.NET

ASP.NET 5 (which was preview, or CTP, or RC, or whatever when Visual Studio 2015 was released—that whole out-of-band, component-based delivery...) is a complete rewrite, for the most part. ASP.NET 5 supports writing web applications for Mac and Linux (as well as continuing to support Windows). This is a huge advance that brings the industry closer to a write-once-run-many paradigm than it's ever been.

One of the concepts that makes ASP.NET write-once-run-many is the reorganization of the .NET Framework. (I'd say "core," but that would only confuse things; as you'll see later.)

Other

In the first few iterations of Visual Studio in the "Metro" era followed the "modern" user experience by using ALL CAPS for menu items. There was, to say the least, a little feedback on that change. Many will be happy to know that Visual Studio 2015 now defaults to Title Case once again for menus (with an option to go back to ALL CAPS if you want to), as shown in Figure 1-15.

Figure 1-15. *Menu items in default title case*

One of the largest complaints about Windows was the poor support for high-resolution screens. Once you got past a dimension over 2000 pixels, font sizes were hard to read. It was easy to tell Windows to use a larger font, but in Windows, control layout was obviously dependent on those sizes. A change in font size often meant that dialogs and form layouts were screwed up. The other problem was that the font size was only related to text-based items (text boxes, buttons with text, etc.). Graphics on dialogs and forms would not be scaled and they would remain the same dimensions and appear smaller. Windows offers the ability to provide larger icons for applications and whatnot so that application icons are "scaled" up in Windows Explorer and the Desktop but did nothing inherently for graphics within applications (like toolbars, etc). So, while text was generally more readable, toolbar buttons were still tiny and unrecognizable or scaled up to the point where they were also unrecognizable. Fortunately, Visual Studio includes higher-resolution images to combat this problem. Figure 1-16 shows an example of Visual Studio on a 3200x1800 screen.

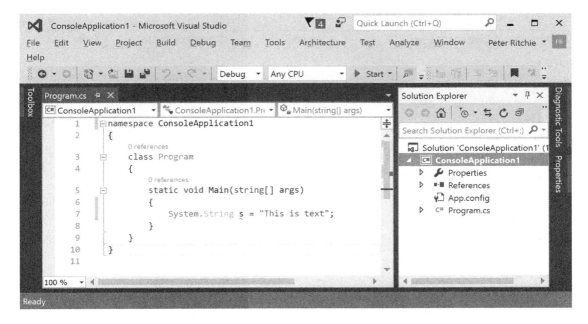

Figure 1-16. *Visual Studio on a 3200x1800 screen*

It's pretty clear that we are well into the touch-enabled technology era. This is a major initiative for Microsoft, supporting touch across almost all of the product groups. Visual Studio 2015 is no different. It now supports touch much better than before. While touching the screen all day while programming seems like a recipe for sore arms, it supports a few touch gestures that I try do on many products despite spending most of my day on the keyboard. Things like touch scrolling and pinch to zoom seem to be better metaphors despite being in a largely textual environment.

Comparing Community, Professional, and Enterprise Editions

Table 1-1 compares the features offered by the Community, Professional, and Enterprise Editions of Visual Studio 2015.

Table 1-1. *Comparison of Community, Professional, and Enterprise Editions*

Debugging and Diagnostics	Community	Professional	Enterprise
IntelliTrace in Production			✓
IntelliTrace (Historical Debugging)			✓
IntelliTrace Performance Indicators			✓
.NET Memory Dump Analysis			✓
Code Map D✓ger Integration			✓
Debugger	✓	✓	✓
Performance and Diagnostics Hub	✓	✓	✓+
Testing Tools			
Web Load and Performance Testing			✓
IntelliTest			✓
Microsoft Fakes (Unit Test Isolation)			✓
Code Coverage			✓
Coded UI Testing			✓
Manual Testing			✓
Exploratory Testing			✓
Test Case Management			✓
Fast-Forward for Manual Testing			✓
Integrated Development Environment			
CodeLens		✓	✓
Code Clone			✓
Development Platform Support			
Office 365, Office, and SharePoint	✓-	✓	✓
Office 365 Cloud Business Apps	✓-	✓	✓
Business Applications (LightSwitch)	✓-	✓	✓
Architecture and Modeling			
Edit Architectural Layer Diagrams			✓
Edit Dependency Graphs			✓
Architecture Validation			✓
UML® 2.0 Compliant Diagrams (Activity, Use Case, Sequence, Class, and Component)			✓
Lab Management			
Virtual Environment Setup and Teardown			✓
Provision Environment from Template			✓
Checkpoint Environment			✓

(*continued*)

Table 1-1. (*continued*)

Debugging and Diagnostics	Community	Professional	Enterprise
Team Foundation Server Features			
Web-Based Test Execution		✓	✓
Web-Based Test Case Management			✓
Agile Portfolio Management		✓	✓
Team (Chat) Rooms		✓	✓
Work Item Charting		✓ -	✓
Request and Manage Feedback		✓	✓
Release Management			✓
Backlog Management		✓	✓
Sprint Planning		✓	✓
Kanban Board		✓	✓
Agile Task Boards		✓	✓
SharePoint integration (Team Project Portal) 4		✓	✓
Reporting and BI		✓	✓
Project and Project Server Integration 5		✓	✓
System Center integration 6		✓	✓
Version Control using TFVC Repositories		✓	✓
Version Control Using Git-Based Repositories		✓	✓
Code Comments on Changesets or Git Commits		✓	✓
Work Item Tracking		✓	✓
Build Automation		✓	✓

Choosing Editions

Despite the number of editions decreasing, choosing which edition to use for your team and your team members can be daunting. Fortunately, using the process of elimination can help you determine your best choice.

Community Edition

It's easy to decide whether you can use Community or not. If you're looking for a no-cost option and have fewer than five developers and fewer than 250 PCs in your organization and your organization has less than US$1 million in annual revenue, you can pick Community. If you're looking for more features or simply cannot use Community, Professional is the next option to consider.

Professional Edition

Visual Studio 2015 Community and Visual Studio 2015 Professional are very similar. Usually you need to choose Visual Studio 2015 Professional if your organization has more than five developers and has more than 250 PCs or has more than US$ 1 million in annual revenue. Visual Studio 2015 Professional does support TFS features and CodeLens, so if you're looking for your team members to collaborate via TFS and Visual Studio 2015, Community is an option, although you might want to choose Visual Studio 2015 Professional instead. If Visual Studio 2015 Community isn't an option and you're looking for a more features than Visual Studio 2015 Professional, Visual Studio 2015 Enterprise is the next option to consider.

Enterprise Edition

One of the biggest features only available in Visual Studio 2015 Enterprise has to do with debugging. Visual Studio 2015 Enterprise has IntelliTrace and .NET Memory Dump Analysis. What this means is that you can more easily dig deeper into production issues. With .NET Memory Dump Analysis, you can get a memory dump of a problem or a crash and dig deeper into what was happening at the time of the problem from your development computer. If that doesn't find your problem, you can install IntelliTrace agents in production to debug the application in real-time and use IntelliTrace Historical Debugging to be able to go backward and forward in your debugging session to home in on the problem. If you've ever had to debug production problems, you'll find that this makes life much easier.

Visual Studio 2015 Enterprise also makes a big leap in the support for testing environments. It is the first edition to include Lab Management. Lab Management is a set of features that manage virtual machines to perform a variety of testing, from UI testing, to load testing, to manual and exploratory testing. Along with Team Foundation Server, you can also perform many of these tests automatically during build processes. Along with this are facilities to manage test cases and managing releases.

If "test environment," "production environment," and "development environment" are terms that you frequently use in your organization, the Visual Studio 2015 Enterprise Edition is likely the one for you.

Although there's nothing stopping you from choosing the Visual Studio 2015 Test Professional Edition along with Visual Studio 2015 Community or Visual Studio 2015 Professional (assuming Visual Studio 2015 Community is an option at all), it likely doesn't make sense unless Visual Studio 2015 Enterprise is an option for at least some of your team members. If no other team members need or will be using Visual Studio 2015 Enterprise, Visual Studio 2015 Test Professional will probably not be used to its fullest potential. Visual Studio 2015 Test Professional is typically used for the testing team members on teams whose developers or architects are using Visual Studio 2015 Enterprise.

Useful Migration Paths

Small Startup

A small startup is likely an organization that has fewer than five developers, has much fewer than 250 PCs, and less than US$ 1 million in annual revenue. This type of organization can easily start out with Visual Studio 2015 Community. This assumes that they are not planning on using any of the Team Foundation Server features and are using hosted source code control providers like GitHub or even Visual Studio Team Services (both are not no cost for private repositories).

As teams ramp up in skill and ability, they may find that upgrading to Visual Studio 2015 Professional is necessary.

If the organization requires testing environments, an MSDN subscription is likely an important product as it contains testing licenses for many Microsoft products, like Windows, Windows Server, SQL Server, etc. that would cost tens of thousands of dollars otherwise if done legally.

Startup

Presumably a startup that is not considered "small" would have at least five developers. In this case, they will likely need to start out with purchasing Visual Studio 2015 Professional for their teams. If the organization has individual roles for testers and architects, the organization can purchase a small number of licenses of Visual Studio 2015 Test Professional and Visual Studio 2015 Enterprise. These editions are typically more expensive than Visual Studio 2015 Professional so they should be purchased only when needed.

Enterprise

It is expected that Enterprise-level application development is very complex and involves many engineers. So, these organizations may purchase Visual Studio 2015 Enterprise by default. To save some money, they could purchase Visual Studio 2015 Professional for junior developers.

Organizations performing enterprise-level development typically have testing and architecture roles so they would purchase Visual Studio 2015 Testing Professionals for their testing roles and use Visual Studio 2015 Enterprise for engineers.

Other Options

Visual Studio Code

Visual Studio Code (currently in Beta) is a cross-platform IDE (Windows, Mac, and Linux) that supports creating ASP.NET 5/DNX, Node.js, Office, and Unity applications.

Visual Studio Code is a much more lightweight IDE that breaks away from the solution/project file structure that Visual Studio uses in favor of JSON files and implied directory structure.

It is currently free and open source and allows users on Windows, Mac, and Linux to work on code. The typical scenario is for ASP.NET 5/DNX projects that support Windows, Mac, and Linux.

If your team works on an ASP.NET 5/DNX application supporting more than Windows, you might want to look at Visual Studio Code.

Figure 1-17 is an example of the UI.

Figure 1-17. *The Visual Studio Code IDE*

Visual Studio Team Services

What used to be Visual Studio Online (which is what used to be called Team Foundation Service) is now called Visual Studio Team Services. (Yes, the acronym is "VSTS" and there was another product with that same acronym from Microsoft called Visual Studio Team System.) I mention it here as an "other option" because Microsoft describes it so: "it's not an IDE, it's everything else". VSTS provides collaboration features for teams to work on various types of applications for various platforms. This is supported by Visual Studio 2015, but it's not required.

VSTS provides features like version control (or source code control) via Git or TFVC (aka TFS), work item tracking, and Kanban boards, continuous integration, and performance testing. It also integrates into Visual Studio and other IDEs and tools (e.g. Eclipse, XCode, etc.). While you can deploy all of these types of features on-premise, VSTS provides a cloud-based alternative with a specific SLA.

OmniSharp

OmniSharp is a toolset that enables editing and editing integrations in the editor of your choice on the operating system of your choice. This allows you to have features like refactoring and IntelliSense in the editor of your choice (assuming there is a plugin for it). Currently Atom, Brackets, Emacs, Sublime, and Vim have supported plugins.

To be clear, this is not a Windows-specific toolset. For example, in the Mac with Sublime and OmniSharp, you can get IDE features like IntelliSense, as shown in Figure 1-18.

```
~/Projects/MyNancyApp/HomeModule.cs
 1
 2  {
 3      using Nancy;
 4
 5      public class HomeModule : NancyModule
 6      {
 7          public HomeModule()
 8          {
 9              Get["/"] = GetMeAResponse;
10          }
11
12          private dynamic GetMeAResponse(dynamic parameters)
13          {
14              string response = "Hello World";
15              response.
16      }
17                  Clone()                                                                 object Clone()
18      }           CompareTo(                                          int CompareTo(object value)
19  }               CompareTo(                                          int CompareTo(string strB)
20                  Contains(                                           bool Contains(string value)
                    CopyTo( void CopyTo(int sourceIndex, char[] destination, int destinationIndex, int count)
                    EndsWith(                                           bool EndsWith(string value)
                    EndsWith(            bool EndsWith(string value, bool ignoreCase, CultureInfo culture)
                    EndsWith(            bool EndsWith(string value, StringComparison comparisonType)
```

Figure 1-18. *The OmniSharp toolset on a Mac*

Compilation and build tasks are typically relegated to the command-line, but with crafty extensions in each editor, that could easily be integrated.

Summary

In this chapter, we introduced the various editions of Visual Studio 2015 (Community, Professional, and Enterprise) and the different features of each. We also looked into most of what is different in Visual Studio 2015 from Visual Studio 2013. Along with some advice on choosing editions, this should provide ample information for you to decide whether to switch from Visual Studio 2013 to Visual Studio 2015, as well as which edition to choose.

Additionally, we looked at the functions of an IDE and some alternatives, such as Visual Studio Code and OmniSharp.

In the next chapter we'll look at working in teams. Chapter 2 will get into some principles and practices of organizing a software project and some software development methodologies like Agile and Scrum and finish off with how Visual Studio can help manage your work.

CHAPTER 2

■ ■ ■

Working in Teams: Tasks and Code

Software systems are generally very complex. Some software designers work with some very simple software, but the majority of the time readers would generally be working on complex systems.

With any complex project, we have to split the work up among multiple people in order to get it done in a reasonable amount of time. Developing software becomes partially knowing about how to work well in teams. In this chapter, we look into some of the generally accepted practices for working in teams and how they apply to Visual Studio.

Applicable Principles

I rarely like to work in isolation, away from the rest of the world. I believe there are lots of ideas, principles, and ways of working, which I can draw on for completing tasks in everyday life. I view software in much the same way (I'm not alone, look at the Lean Software movement, Kanban, etc.). In any case, there are a few principles that for years I've found aid in software projects. Here are some that I believe help on the context of this chapter.

Project Management Triangle

In project management circles, there is the concept of the *project management triangle*. It basically distills the constraints of a project down to three attributes: scope, cost, and time. A combination of these constraints leads to quality and any change in any of the three attributes affects quality. It also details that you can't have all three with the values you require; you can have at most two. You have to concede one of the three attributes to get the other two. For example, if you want a certain number of features (scope) and for those features to be done on a certain date (time), you have to be flexible on cost. Or, if you want a certain number of features (scope) within a specific budget (cost), you have to be flexible on when that will be done (time). Figure 2-1 shows the typical project management triangle.

© Peter Ritchie 2016
P. Ritchie, *Practical Microsoft Visual Studio 2015*, DOI 10.1007/978-1-4842-2313-0_2

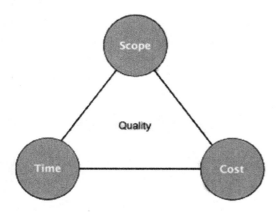

Figure 2-1. *The typical project management triangle*

This also applies to change throughout the life of a software project. Despite our best efforts, we empirically discover things along the path to producing that software. The things we discover can affect all of the constraints, leaving us to make concessions on at least one of these constraints. For example, if we discover that what we wanted to produce (scope) was actually more work (time), we have to reduce the scope, extend the time, or spend more money (cost) to keep scope and time.

This concept isn't specific to producing software, but it is very applicable and I find it very useful to remember when talking about software tasks.

Vision

A vision is a widely used concept to help focus effort. It can be seen in many disciplines outside of software as well as inside (see Chapter 4 for more information).

A vision details the what, not the how. In project management circles, a vision is defined as "…the picturing of the project's deliverable as the solution to the stated need or problem." Not overly enlightening and possibly even more confusing to some people. A vision may simply state a goal, or it may allude to strategy or mission. It should, at the very least, describe a goal. It should also provide enough detail and inspiration to be able to evaluate any and all work to be done on a project so that it can be categorized as in or out of scope.

It's useful to devise a vision at some point in the life for your software project. If everyone agrees, it helps communicate purpose as well as focus the work that goes into the software. Sometimes it even helps you make decisions about what may be the right or wrong thing to do for the project.

Charter

Another project management concept, the *project charter* is part of a formal ceremony kicking off a project and formally defining the people who will fulfill the roles involved in the project. It also details scope, potential deliverables, business needs, business problems, opportunities, etc. A charter may also include milestones.

A project charter defines and introduces the people involved in the project, identifies the necessary roles, and empowers those involved to get things done.

I find that a charter provides vital information about roles on the project as well as information that will help keep the project focused on its goals. This can help some projects from getting off the rails on work that might seem related but really isn't.

It's a fairly simple thing to do but provides value to many software projects. If you have a project manager on the team, they should be able to facilitate this fairly quickly.

Sponsor

One of the things that comes out of a project charter is a *project sponsor* (or just sponsor). The sponsor acts as a link between the project and the organization. Typically, between the project management and the executive management.

The sponsor should be viewed by the executive management as the owner and is responsible for the success (or failure) of the project. The sponsor should understand the business aspects of why the project exists and the solution it is proposing. The sponsor should also ensure that the project remains true to its business goals. The sponsor should be key to ensuring impediments are removed or more importantly avoided. Sponsors are the voice of the project with the rest of the organization.

I find that without a sponsor project, teams can easily progress into working in a silo (or start by working in a silo and not get out). A sponsor can either help a project get out of a silo or help keep it from progressing to a silo by providing the voice outside of the project team. A project that works in a silo will have a hard time gaining adoption when it's complete.

Delivering Software

Types of Work

There are effectively two types of processes: defined processes and empirical processes.

Defined Processes

A *defined process* is the easier of the two processes to understand. "Defined" is a much more common word to most people. A defined process is one that can be defined before work begins. It's generally a set of sequential steps. One step may be dependent on the previous, or their sequence is inconsequential. The important part is that the steps are, or could be, known ahead of time and it's a simple matter of performing the steps one by one.

Defined processes are important in delivering software. Not all processes can be defined when developing software, but some are, and it's important to make the distinction between the two. When a defined process is discovered, it's important to formally define it (which can simply be a list of the steps). Once defined, team members should strive to automate defined processes whenever possible (at least the ones who need to be repeated—and let's face it, that should be all of them).

Manually following a set of steps is prone to error and when defined processes are not automated, we introduce unnecessary risk to the delivery of software. When a defined process is automated, that automation is human readable and can then be reviewed by another team member for errors before executing. This is vital to reduce risk and reduce error but also provides documentation of the process and promotes knowledge sharing among team members.

The describable nature of defined processes contrasts with empirical processes.

Empirical Processes

Although an empirical process has a formal meaning just like a defined process, it seems less understood. Empirical is defined by Wiktionary as "pertaining to, derived from, or testable by observation made using physical senses or using instruments which extend the senses." Basically empirical means *making observations*.

Empirical processes are processes that do not have an entirely defined set of steps that need to be performed. Instead, the choice of some steps or the discovery of some steps is based on observation.

Developing and delivering software involves a mix of defined and empirical processes.

Systems Development Lifecycle

The Systems Development Lifecycle (or SDLC) defines some essential and often necessary steps in the process of developing software. I wouldn't call it its own methodology or a process in and of itself because it really only outlines some various actions that are normally performed during the development of software. Those actions are often outlined as analysis, design, implementation, maintenance, and planning, but often include other actions such as requirements gathering, integration, testing, etc. Defined methodologies detail how these actions interrelate and prescribe processes around how they overlap, how they feed from one into another, etc.

We'll get into a couple useful methodologies, so it's important to understand the basic tasks that these methodologies use.

Iterative Development

Although often referred to simply as "iterative development," this often refers to "iterative and incremental development". Although the incremental part is left off, it's a critical part of iterative development.

As detailed earlier, software development at many levels is an empirical process. You need to perform actions (or small experiments) and observe results before you can choose the next step. You could actually view performing actions, observing results, and choosing the next step as *iterative*. Iterative and incremental development recognizes the empirical nature of software to systematize the observance and decision-making process.

The incremental aspect of iterative and incremental development builds on the empirical nature of software development by facilitating the information learned through prior iterations. The software is developed incrementally, meaning that it only fulfills the requirements known at the time and that apply to the current story or stories. It does not try to predict the future and guess at requirements that have not yet been communicated or are not complete. You can apply lessons learned from prior iterations along with clearer requirements to incrementally increase functionality rather than changing or correcting functionality that didn't fulfill requirements not known at the time. This allows for higher-quality software because you'll spend less time pulling out code (making corrections) that's prone to error as well as not ever being coupled to that code.

The basic process of iterative development is to 1) gather some set of requirements, 2) perform planning to choose which requirements can be developed in the next iteration, 3) perform analysis to gather information for 4) design and implementation, which is then used in 5) testing. Somewhere between design and implementation, working software is deployed so that it can be tested and viewed. All the knowledge and source code then feeds into the next iteration, which pulls in more requirements and starts again. This process can be seen visually in the typical iterative development diagram in Figure 2-2.

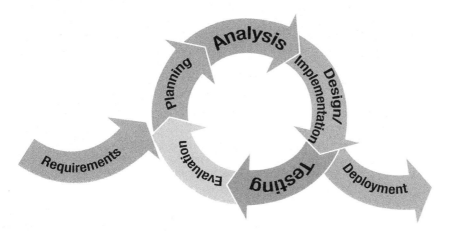

Figure 2-2. *The process of iterative development*

Domain Experts

A *domain* is a focused business area with unique (but common within the domain) requirements and terminology. Typically a domain is focused on a specific type of business or a specific context within a business.

Domain experts are experts within a specific business domain. They are experts in the process, the requirements, the terminology, the information, the people, events, etc. involved with that domain. Ideally on any software project there should be at least one person recognized as the domain expert. A domain expert helps ensure the project is solving the business problems it is supposed to solve and maintains a scope within the domain. The domain expert helps to refine a conceptual model that addresses the solution to the problem domain.

Sometimes domain experts are referred to subject matter experts (SMEs). In either case, these experts are generally technical (often senior). A team member who is an expert in accounting when working on an accounting system would be a domain expert or subject matter expert, for example.

It is best to have at least one domain expert or subject matter expert on a project. When projects are just starting, there may not be one. Eventually a domain expert or subject matter expert will become necessary. They will be the team member with the greatest amount of knowledge on the business or business domain relating to what the software is trying to accomplish. It's best that all the team members know who the domain expert (or experts) are so that person's expertise can be used whenever needed.

Agile

Agile defines the principles related to software development methodologies. It doesn't prescribe much in the way of actual process other than delivering working software frequently (weeks rather than months) through continuous delivery and using iterative and incremental development. It typically guides you about how to make process choices. It assumes that the process is evolving and unique to a particular team or organization.

Agile was codified in the *Agile Manifesto*. The manifesto has four policies:

- Individuals and interactions over process and tools

- Working software over comprehensive documentation

- Customer collaboration over contract negotiation

- Responding to change over following a plan

Let's look at each of these in more detail in the following sections.

Individuals and Interactions Over Process and Tools

The creators of Agile recognize that for software teams (or any team producing artifacts for someone else) to be successful they need to be self-organizing. The empirical nature of software means people need to think, they need to be self-motivated to think, they need to feel empowered to think. They can't simply follow a bunch of steps and produce good software. Teams need to value those personal interactions between team members and utilize that to make great software.

Working Software Over Comprehensive Documentation

No matter how much process you throw at producing software, the end goal is always to produce software. You can mandate that comprehensive requirements documents be produced, or analysis reports be produced for all analysis work, or diagrams and descriptions be produced for design, or test plans that cover 100% of the functional be documented. What all of those things try to accomplish is to produce the software. When choosing to produce working software over comprehensive documentation, always choose to produce working software.

That's not to say that documentation should not be done, far from it. It's part of the artifacts that are usually required by any software. Software often lives beyond the team that created it and requires care and maintenance. That care and maintenance requires context and instruction that can only be truly communicated via documentation. Plan to produce the documentation required, but only as much as is required. It should never be more important than working software.

Customer Collaboration Over Contract Negotiation

This policy details that as much as we'd like to get on paper (documentation) what a customer wants or needs, that is almost always flawed. Contracts just contradict iterative development and suggest you can define exactly what is needed in any piece of software before you start producing it. We know the process is empirical, we know we discover things along the journey, we know we have project constraints and how to deal with change. This policy is telling you to maintain customer collaboration throughout the journey.

That's not to say you can't do iterative development and you can't recognize the empirical process, etc. and not have *contracts*. In fact, there are techniques that help promote contract-like responsibility and accountability. Project charters, for example, help define the responsibilities and goals and hold team members accountable.

Responding to Change Over Following a Plan

Nothing is more annoying than dealing with someone who's a stickler for their process over providing value to customers. "Fill out this form in triplicate" when you simply want to provide feedback or get a refund. This can get out of hand during software projects. Waterfall-based methodologies often demand that certain phases be complete before others. So, if requirements change, for example, the process demands everything start from scratch. Customers don't find this particularly useful.

This policy is detailing that you should recognize that change happens, either as a result of software development work or as a result of changing customer needs, so you need to embrace and support it.

Agile Principles

In addition to the policies in the Agile Manifesto, there are several Agile principles that help guide the creation and evolution of software process or methodology.

> *Our highest priority is to satisfy the customer through early and continuous delivery of valuable software.*

This principle reinforces policy two—that working software is the value that a software project produces. It also introduces the concept of *continuous delivery*. Continuous delivery alludes to the interactive and incremental nature of Agile.

Welcome changing requirements, even late in development. Agile processes harness change for the customer's competitive advantage.

This principle reinforces that individuals and collaboration are valued in Agile projects. The value is working software and it must have value to stakeholders. If requirements change, the value changes and if the software cannot accommodate those requirements, it has less value.

Deliver working software frequently, from a couple of weeks to a couple of months, with a preference to the shorter timescale.

This further clarifies the time-boxed nature of Agile iterations and starts to define specifics. For the most part, the timeframe has evolved to one to three weeks, but that depends on the project.

Business people and developers must work together daily throughout the project.

This principle reinforces customer collaboration and hints at daily stand-ups or describes the *daily scrum*.

Build projects around motivated individuals. Give them the environment and support they need, and trust them to get the job done.

Agile is about treating team members with respect. They are adults and skilled at their profession. They should be empowered to utilize their skills and experience. This speaks to self-organizing and autonomous teams.

The most efficient and effective method of conveying information to and within a development team is face-to-face conversation.

Reinforcing collaboration and valuing that collaboration over reams of documentation.

Working software is the primary measure of progress.

Reinforces the working software idea, but also points out that working software should be a metric.

Agile processes promote sustainable development. The sponsors, developers, and users should be able to maintain a constant pace indefinitely.

Calls out that a software project is a team effort that should involve more than just the development team.

Continuous attention to technical excellence and good design enhances agility.

Team members should always be striving for continuous improvement and the organization should promote that.

> *Simplicity—the art of maximizing the amount of work not done—is essential.*

Introducing complexity when it is not needed does not add value. This reinforces the incremental nature of Agile iterations.

> *The best architectures, requirements, and designs emerge from self-organizing teams.*

This describes one of the reasons for self-organizing and autonomous teams.

> *At regular intervals, the team reflects on how to become more effective, then tunes and adjusts its behavior accordingly.*

In order to continuously improve and evolve to changing needs, it's vital that teams be reflective and introspective and continuously look for ways to improve their work.

Scrum

The basic flow of the scrum process is detailed in Figure 2-3.

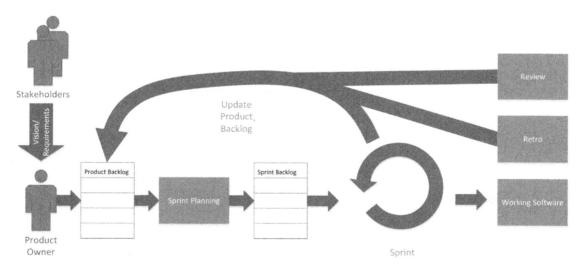

Figure 2-3. *The basic flow of the scrum process*

From an iteration-to-iteration point of view (this ignores how the project gets started, initiated, envisioned, etc.), a product owner works with stakeholders to consume and understand requirements or work required for a particular project. The product owner works with the stakeholders to clarify that information before adding it to the product backlog, which is the living list of estimable work items.

At the start of each sprint, the software development team analyzes the product backlog in the current state to choose a subset of backlog items, based on priorities, how much work the team can get done in the sprint, etc. That process means that the team estimates the work for backlog items and the ones they choose to work on are added to a sprint backlog. Backlog item estimates are by point or size (small, medium, large, etc.), not by days of work.

The development team then begins the sprint and starts working on the items in the sprint backlog. As the team completes the backlog items, the rate at which they are complete work is tracked and a velocity is calculated (or updated, if this isn't their first sprint) and used to forecast completion.

Estimates

When we talk about estimates in a process where we discover some of the actual work as work is performed, we talk about high-level estimates (sometimes called *points* or *t-shirt sizes*). Because we know that we don't know all the work involved, we don't estimate by timeframes because we can't possibly be correct.

As teams work together, they get better at estimating points. As they work together, their velocity improves. So, over time we can better estimate whether a team will be able to complete a specific number of points within a sprint.

Sprint

Although originally a scrum term, the term *sprint* has become known across Agile, not just with scrum.

A *sprint* is the timeframe in iterative and incremental software development where the non-planning work is performed by a software development team. A sprint is typically one to three weeks in duration.

During the sprint, the team generally meets once a day (typically in the morning) to give a status about the backlog items being worked on and to communicate whether there are any impediments to that work.

Stakeholders

Stakeholder is not a term unique to scrum. From a project management perspective, it's an individual or group who may affect or be affected by decisions, activities, and the outcome of a project.

That's not too different in the scrum context. Scrum further delineates certain types of stakeholders—business owner, product owner, scrum team members, and scrum master.

Business Owner

In scrum, the business owner is often the person responsible for creating a team or instigating the project. This person ultimately owns the budget of the effort and has needs as a stakeholder.

Typically the scrum master manages the relationship and communication among the business owner, the product owner, other stakeholders, and the scrum team.

Product Owner

Scrum typically uses the term *product owner* to refer to the project sponsor, but this could be an end user rather than leadership. If this is not a system user, they might be a member of product management or marketing teams. The product owner is an expert in user needs and usage patterns. The product owner is an expert in the marketplace and competition (if a commercial software package). The product owner also understands the market and the future trends of the domain.

A product owner is a stakeholder and understands and owns the vision of the software project. This person typically has frontline experience in the business domain.

A product owner is vital to the success of scrum projects. The product owner also owns and manages (adds, clarifies, and prioritizes) the product backlog. The product owner effectively provides direction to the scrum team.

The product owner prioritizes the product backlog, but they are neither a project manager nor a development lead. The software development teams have ultimate say in what they believe is the best choice of backlog items to work on during any given sprint. Of course, the development team must make intelligent choices to maintain credibility with the product owner. With that credibility comes respect by the product owner; they try to allow the team to focus on the sprint backlog during the sprint and introduce new requirements only during planning, high-priority items notwithstanding.

Daily Scrum

As mentioned earlier, the daily scrum or the stand-up is the daily ceremony that the development team performs. The stand-up is often focused on three questions for each team member:

- What did I do yesterday?

- What will I do today?

- Are there any impediments in my way?

Metronomic adherence to the questions is good for young or newly formed teams. The end goal of the stand-up is that status and the velocity of work on backlog items be verified. A backlog-item-focused approach of answering the three questions for each backlog items is another way teams can perform the daily scrum.

Although anyone is welcome to attend the daily scrum, there is the concept of committed team members and involved team members. The development team and the scrum master are considered committed. In the spirit of self-organizing, autonomous teams, only committed team members may participate in and non-committed (involved) team members should only watch and listen. (See the "Pigs and Chickens" sidebar). Committed team members are required to attend each daily scrum.

Over and above keeping the backlog status up to date and under control, the daily scrum ensures openness and transparency within the team. Team members are encouraged to be involved, knowledgeable, and participatory in the work of other team members. Helping other team members or work involved in removing impediments should be done after the daily scrum.

The daily scrum should last only about 15 minutes and is often referred to a stand-up because people should not need to sit if it's kept short. Typically a scrum master chairs the meeting and is responsible for ensuring that the sprint backlog items are discussed and their exact status is up to date. The scrum master should also ensure that the team's velocity is still able to complete the sprint backlog in the remaining sprint timeframe. The scrum master is also responsible for resolving (or helping to resolve) any impediments the team has communicated (include if the sprint backlog cannot be completed with the given velocity).

> ## PIGS AND CHICKENS
>
> The story of the pig and chicken is meant to communicate the difference between team members who are *committed* and team members who are only *involved*. The story goes something like this:
>
> A pig and chicken are walking down the road.
>
> The chicken says, "Hey pig, I was thinking we should open a restaurant."
>
> The pig replies, "Hmm, maybe, what would we call it?"
>
> The chicken responds, "How about 'Ham-n-eggs'?"
>
> The pig thinks for a moment and says, "No thanks. I'd be committed, but you'd only be involved."
>
> What the story is trying to communicate is that the pig gives up more for the project (ham, bacon, or otherwise itself) whereas the chicken merely provides eggs.
>
> The analogy is that development team members are pigs and are totally committed to the project. They are accountable to the outcome. Chickens are other team members and merely consult or are involved and are not accountable to the outcome of the project.

User Stories

Backlog items are often called *user stories*. Scrum recognizes that backlog items can be more than user stories, but Agile typically views backlogs as containing user stories.

A user story is a written sentence in the context of a particular user. It's meant to tightly bind the work involved with the fact that the work should ultimately fulfill the needs of a person. It has the form

As a <type of user>, I want <some goal> so that <some reason>.

Epics

An *epic* is effectively a user story that has a complexity level that can't be accurately tracked as just one user story. It should include two or more related user stories as children. For example, a story such as, "As a user, I would like to set a password so that I may log into the system" could actually result in a fair amount of work. First, you have to be able to track users. You also need to enable the user to log in, have a profile, and edit a profile (change a password). It also may mean that an administer needs to be able to manage the users: validate them, change their authentication, change their authorization, etc.

Visual Studio doesn't support promoting a backlog item to a feature. If you find that you've added a backlog item, you'll have to resort to removing it (adding a reason that it is being converted to an epic) and creating a new epic. You'll have to copy the details and probably redistribute the tasks once you create the new stories under the epic.

Review

The sprint review meeting is held at the end of each sprint. During the sprint review meeting, the team members show the work they accomplished since the last sprint. As the focus of scrum is the delivery of working software, this should almost always be the demonstration of working software. The meeting should be informal and focus mostly on the software and the work accomplished. The meeting should include the product owner, the scrum team, scrum master, and leadership. Developers from other teams or projects can attend, but it should not be mandatory.

The outcome of the sprint review meeting should be an assessment of the project against the sprint goal. Was the goal reached? Why not? What may need to change in the backlog? (The goal of the sprint is typically decided in the sprint planning meeting.) This assessment should be used to plan the next sprint.

Retro

The sprint *retro*, or the sprint retrospective, focuses on what the team feels they have done well and where they could improve. Much like a stand-up, the retro attempts to answer three basic questions:

- What went well during the sprint?

- What went wrong during the sprint?

- What could be done differently to improve?

The retro tries to focus on solution to problems when possible. At the very least, the team should be taking responsibility for what they feel has or has not gone well during the sprint, despite possibly having no solution to a particular problem.

The sprint review focuses on the *what* the team is building, whereas the retro focuses on how the team is building software.

Tasks in Visual Studio

Agile versus Scrum

In Visual Studio, there are several process templates, two of which are scrum and Agile. Both templates have the same basic flow, and each has a slightly different terminology for certain things. Scrum uses *product backlog item* whereas Agile uses *user story*; Scrum uses *impediment* whereas Agile uses *issue*. I don't recommend getting too hung up on the terminology. You should focus on your process. If YOU'RE doing scrum, choose scrum. Don't choose Agile if you're really doing Scrum but then call "product backlog items" "user stories".

When should you choose one over the other? The easiest way to choose is if your team practices scrum, pick the scrum template. I do recommend choosing a *process* before you choose a template. Don't decide on a template and then try to change or create your process around the template. Understand scrum before making a process choice then pick the template that best suits your process. Scrum typically tracks remaining work and includes bugs within that work.

The Agile template is different from the scrum template. The Agile template allows tracking bugs separately from other tasks. The Agile template allows tracking remaining work like the scrum template, but you can also choose to track original work or completed work instead.

For the most part, the examples I show specifically with Visual Studio use scrum. Just be aware of the differences if you want to apply this chapter to an Agile project/template.

Managing Work Items

Depending on how your TFS server is configured, you'll be able to track a variety of work items. The lowest level of work item is a task or a bug. Tasks are generally children of a product backlog item but a bug could also have child tasks. Depending on your TFS configuration, product backlog items can be associated with (or effectively grouped under) a feature. Likewise, a feature or a product backlog item could be associated with (or effectively grouped under) an epic.

Within Visual Studio, the way you work with tasks and work items is via the Team Explorer. Figure 2-4 shows the Team Explorer.

Figure 2-4. *The Team Explorer in Visual Studio*

Clicking Work Items brings you to the Work Items tab of the Team Explorer, as shown in Figure 2-5.

Figure 2-5. *The Work Items tab in Team Explorer*

From the Work Items tab, you can perform queries or create work items. Work items include bugs, tasks, product backlog items, epics, features, impediments, and test cases. Availability of these will depend on your edition of Visual Studio. You can also manage work items from within Microsoft Excel from the New Work Item drop-down. This is useful for adding or editing things in bulk, but we won't discuss it in this book.

In an ideal world, you'd create epics then define features and their timeframes, then create product backlog items and added them to a feature or epic. And as work is broken down for each product backlog item, tasks are added to the product backlog item. Bugs normally come in out of band as they are discovered and brought into a sprint to be worked on during sprint planning. If a bug need to be addressed before the next sprint planning, the team effectively needs to replan the current sprint. This could effectively be as simple as deciding if the bug can be fixed in the current sprint. If not, the worst case is that work on the current sprint is abandoned and replanned to include the bug. This also has varying degrees of complexity from being as simple as deciding which backlog items will be removed from the sprint, to something more complex in terms of discussions around work and priorities.

Figure 2-6 shows the form in Visual Studio used to create an epic.

Figure 2-6. *Creating an epic in Visual Studio*

Notice the Iteration field. When you want to perform the work, you can change this field to the sprint the work will be performed in.

You can create features independently, but if you want to actually create a feature that will be a child of an epic, it's often easier to create it as a child. You can do this from a query list by right-clicking the epic you want to add it to and then selecting New Linked Work Item, as shown in Figure 2-7. This brings up the New Linked Work Item form shown in Figure 2-8, where you can set the work item type of feature and enter a title and comment.

Figure 2-7. *Creating a feature that will be a child of an epic*

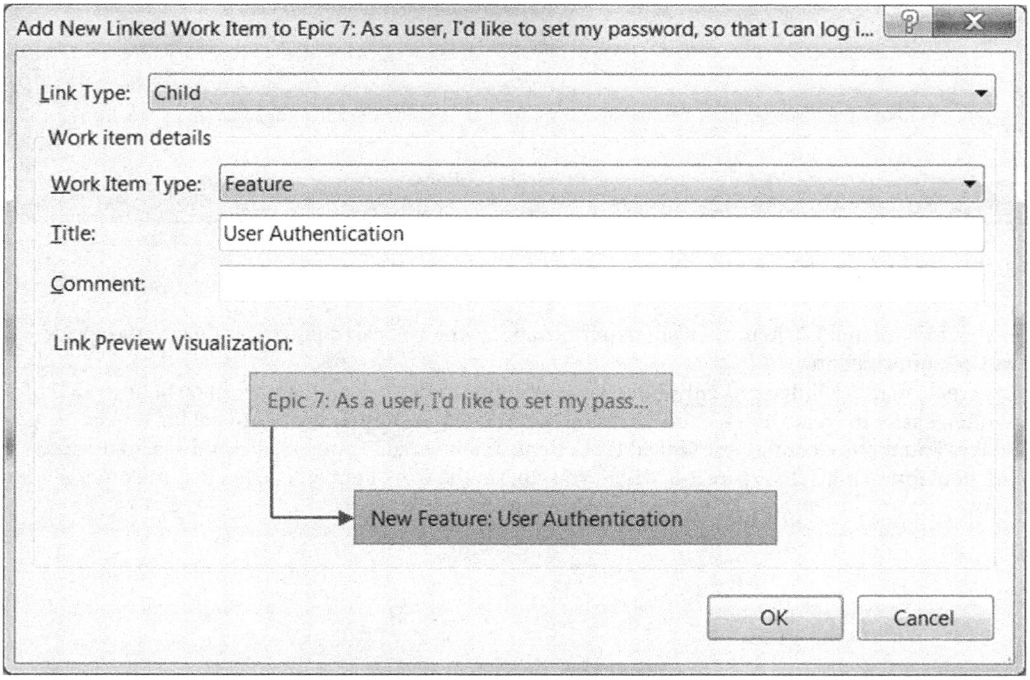

Figure 2-8. *The New Linked Work Item form*

Figure 2-9 shows the form in Visual Studio to create a feature.

Figure 2-9. *The Create a Feature form in Visual Studio*

Notice the Target Date field. A feature typically has a target date associated with it. A feature has the identical fields that an epic does, so they can be used identically. You pick a feature over and epic for semantic reasons. Choose a feature when you have multiple backlog items (grouped by epics) that might not all relate but are related to a "feature". Use an epic when you want to have multiple backlog items that are related.

You can create a backlog item with a specific parent from a query list by right-clicking a feature and selecting New Linked Work Item. This brings up the New Linked Work Item form shown in Figure 2-10, where you can set the type of work item to product backlog item and add a title and comment.

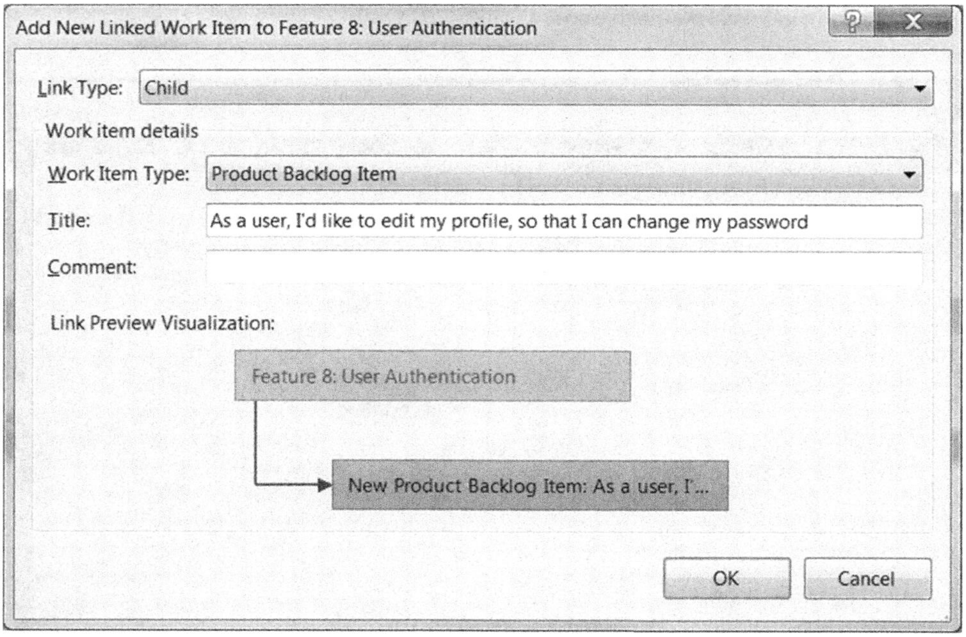

Figure 2-10. Setting the type of Work item to product backlog item and adding a title and comment

Once you click OK, you'll have the Product Backlog Item detail, as shown in Figure 2-11.

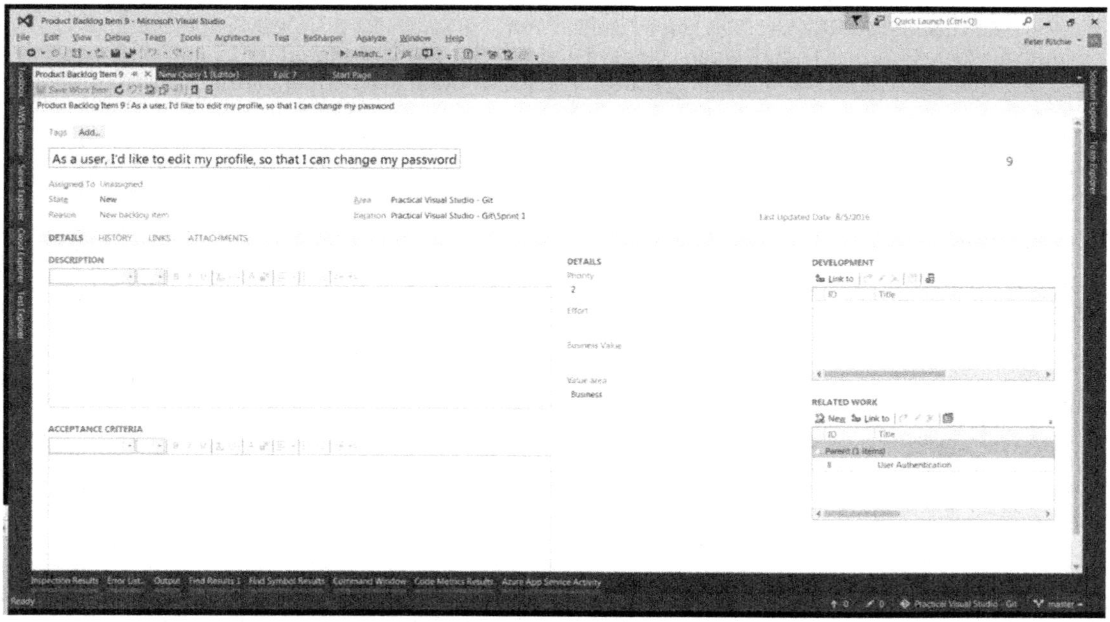

Figure 2-11. The Product Backlog Item detail

Notice that unlike with a feature or epic, there is no target date. Instead you'll see *effort*. This is where things like story points or t-shirt sizes can be placed to assign an effort in relation to other backlog items. The effort does not directly detail how long a backlog item will take to complete; it just describes its effort in relation to other backlog items.

CodeLens

Visual Studio supports tasks and process in another way. CodeLens is a Visual Studio Professional 2015 and above feature (previously only Visual Studio Enterprise). CodeLens displays information above classes and methods. For example, Figure 2-12 shows 0 references|0 changes|0 authors, 0 changes above the Main method on line 11.

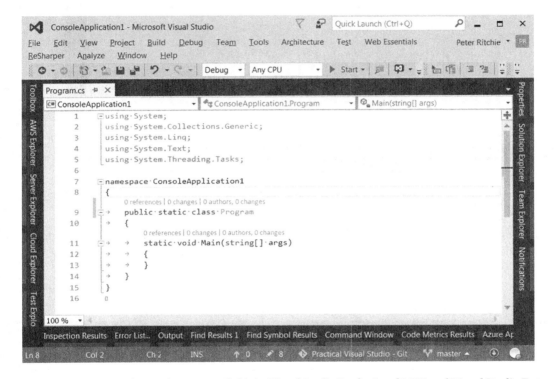

Figure 2-12. *The CodeLens feature, available in Visual Studio Professional 2015 and Visual Studio Enterprise*

As work items are completed and code is committed, CodeLens includes information about the commit, including the author. For example, after a developer commits a change, CodeLens displays who made the last commit and when (Peter Ritchie Less than 5 minutes ago) and the number of authors and changes (1 author, 1 change), as seen in Figure 2-13 above line 11.

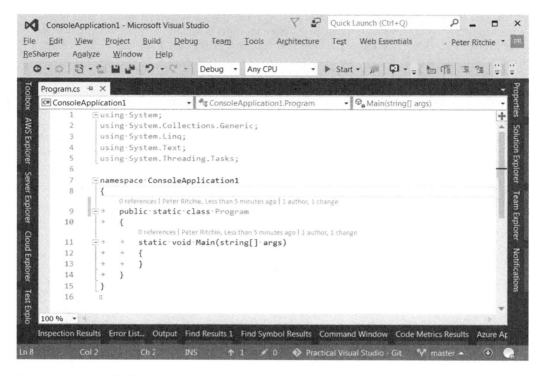

Figure 2-13. *Details about a commit recorded in CodeLens*

The changes can also be viewed by clicking the author/change quantity. See Figure 2-14 for an example of the commits in CodeLens.

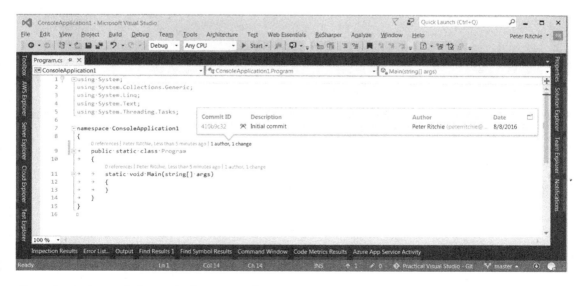

Figure 2-14. *A record of commits shown in CodeLens*

As work items are completed and associated to commits, the work item detail can also be seen in CodeLens. Figure 2-15 shows that a work item is associated with `Program.Main` and that the detail of the work item (when the one work item is clicked) shows the task information. This can be drilled down by clicking the task.

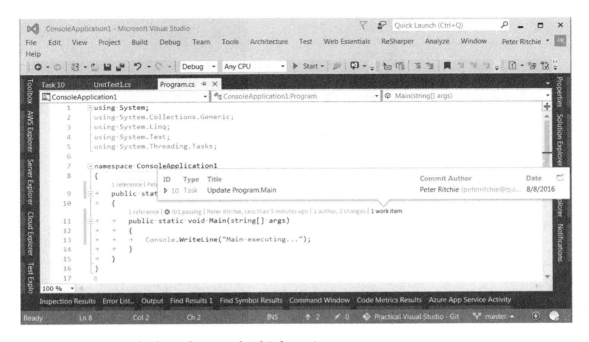

Figure 2-15. *The details of a work item and task information*

Waterfall Processes

I wanted to add a short note about Waterfall processes. Anyone familiar with the Systems Development Lifecycle (SDLC) will note various tasks relating to producing software, which typically include analysis, design, implementation, maintenance, and planning. (There are in fact many more, including initiation/ elicitation, requirements gathering, integration, testing, etc.) Needless to say, many of these tasks take in artifacts from another task and produce artifacts used by another task. These facts were detailed by Dr. Winston W. Royce in his paper, "Managing the Development of Large Software Systems."[1] Dr. Royce detailed the relationship of those tasks in a diagram similar to Figure 12-16.

---

[1]`https://www.cs.umd.edu/class/spring2003/cmsc838p/Process/waterfall.pdf`

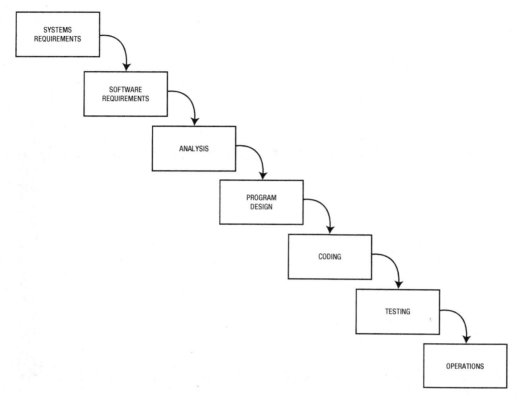

Figure 2-16. *The Systems Development Lifecycle shown as a Waterfall process*

It is in this paper and likely in this diagram that many people mistake the Waterfall process as a viable process. In the paper Dr. Royce, describes the diagram as "risky and invites failure". He goes on to describe the "iterative relationship between successive development phases" and goes on to diagram something more iterative, described as "fundamentally sound," similar to Figure 2-17.

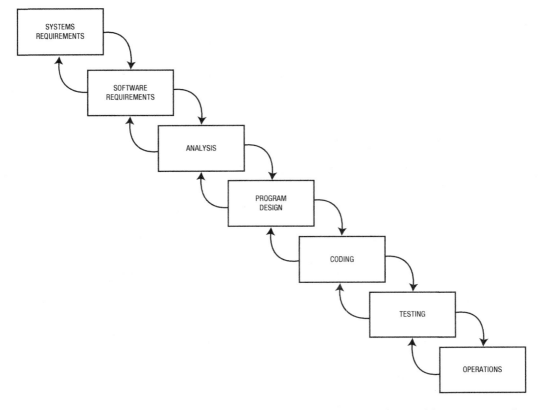

Figure 2-17. *The iterative relationship between successive development phases of the Systems Development Lifecycle*

What Dr. Royce was describing was that a fundamentally iterative process is required to develop software systems, not a successful "Waterfall process".

Summary

In this chapter, we dug deep into a couple of the most common software development methodologies. As you can see, you need a methodology that addresses the fact that many aspects of writing never-before-written software is comprised of yet-to-be-known and unplannable work. Agile has become more or less the de facto standard methodology for planning and process guidance for delivering software projects.

Delivering software is hard. It is even harder when you don't have a good methodology or a methodology doesn't recognize that software is mostly an empirical process. This chapter details how you can use those appropriate methodologies with Visual Studio.

One thing we didn't discuss much in a team context is source code control. This topic is very broad and could not be covered appropriately as a part of this chapter. Source code control in the context of team is covered in the next chapter, so let's have a look at that.

CHAPTER 3

■ ■ ■

Version Control

Version control is fundamental to working with software. It's not just something that teams require, it should be fundamental to working in the software industry.

This chapter will quickly delve into some source code fundamentals. We'll then dig a little deeper into Git and Team Foundation Version Control (TFVC) and provide some guidance on using the two version control systems (VCS) included with Visual Studio 2015. The chapter covers branching, basic usage, terminology, working with work items, generally accepted practices, and usage strategies.

Version Control Fundamentals

Version control, also known as *revision control*, is primarily concerned with tracking changes to source code, or *versioning* of source code. This allows you to track revisions to source code for a multitude of reasons. You can track who made the changes, when the changes were made, and revert to a prior state. Systems that implement version control are called version control systems. Some of those systems are called *revision control systems* (RCS), but for this book, I will use *version control systems* to refer these systems as a whole and *version control* to refer to the concept.

Version control is used by teams and one of the issues that version control systems need to deal with are cases when there are concurrent changes to source code. There are two basic models for being able to track these changes. One is the *lock-modify-unlock* model and the other is the *copy-modify-merge* model.

The Lock-Modify-Unlock Model

The lock-modify-unlock model allows one person to work on a *file* at a time. The developer must first try to lock a file. If they are able to lock the file, they can modify it and then should unlock it (after checking it in) when done.

This model has a few issues. The first and foremost is the complete lack of concurrency in which developers can work on files. As much as we'd like to be able to structure files to make it possible for one person to work on a file at a time, it's unrealistic. One of the other issues is the fact that unlock is a manual operation. It's possible that someone might forget to unlock a file and no other developer can work on it in the meantime. Version control systems that employ this model have ways of circumventing this by allowing merges to check modified files in, but they're cumbersome and prone to error.

Team Foundation Version Control (TFVC) is a centralized version control system, which means it effectively uses the lock-modify-unlock model. You can see this in prior versions of TFVC if you ever get disconnected from your Team Foundation Server. All source files are read-only and must be "unlocked" on the server before they can be modified.

TFVC has "local workspaces" but it simply tracks whether files are modified. You can't "check in" until you have a connection to the Team Foundation Server.

© Peter Ritchie 2016

P. Ritchie, *Practical Microsoft Visual Studio 2015*, DOI 10.1007/978-1-4842-2313-0_3

The Copy-Modify-Merge Model

Copy-modify-merge is the prevalent model. In this case, developers work with a copy of the source code from the repository and perform a merge whenever they want the changes placed into the repository. Depending on the merge algorithms, this puts potential conflicts at the line level, not the file level. This also means concurrency is also at the line level. It's fairly rare (certainly rarer than at the file level) that there would be line-level conflicts in any well communicating team. This is the model that Git uses.

As version control systems moved toward distributed models, it was clear that the copy-modify-merge model had to be used. For a distributed repo that might not have access to the server that it is based from, moving changes to the source repository must involve a merge model and not use server-based locks.

Locking Binary Files

One concern that comes up from people experienced with the lock-modify-unlock model is the ability to lock binary files. Since binary files often cannot be merged, it's ideal for one developer to lock out changes by other developers. Some version control systems allow for this (like TFVC) and some don't. In any decent version control system, binary files simply aren't merged. In the *rare* case that two people modify a binary file *at the same time*, the version control system would warn you and you would have to pick a version. At the "same time" really just means one person edited a file after another, before that edit was committed to the repository.

For the most part, you should avoid putting binary files into revision control. If those binary files can be generated, what generates them should be placed in version control, not the binary files. But, that's not always the case; assets like bitmaps still need to be version controlled (although not necessarily to the same degree as content files, mind you).

Version Control Terminology

Knowing the meanings of some various terms generally used in version control is vital to understanding the content in the rest of this chapter. Let's look at some of those terms.

Branch

A *branch* is a physical or theoretical copy of source code that can be worked on independently with the goal of merging back into the source of the branch.

Mainline

A *mainline* is the main path of a given branch, i.e., the source of a branch and in to which changes within that branch will be merged. There can be more than one mainline in a repository.

Trunk

A *trunk* is a form of mainline, but the lowest level mainline. There is only one trunk and it's the source of all other branches, directly or indirectly.

Branching

Branching is probably the biggest source of friction and consternation when it comes to version control. That friction is almost entirely due to a lack of a branching plan. If team members are not on the same page when it comes to branching, they'll all do different and disparate things. This makes the branching landscape confusing and very prone to error.

The first place to start is to recognize that source code is "evergreen". The source code is never "released," a snapshot in time of the source code is used for a particular release version. This means there is at least one copy of the source code that is modified over time and is never "done". This concept is called a *trunk*. Some may call this the mainline, but mainline can also be used to describe a branch that is branched from, so I prefer trunk.

The trunk is the source of truth; it *is* the source code. When work needs to be done with that source code that needs to be independent until merged back in, a copy is made via a branch and worked on independently. The reasons to branch are varied, so let's look at some important reasons.

Development Isolation

With most teams, what is built is based on a specific branch. In the normal case, this branch is the trunk. Releases are built from the trunk and released. This means that while development occurs it's important that the trunk remain consistent—devoid of half-done features, untested code, etc. This is handled with a development branch, also called a develop branch.

Developers work in the develop branch and when all involved agree that what's in develop is good enough to release to clients, it can be merged into the trunk.

Hotfix Isolation

Inevitably, something needs to be fixed in the software. Branching for hotfix is vital to work on fixes in isolation and be able to release them independently of other work. Hotfixes are a change to fix a specific client bug or service disruption. They are meant to enable a quick response to clients in need, have a different quality bar, and can be one-off compared to how the fix relates to the rest of the code. A hotfix is generally refined further before the fix is applied back to the trunk—a refinement that would otherwise hinder a quick response to a client (broader side-effect checks, translation, audits, etc.).

This means hotfix branches are also used as the source for builds. The code that went into the hotfix can then be merged back into the develop branch for further refinement and eventually merged into the trunk.

Feature Isolation

It's quite common that there are known unknowns and unknown unknowns in any project. It's impossible to know up front how software needs to be written until it's written. This fact means that for any given feature, how it will impact the rest of the source code is unknown. To mitigate the risk of a feature adversely impacting other source code and the viability of the product, individual features need to be worked on in isolation until they have a level of quality that makes them realistic to be part of the product. It's not until then that the risk of the feature impacting the rest of the source code and project is acceptable.

A feature branch is used to isolate the work so it can be merged back into the source branch (develop). This can often be used with *feature toggles* to minimize the impact on the rest of the source code when the branch is merged.

The Branching Big Picture

The most important practice with branching is to branch based on need. If you don't have a need for the branches at any given time, don't use them. It's acceptable to start with a trunk and work from there. As needs to branch arise, make sure you're doing the right thing.

A well-designed diagram can help drive the concepts home, as shown in Figure 3-1.

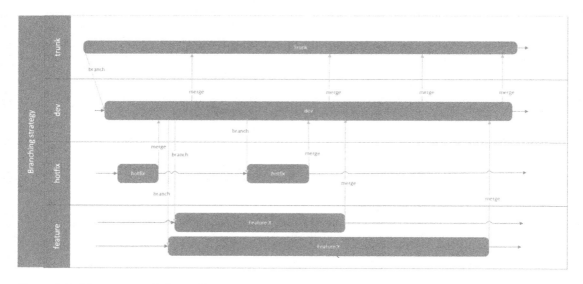

Figure 3-1. *The concepts of a branching strategy*

Using Git

Since Git is an included add-on to Visual Studio 2015 and is quickly becoming one of the most popular version control systems, I think it's important to provide detail about using Git. The concepts of Git and its usage flow differs from the version control systems that have integrated into Visual Studio in the past, so while it's integrated into Visual Studio 2015, it's not fully integrated. There are certain tasks with Git that need to be performed outside of Visual Studio 2015. Fortunately, with each release of Visual Studio that integration is getting better and better.

Intro to Git

Git is one of the first mainstream version control systems designed inherently to be distributed. It was originally designed for Linux so Linux developers around the world could work on and contribute changes to the Linux source code.

Distributed in Git (and any other distributed VCS system that I'm aware of) means that there is more than one repository on multiple computers. Changes are added to a particular repository and then pushed to other repositories, usually in a batch fashion (pulling several commits at a time from one repository to another).

Since Git comes out of the gate being a distributed VCS, there is some unique terminology involved that we should cover first.

Repo

A common colloquialism for repository.

Fork

Since *distributed* infers multiple repositories, copies of an original or source repository need to be made. Since the usual intention is that changes may be merged back into the original, the term *fork* is used here to mean that the new repository is forking off from the original and your changes may or may not be merged back into the original.

Depending on your version control provider, forking is done in a UI, such as GitHub or GitHub Enterprise, as shown in Figure 3-2.

Figure 3-2. *Creating a forked repository in GitHub*

Remote

Again relating to distributed nature, forking an original repository usually means that the original is in a remote location. In Git parlance, all other repos are considered remotes. Normally a "remote" refers to a related repository. In our example of forking, the original repo is tracked as a remote to the new repo.

Clone

Although this is not required, when working with a fork of a repo, the fork is usually kept in a remote location and work is done on a local copy of the repository. Rather than forking that remote repository, you copy a remote repository to your local computer, which is called *cloning*. You're not really forking from this remote; you're using the remote as the source of truth (backups, working offline, etc.). So, once you fork an original you generally make a clone of the fork and work with the clone.

You clone a repository using the clone command:

```
git clone https://github.com/peteraritchie/LongPath.git
```

Upstream

When you clone a repo, the clone is considered the *upstream* repo. Your local Git repo will be configured to track the source of the clone as the upstream version so that when you want to copy all your local changes to the source of the clone, you don't have to remember the location of the clone. Another way to look at this is that an upstream version is the default remote version.

Working Directory

The Git repository lives in a particular directory (.git), and the files in the repository are copied to the local directory so that you can work with them. This local directory is called the *working directory*. You make changes to files in the working directory and Git knows the files have changed, but does not track them until you tell Git to put those changes in the repository.

Staging Area

As we described in the working directory section, Git does not track changes in the working directory (although it tracks files that are different from the repository). You have to tell Git about those changes and to track them. Git takes an opt-in approach in terms of what changes to track. In order to tell Git which changes to track, you *add* which files you want to track to a staging area. Once you have all the files in the staging area, you can tell Git to start tracking those changes. The files are then removed from the staging area and Git will begin tracking those files. (And not changing anything in your working folder unless a merge occurs, which should be rare because this is your local repository.)

To tell Git you want changed files in the staging area, you use the add command. Or if files are to be removed, you could use the rm command. For example:

```
git add
```

Or:

```
git rm oldfile.txt
```

To understand the relationship between the working directory and the staging area, Figure 3-3 may be helpful.

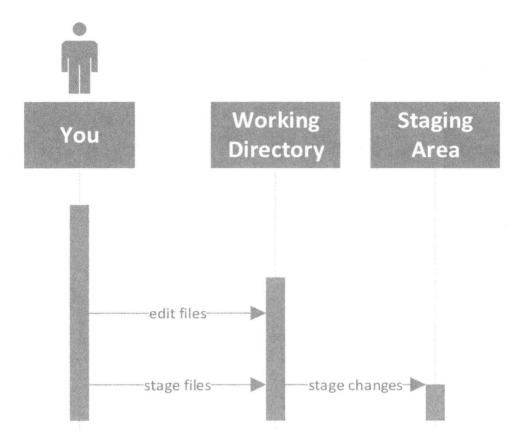

Figure 3-3. *The relationship between the working directory and the staging area*

Commit

After you make changes locally, you put those changes into the Git repository by committing them to the repository. Once you tell Git which files to commit by putting them in the staging area, you tell Git to commit the changes to the files in the staging area to the repository.

This is done with the commit command or using the commit feature in Team Explorer.

Although the add command exists to add files first to the staging area so that their changes can be committed, you can do that in one step with the commit command and the -a option. This will add all changed files to the staging area before committing them. For example:

```
git commit -a -m "refactored to the circuit breaker pattern"
```

Origin

When using Git you will frequently encounter the term *origin*. By default, the *name* of the remote that is cloned is called the origin, for fairly obvious reasons. You can rename that origin remote anything you want.

Pull

Since any repo can be the upstream for many different clones, that upstream repo can be updated by other team members after you clone that upstream repo. You might not have made changes since those upstream changes were saved. If you have made changes since then (or you simply want the latest code from your upstream), you need to pull those changes down to your local repo, unlike with some other version control systems. This is done with the `pull` command and will automatically perform a merge (i.e., it will inform you of merge conflicts that you will have to resolve before you can save your changes to the upstream repo). See the section on push for more details on pull when working in Visual Studio 2015 Team Explorer.

Push

When you have completed the changes you want and you get your source code into a state that is safe to share with other team members (see later chapters on unit testing, etc.), you can save your commits to the upstream remote. The act of doing this is called *pushing* and is done with the `push` command or using the Sync feature in Visual Studio 2015 Team Explorer. It performs a pull and then a push (only the push if there are no merge conflicts). By default, the `push` command pushes to the upstream (if you remember, usually named origin), but the `push` command has the option to push to *any* remote that you have configured. More on pushing to other remotes later.

Master

With Git, the default name of the *trunk* branch or the *mainline* is *master*. Although you can rename it, master is a convention used in Git repositories. Not using *master* might be confusing to new team members and violates the principle of least astonishment.

Basic Flow

What I've described so far is the basic flow. The simplest useful usage flow with Git (you could never use remotes and upstreams, but I don't consider that a normal flow) is effectively to clone, change, commit, and push. That flow is outlined in Figure 3-4.

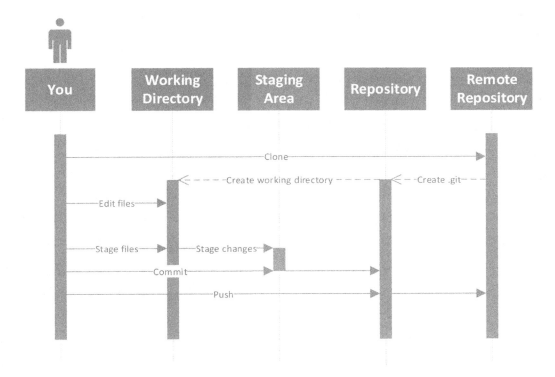

Figure 3-4. *The clone, change, commit, and push flow*

If you use Team Explorer in Visual Studio 2015 to perform commits, you need to think about the opt-out approach. Visual Studio 2015 automatically just takes all local changes (that aren't automatically excluded) and includes them when you tell it to commit to a Git repository. You must manually exclude files you don't want to be placed in the staging area when Visual Studio commits (i.e., opt-out). If you're familiar with Team Explorer, that won't be anything new to you.

Advanced Flow

The basic flow assumes that you're pushing changes into the upstream with no formal review. When you're working in teams, this is rarely the case. When you're working in teams, changes are generally reviewed and accepted before they are merged into the repo that is considered the source of truth. Git supports that model with an additional repo (the repo used to fork from) and changes required you to you make requests to put changes into that higher-level repo by sending your team members a pull request.

A *pull request* simply tells your team members that you would like a certain commit, or set of commits, to be merged (or pulled) into that higher-level repo. This can be done with the `request-pull` command, but more typically pull requests are created within the user interface of your Git provider, like GitHub or GitHub Enterprise. The owners of that repo would ultimately merge into their repo by invoking the `pull` command (remember when I explained that it supported a number of remotes?), but can often be done in the provider UI.

Ideally the owners would review the changes before accepting them and pulling them into their repo, but that's as far as Git supports the code review process. The flow is outlined in Figure 3-5.

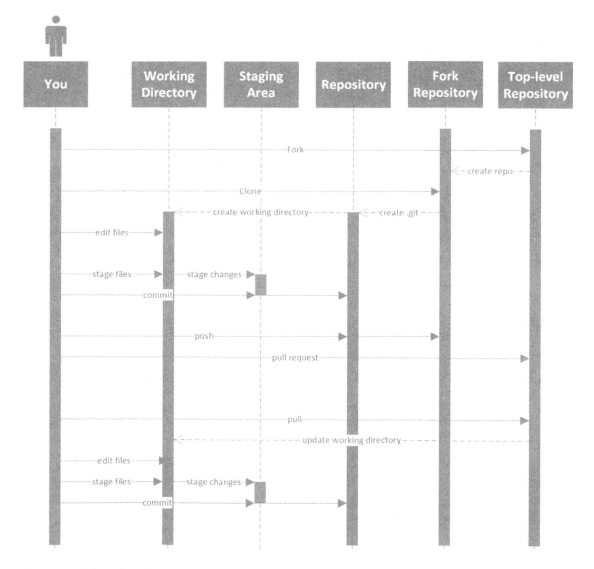

Figure 3-5. *The code review process as supported in Git*

This advanced flow introduces a bit of complexity and some extra steps/commands that you'll likely need to be able to handle. I generally drop down to using Git in the command line to perform these actions because Visual Studio 2015 doesn't have a user interface to do these sorts of things. I'll get into these actions based on what you want to accomplish rather than by each command.

Configure Higher-Level Upstream

When you clone a repo, you only clone the original repo and Git only knows about that remote (named origin) as the *upstream* repo. If you've forked from another repo and you're cloning that fork to your local machine, you'll often need to pull down changes from that higher-level upstream and push them up to the direct upstream (either without or with your changes). In order to do that, you need to configure that higher-level upstream as a remote in order for the push command to know what to push to. This is done with the remote command.

A remote in Git is reference as a URL, but we don't want to have to remember or type that URL when we want to push, so we add named remotes to the local repo's configuration. The remote command allows you to add a remote with the add sub-command. Now, I generally refer to that higher-level upstream as *upstream*, and the local Git repo is configured to consider the upstream as the "origin". If that confuses you, use something other than "upstream" in the following commands.

To add that higher-level upstream remote, invoke the following Git command:

```
git remote add upstream https://github.com/contoso/LongPath.git
```

You can view the configured remotes with the remote -v command, which would result in something similar to the following once you invoke git remote add:

```
origin      http://gitub.com/peteraritchie/LongPath.git (fetch)
origin      http://github.com/peteraritchie/LongPath.git (push)
upstream    https://github.com/contoso/LongPath.git git (fetch)
upstream    https://github.com/contoso/LongPath.git (push)
```

Get Updates from Higher-Level Upstream

Once you have configured the higher-level upstream, to get updates made by other team members to that repo, you can simply use the pull command. Since Git defaults to the configured upstream, to get it to pull from the higher-level upstream, you have to specify the name of the remote and the branch. For example:

```
git pull upstream master
```

Where upstream is the name of the remote and master is the name of the branch. If your working directory is checked out to master, your working directory will be updated as well, showing any merge conflicts you might have (which will need to be resolved before pushing). This updates your clone with the changes from the top-level repo and if you simply wanted to get your fork to the same point, you just need to invoke Git push or use Sync in Team Explorer.

Get Updates to Higher-Level Upstream

In scenarios where you do have higher-level upstreams, you almost always want to follow the pull-request model and have your changes reviewed before they are added to the higher-level (or top-level) repo. In which case, ignore the rest of this section.

In the off chance that you do need to avoid the pull-request flow, getting updates to the higher-level upstream is just a matter of invoking the push command, but including the name and fork to explicitly push to the non-default remote:

```
git push upstream master
```

OSS Flow

In open source software (OSS) projects, there's really no hard and fast rule about a particular flow.

If the project was started by one person and that person is really the only committer, they're probably using a flow identical or very similar to the basic flow described previously.

If the project was started by several people or is committed to by several people, they're likely using the advanced flow, or something very similar.

If you're thinking of creating your own OSS project, you might want to think about using the advanced flow to avoid having to move away from the basic flow when you add team members and want them to review your changes via pull requests.

It's easy to move from the basic flow to the advanced flow, it's just extra work. To move away from the basic flow to the advanced flow, you just need to consider what you've cloned to be the higher-level upstream, fork from that, update your Git remotes, and then continue committing to your fork and issuing pull requests to the original repository. Once you've forked the original repository (say http://github.com/ peter-ritchie/LongPath.git), you can get things set up like this:

```
git remote rename origin upstream
git remote add origin http://github.com/peter-ritchie/LongPath.git
git config branch.master.remote origin
```

If you've worked on multiple branches, you may have to remap those branches to origin again with more git config commands.

Using TFVC

Team Foundtioan Version Control (TFVC) is typically used from within Visual Studio. There are various options for working from the command line, like the TF command, but I find using those to be the exception rather than the rule. So, we'll talk about using TFVC from within Visual Studio 2015 for the most part.

Prior versions of TFS only supported being connected to the TFS server 100% of the time (and we all know how often we have 100% connection to any computer). Files tracked by TFVC would be read-only by default and they had to be checked out in Visual Studio in order to edit them. Visual Studio would handle that read-write change for you, if it had a connection to the TFS server. Editing them outside of Visual Studio often caused issues because Visual Studio couldn't know there were any changes to the file. If you were disconnected from the TFS server (e.g., working on a plane), you had to manually make the file read-write and face the consequences when you regained your connection to TFS.

Fortunately, a prior version of Visual Studio introduced an offline mode, known as *local workspaces*. A local workspace is a copy of the files as they existed in TFS when retrieved. Files are no longer read-only until checked out and TFVC monitors changes to files in order to synchronize correctly with the TFS server. The check-out and check-in processes still require a connection to TFS, as TFVC is still centralized.

For the most part, TFVC is easy to use. From the standpoint of Visual Studio 2015, you perform all the actions you want to perform on the files within Visual Studio. Apart from this, there are some caveats. Let's look at some generally accepted practices for dealing with these caveats.

Files Added to TFVC Must Be Part of the Project

The ease of use of Visual Studio 2015 being the frontend to your revision control has a slight caveat: all the files you want to track in revision control must be added to the project or the solution. For project-level files, that's pretty straight-forward. You just right-click the project or a folder within the project and choose Add ➤ Existing Item, as shown in Figure 3-6. The file will be added to the Solution Items folder (or created if it doesn't exist).

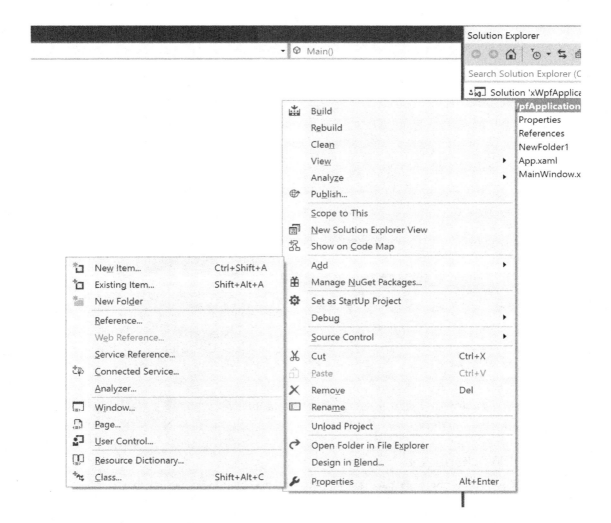

Figure 3-6. *For solution-level files, right-click the solution and click Add Existing Item*

If the name Solution Items doesn't do it for you, you can rename it or add a new Solution Item folder to the solution and then add files by right-clicking that folder instead (see Figure 3-7).

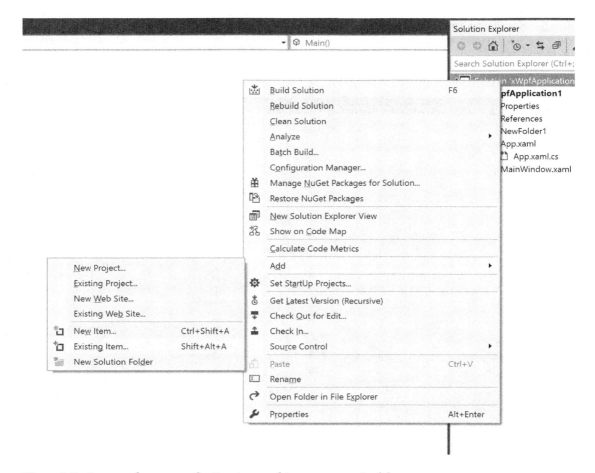

Figure 3-7. *You can also rename the item to something more meaningful*

Use Local Workspaces

The *local* workspace is the only workspace that supports working offline in any fashion that is close to useful. Fortunately it is the default type of workspace since Visual Studio 2012, so you just need to make sure you don't choose a server workspace. You still need a connection to a TFS server in order to create workspaces, local or not. But, once you create one, you can work offline and check in your files when you have a connection to the TFS server again.

Choosing TFVC or Git

Visual Studio 2015 includes some variety of TFVC (or Team Foundation Server) and includes Git integration. So, which one do you choose? Fortunately it's fairly easy to choose.

If you want the following features, consider using TFVC:

- Integration with TFS

- Gated check-ins

- Integration with work item tracking

If you need the following abilities, consider Git:

- Don't want to allocate TFS server

- Don't want to use hosted TFS

- Working offline

- Local commits

Git-tfs

Even if you need to use TFS on your backend for whatever reason (migrating away, forced upon you, etc.), you can still use Git locally or in addition to a hosted TFS repository. You can use tools like git-tfs to treat the TFVC repository as a remote and simply push changes up to TFVC the same way as with Git remotes.

Work Items

Visual Studio 2015 and TFVC give first class status to work items. However, the only work items that Visual Studio 2015 supports are via TFVC. If you're using TFCS, there are some generally accepted practices you can follow.

Know Your Team Template

Know your team template. Know if your team uses the Agile template, the Scrum template, or the CMMI template.

Don't try to work outside the work item flows. Working outside of the flow means the end result won't be what you want. Plus, it just confuses everyone.

Track Your Work

Just because you're using the Scrum or Agile template and you're working from a fixed set of work items on the sprint backlog doesn't mean the work items are perfect. One of the reasons Agile methodologies are used is because it's impossible to define all the steps needed to write or create software ahead of time. Each step you take in software can viewed scientifically, as a theory. You *think* what you've just created will work or is the right thing to do. The proof is whether it does actually work. If it doesn't, your theory is wrong and you have to backtrack. Clearly you can't predict that work, or the actual series of steps to take to get to where you need to be. In cases like that, be sure to track those differences with work items.

What you need to do to get the work done is what needs to be done; no one can argue against that. The biggest issue is the time it takes. If you estimated that story X would take five tasks and would take roughly five days and it ends up taking 15 days, you need to be able explain why. The more you do this, the better you will get at estimating work and the less likely that you'll need to add more work items.

Each project is different. Despite past experiences, there is some ramp up time to getting good at estimating all tasks for any specific project. Keeping track of actual work compared to estimated work will help you improve.

Associate Work Done with Work Items

As you do work, it should be to fulfill a work item in TFVC. As you commit work, it's best to associate that commit with the one work item that the work applies to.

You could, of course, do work for several work items before committing the changes. But one reason to use version control is to go backward in the history of the code to get back to a point in time. If you have multiple work items in one commit, going back to a state in the code cannot differentiate between those work items. If one work item was done correctly but the other wasn't (they should have independent acceptance criteria), you're forced to back out both and redo or remerge the other. That's a waste of time.

Integrate with Git

Unlike TFVC, Git doesn't inherently support any sort of work item. Fortunately when Visual Studio 2015 is integrated with Git, you can associate work items with a commit using a handy convention.

To associate a commit with a work item, simply end the commit comment with # and the number of the work item. For example:

```
git commit -a -m "Added correct object disposal logic #29174"
```

Reviewing Code

TFVC offers a distinct flow for team members to review code. Essentially Visual Studio 2015 creates a shelveset of the changes you want reviewed, and then you select who you want to review the code (and any comments you want to also include). Visual Studio 2015 then alerts the other team member (or members) that you are requesting a code view.

If you're used to Git, this is much the same as a pull request. After all, what's the point of reviewing the code if you aren't going to pull the changes into the mainline?

As with most things related to working with other team members, you request a review from Team Explorer. Once you open Team Explorer, if you are not at the home, you click the Home button. Then click the My Work button to see your current work. There are a few options you have in the My Work pane; the one we're interested in here is the Request Review link (right under the Suspend button). Clicking this link takes you to the New Code Review pane, as illustrated in Figure 3-8.

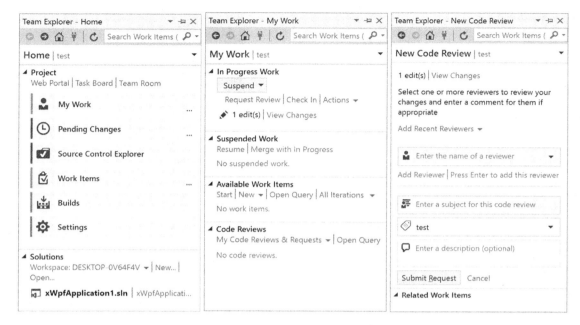

Figure 3-8. *Accessing the New Code Review pane in Team Explorer*

To create the request, enter the names of the reviewers who you want to review your code and add a subject and a description. Click Submit Request; the code will be packaged up as a shelveset (the same thing that Suspend does in the My Work pane). It then sends an alert to the reviewers so that they can review the code.

The review request can then be received by the requested reviewers and viewed within their Team Explorer, as shown in Figure 3-9.

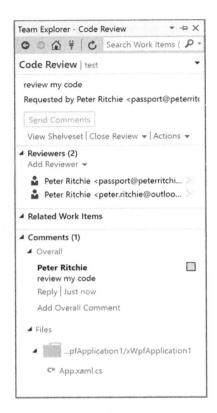

Figure 3-9. *A review request received by the requested reviewer*

The reviewer can then view the changes by clicking the View Shelveset link to see the files involved in the change, as shown in Figure 3-10.

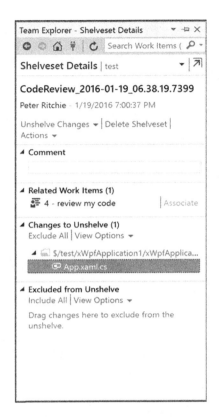

Figure 3-10. *Details of files involved in a change, accessed by clicking the View Shelveset link*

Double-clicking a file allows the reviewer to see the changes to that file, shown as a *Diff*. See Figure 3-11 for an example.

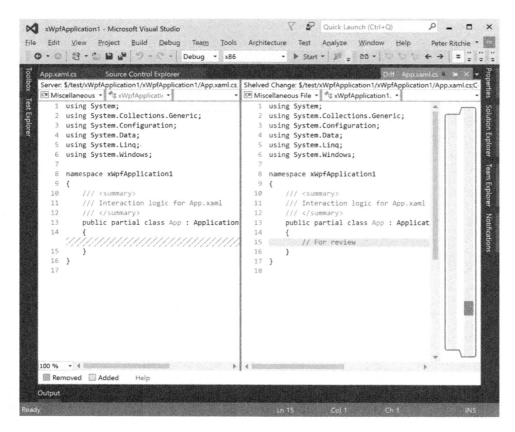

Figure 3-11. *Details of changes made to a file*

Once the reviewers have reviewed the code and checked the various criteria that a review should check, they can make edits to the file or, back in Team Explorer, they can add comments about the shelveset. Figure 3-12 illustrates this.

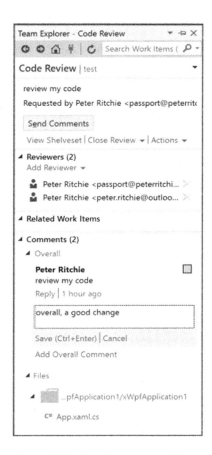

Figure 3-12. *A reviewer can add overall comments about a shelveset in Team Explorer*

Figure 3-13 shows that once the Send Comments button is clicked, the comments are available to the author of the change.

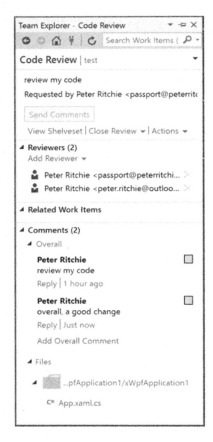

Figure 3-13. *A reviewer's comments available to the author*

What to Review

Visual Studio 2015 enables you to get a code review and or perform a code view, but it doesn't help you decide what to review. Each team needs to work out what is and isn't important to them, the level of detail involved in a review, and have it as detailed as needed. We won't possibly get into all possible things that *could* be reviewed, but let's look at some generally accepted code reviewing practices.

Style

I put style first only to get it out of the way. Conceptually there isn't much use to getting finicky about style—it's a religious issue to many people and can easily deviate into a religious argument that no one really wins. Braces at end of line, braces on own line, etc. don't really do anything about the quality of the code (despite what some may say) or its functionality. The style, however, is one way that team members communicate with one another. I won't get into specific styles that should or should not be chosen, I'll only say that team should collectively decide on the style that is acceptable.

A code reviewer should be fluent in this style and check to make sure that the code abides by that style. For the most part, I recommend using code reformatters that are configurable so that style choices can be checked/reformatted with the tool (such as JetBrains ReSharper). The code reviewer should simply check if the style is used and comment with something like "Please run the code reformatter" or something similar.

Static Analysis

There are a lot of really good static code analysis tools out there. Visual Studio 2015 has one. If there is no gated check-in policy to ensure a certain ruleset passes before check-in, a code reviewer should run static analysis on the code. If you're using the code review feature of Visual Studio and TFS, this won't be checked when a shelveset is made or received for review, so it might be worth checking despite being part of a gated check-in in the future.

Code Analysis is highly configurable. I do not recommend enabling all the rules. The complete ruleset is simply the complete ruleset; there are subsets of rules for different types of projects and applications. I do recommend at least the Minimum Recommended Rules ruleset, with one addition: enable CA2000. CA2000 ensures that objects are disposed of properly. If objects are not being disposed of properly, this can open a can of hard-to-reproduce worms.

Architecture

The code reviewer should be familiar with the architecture of the system. The reviewer should make sure that the code change does not violate the architecture in some way.

For example, in a layered architecture, lower-level layers should never directly reference higher-level layers. This double reference is called a *dependency cycle*. In the simplest case of this it should generate a build error because Visual Studio 2015 won't know which project to build first, or it chooses one and the other is out of date. In more complex cases, such as when a lower-level layer accesses a layer more than one layer higher, the build will work fine most of the time (maybe it will fail on the first build). But in this complex case, there will be occasional issues, such as code changes are ignored (an implicitly dependent assembly wasn't built before an explicitly dependent assembly), as well as occasional build errors. The only way to fix such problems is to remove the cycle.

Framework Usage

Every project uses at least one framework (e.g., the .NET Framework or jQuery). The reviewer should be fluent in the frameworks used and be able to see semantic errors or problems in the code (code that compiles without error but might have unobvious problems).

Although I pointed out that CA2000 should be enabled, proper disposal is a good example of this. The reviewer should know about disposing objects in .NET, know how to do it right, and be able to notice when it's not done right. In terms of framework usage, there's a short list of things the reviewer should be checking, discussed next.

Thread Safety

A framework makes certain assumptions about thread safety, and it's important that your code not conflict with those assumptions. If they do conflict, a hard-to-detect bug will likely be introduced. Just because thread-unsafe code runs once doesn't mean it will work all the time or is the right thing to do.

Thread-safety issues should be found and corrected as soon as possible, because they *will* cause problems later., perhaps on a computer with a different type of processor, a different number of cores, with a slower network, etc. When that happens it will be hard to track down and you won't know exactly which thread-safety issue is the cause if you don't catch them during code review.

73

Race Conditions

I brought up race conditions with thread safety, but race conditions also live outside of multi-threading. Your application can have a message-oriented design, for example. A message could be sent and the sending application could make assumptions on side-effects that the receiving application will apply and when they will be applied. If that's the case, *that's* a race condition.

The code reviewer must think about the side-effects and think about what's going on in the code, what the code expects, and what is going on in the rest of the system. Think about potential race conditions and point them out in the code review.

Sometimes fixing race conditions can be extremely complex. In the messaging example, one solution may be to employ a request-response pattern and require that the receiver send a response or an event when it completes processing the message. Adding that response could involve a lot of coding. If an event is a better choice, and there is no back channel to the requesting application, that could mean implementing and deploying a completely new channel. However, these options are better than having the system fail and lose data.

Pattern Usage

Code reviewers need to be fluent in patterns. They need to be able to detect partial or incorrect pattern usage and tell the author how to implement the pattern better.

In cases where a pattern is correctly used, they may want to suggest better naming. For example, if the adapter pattern is used and the name of the class involved is called `SomeManager`, they might want to suggest that the class be named `SomeAdapter` instead. When code naming corresponds to the pattern, there's better communication with the reader. It also tells the reader the intent of the code. `SomeAdapter` tells the reader, "yes, I *did* intend to implement an adapter pattern here". If the team has a habit of explicit pattern naming, it's that much easier to detect usage in the future. It's also a whole lot easier to detect incorrect usage. If the author created a class called `SomeAdapter` and it wasn't an adapter, you can enlighten them on the adapter pattern and make your team better for it.

Code reviewers should also be fluent in anti-patterns. These are patterns that may seem like they're a good idea, but aren't really. Singleton is an example of an anti-pattern.

Object-Oriented Design

In cases where code written in an object-oriented language is being reviewed, the code reviewers should be fluent in object-oriented design. The code should abide by object-oriented design and the code reviewers should point out when it's not following proper design or where it could be better.

There are all sorts of object-oriented design violations. The code viewer should be aware of some common ones, such as Liskov violations, exposing privates, multiple inheritance, God classes, etc.

Being fluent in patterns also helps with this; there are many anti-patterns based on object-oriented design.

Technical Debt

For the most part, everything described up to this point is technical debt if it's not changed. But it's important not to limit a review to a fixed set of criteria. Look for anything that you think will end up needing change in the future (for a tangible reason—we don't want code reviews to turn into a future-proofing exercise) and point it out in a code review.

If it's more of a gut feeling, verbally discuss it with the author or pair with the author. It never hurts to bring in someone more senior as a sounding board for your concerns. The less technical debt that can be introduced, the more maintainable to code will be later.

Propose Solutions

It's one thing to review code and point out problems, but it's also important to include solutions. If you want your team to learn rather than tell them how to do things, you might want to pair with them instead of providing a written code view and work with them to get a better understanding of the solutions. There's no hard-and-fast-rule that code reviewers need (i.e., with Visual Studio 2015 request code review). Go talk with them, pair with them, and/or have them walk through the code with you.

As time goes on, your team should require less and less help finding solutions.

There Are Exceptions

A good code reviewer is flexible. It's easy to be the difficult guy and demand that the code abide by your every rule, but many rules have exceptions. A good code reviewer knows when exceptions make sense and when they do not.

I mentioned the singleton anti-pattern earlier. The singleton is an anti-pattern because many feel it's just a glorified global variable. Object-oriented design is about encapsulating data and behavior in one class. Global variables violate that rule. But, almost every system needs a singleton or two. There may be a service pattern implementation that provides one and only one instance of a type of object. Technically that's a singleton, but when it makes sense in the context and in an object-oriented way, it might be acceptable.

Always think of solutions. If you can't come up with a solution yourself, maybe you're being critical for the sake of being critical.

Generally Accepted Version Control Practices

The following sections outline the version control practices you should follow for best results.

Commit Early, Commit Often

The longer modified source code lives outside the team unmerged, the greater the risk of merge conflicts.

Merge conflicts, although a fact of working in teams, should be avoided. Committing early and often minimizes that risk and frees team members to focus on more productive endeavors.

Do Not Commit Broken Code

This is the #1 rule of working with version control systems. Committing broken code causes friction for your team members. This applies to code that does not compile and code that does not pass unit tests. Code that does not have at least one unit test is code that does not pass unit tests.

Do Not Commit Commented-Out Code

Version control *is* your revision tracking mechanism. There is no need to commit commented-out code (unless it was always commented out and is an example, not something that was compiled in prior commits).

Commented-out code in the repo simply generates noise. Many version control systems allow for searches. Commented-out code increases the likelihood of false positives and slows your team members down. Do not commit commented-out code.

Do Not Commit Fewer Unit Tests

This is a bit subjective and could better be described as "do not commit with unit test code coverage lower than before," but that's a bit wordy. Do not commit fewer unit tests means if you've changed code the existing tests must pass, removing tests doesn't make the code "pass". If you've added code, there should be *more* tests.

The only scenario in which the code coverage is more important is when you remove code. If you remove code you likely have to remove tests; in this case, make sure the coverage of the unit tests does not get smaller.

In other words, always look for positive deltas in code coverage upon commit.

Avoid Version Branches

It seems like a logical thing, the next version is 2.3, let's make a branch for that and move forward. But, the version number is not tied to the code, it's tied to *when* that code is released and you can't know that when you start working on the code (i.e., when you *branch*). In many cases, *when* 2.3 is delivered (and thus *what* is in 2.3) is decided completely independently from the developers.

The worst case is when the release date changes and the version number is no longer meaningful. Developers will push back on changing the version number because of the impact on the branch, and this is natural. But the developers are no longer considering the best interests of the clients or the source code.

Choose feature branches instead and consider version milestones.

Tag Milestones, Don't Branch Them

This brings us to how to deal with version or releases. Simple, you use the tagging mechanism of the VCS. As soon as a release is accepted and deployed/delivered, tag the last commit from which the build was based.

The most common milestones are versions, but your team may have several other milestones, including end-of-sprint, feature completed, etc. It's up to your team to decide what its milestones are, obviously, but the previous sentence might offer a hint at a minimum. Any time you merge a branch (and especially if the branch is deleted afterward) is a good candidate for a tag. Although you can always find the commit from the merge, it's easier if you explicitly tag it with a meaningful name.

Use Feature Branches

Whenever new work starts, it is based on a feature or set of features. You could take the view that "vNext" will contain a set of features. That's a noble goal, but there are so many external factors that can change what features will be in vNext that lumping several features into one branch means you eventually have to figure out how to remove one or two. Feature branches maintain that separation and you can then merge the feature back in the development branch only when it's ready (quality-wise, delivery-wise, etc.).

Feature branches should use the development branch as the source branch because the development branch should include anything developers consider ready, not necessarily what was last deployed. (Although those two might be the same, branching from the development branch ensures that work that's in progress is not lost.)

Alternatively, you could use sprint branches so that work done in a sprint is independent and can be merged when it's complete. The branch would then be deleted once it's been merged.

Be Explicit with Source Branch When Branching (Git)

Git defaults to branching from the current branch when you invoke the branch command. This seems like a convenience but it's more of a burden. Normally you want to branch from a source branch that does not have a limited lifespan. For example, you'd rarely branch from a hotfix branch—that branch is there for you to get in, fix it, and then get out as quickly as possible. You normally want to branch from the "latest" code, which is the trunk or the development branch. While the Git branch command will branch from whatever the current branch is (or the checked-out), explicitly including the source branch name when branching will always ensure that you get what you want. For example:

```
git branch hotfix-1-jan-2016 master
```

Include Descriptive Commit Comments

Don't just add a comment like "see commits" or "see code". Review the commit early, commit often section. Your commits should be granular enough to easily describe in a sentence or two. If not, you're waiting too long to commit.

Summary

Working with revision control is a fundamental part of working with source code. In fact, it's become social media with sites like GitHub, Bitbucket, and Visual Studio Team Services. It's important to have a good understanding of the version control system that your team uses, both conceptually and syntactically. Understand the concepts, understand how to use it correctly, and understand how to get the most out of it.

Version control is used for specific reasons, and those reasons can facilitate other tasks that software development teams need to perform, such as working in parallel, merging concurrent work, code reviews, etc. Make sure that you're not making your revision control tool work against you by making an effort to do those other tasks in the most acceptable way recognized.

Next up, let's expand these patterns and think about patterns and practices from an architectural perspective.

CHAPTER 4

■ ■ ■

Design and Architecture: Patterns and Practices

Two things are clear about software. One is that the term *architecture* is often misunderstood, and the second is that every software system has an architecture. Many authors have written tomes of books on architecture, including what it means, how to do it, who should do it, when you should do it. This chapter really just scratches the surface of architecture and distills it down to what it is, what it tries to address, and some of its attributes. The chapter presents some patterns and practices when it comes to architecture.

Architecture

Every system has an architecture. A system has elements, there are relationships among the elements (structure), and there are principles that constrain the system's design and evolution. Some architectures can be simple because they reuse common architectures, designs, or language and thus require less description. Other systems are more complex as they may use a less common language to describe a new architecture or design. Whether a system is simple or complex, it has an architecture.

Historically, software architecture has been somewhat neglected. The formal description of the architecture is sometimes ignored, despite architecture being a property of every system. In situations like this, the architecture is assumed, leading the inability to follow any principles or constraints. This lack of communication of the high-level design often leads to a poorly designed system and the decisions about system constraints are not taken into consideration for lower-level design decisions.

Let's look at an example of where the architecture may be ignored. When someone creates a Windows application in Visual Studio they choose a template. Sometimes they might add class libraries to contain some of the code, but for all intents and purposes it is just a Windows application project (be it WinForms, WPF, Console, etc.). There is still an architecture to that application that should constrain all future design decisions.

In a Windows application, typically, all the logic resides in the application; there are no external services that perform logic, which limits the scalability of the system to vertically scalable. If the application is GUI-based, there is a limited ability to interact with the system and the ability of the system to interact with the external system. The system must run on a Windows computer and probably requires specific versions of Windows. There are sorts of other implicit decisions that have been pre-made when choosing a Visual Studio project template, decisions that define the elements of the system, their relationships, and constraints of future design decisions.

Not all templates are limited to the implied architecture. You can make additional architectural decisions and still use an application template in Visual Studio. For example, you may choose to create a WPF application but have it communicate with a REST service to perform certain logic or to access certain data. That is a decision that results in a different architecture. You may choose a formal description of that architecture. The description often comes in the form of architecture diagrams. We will get into more detail about architecture diagrams in Chapter 5.

© Peter Ritchie 2016

P. Ritchie, *Practical Microsoft Visual Studio 2015*, DOI 10.1007/978-1-4842-2313-0_4

In any system, it is important to describe the architecture. In systems that use a common architecture (or someone else's decisions) it is less important. However, in systems where there are significant decisions made about the focus of the system outwardly, it is vital to describe that architecture. The architecture *is* how the system constrains to those decisions; if it does not constrain to those decisions then the result is a *different* architecture. That different architecture may still be valid, it is just not the one that was decided upon. How well a design abides by those constraints defines how well the system meets the needs it was supposed to solve.

To a certain extent, architecture is about the high-level *what*s and *how* the system outwardly communicates.

Design

There are still design decisions that need to be made about any system, despite there being an architecture, either implied or explicit. Those decisions are equally important in a system and are ultimately constrained by the architecture of the system, whether it is implied or explicit.

Design embodies the internals, or is inwardly focused. It focuses on the algorithms, the internal data structures, etc. The design must take into account the architectural decisions and constraints of the system in order to correctly implement the system.

The design is concerned how about the *how*s and inwardly-focused concepts: the algorithms, data structures, etc.

Patterns and Practices

A maintainable system is consistent in its architecture and design. The architecture and design follow and promote certain patterns and practices. In order to achieve maintainability and quality and complete in a reasonable amount of time, an architecture defines some of the patterns and practices that should be followed in the design and implementation of the system in order to reduce the scope of technology. It's not that any other technologies are bad, but at some point you can't just have a patchwork of technologies, each following different patterns and practices. There should be a theme to the use of technology and the architecture should describe that constraint.

A design is often focused on how it implements the functionality of the system—the functional requirements. There are aspects of a system that don't pertain to the behavior of the system; they pertain to the non-functional requirements. The architecture of a system generally ensures that the non-functional requirements are fulfilled. Let's have a look at some patterns and practices relating to non-functional requirements.

Non-Functional Requirements

When we think of architecture, some very common non-functional requirements come to mind, such as scalability, availability, and operability. But those are just some of the more exciting non-functional requirements. Truth be told, the architecture has to take into account many non-functional requirements. Some non-functional requirements like accessibility are often implied by other architectural decisions (like choice of framework). Other non-functional requirements like backup and documentation are more procedural or follow already-defined policies or procedures.

Let's look at many common non-functional requirements to see how they relate to architecture and architectural patterns.

Accessibility

As noted, accessibility is often implied from other architecture decisions. Accessibility is design and user experience geared toward supporting people with disabilities. As most applications use frameworks for the user experience, this "design" is usually just the acceptance of a framework that has accessibility features. A system is almost never the only software running on a system and the accessibility features usually must be common or consistent across the operating system.

Fortunately, there is great support for accessibility across many frameworks. Accessibility rarely needs much thought in modern software systems. The great support in the frameworks really just means that designers and developers need to do the right thing—the framework supports most or all of the required accessibility features.

Auditability

Auditability is the ability of an auditor to inspect the interactions within a system by users.

What is audit data? That can vary from project to project. This can be heavily affected by regulatory requirements. Some businesses are required to audit specific user actions, in which case these actions should be auditable. In general, who accessed what data and when and what they did to the data needs to be audited. Auditability could be as simple as logging all that information each time data is accessed.

Practices

What is involved in collecting audit data? That also varies from project to project. For some projects, it's sufficient to simply log information to the system logs. This could be as simple as including "audit" in the log message, it could be the use of a custom log level (like "AUDIT"), or it could be that audit log entries are logged to a specific destination (like an EventLog).

Data access, especially in systems requiring auditability (those with some level of regulation), often involves personal information. In these cases, it's important to be able to log who accessed the personal information but to not log the personal information. Personal information in a log is open to anyone who can read the log and thus who accessed it in the log cannot be audited. This means logging a *representation* of the personal information, like a database key ID or some other impersonal information. This can be a variety of things and what is and isn't personal information may be specific to your organization (e.g., a name by itself may be considered impersonal, whereas a name and address would be personal). The practice here is to understand and recognize what is and isn't personal information, log access to personal information, and not include personal information in the log.

Patterns

Aspect-Oriented Programming

Aspect-oriented programming (or AOP) is a pattern of design that separates cross-cutting concerns from the business logic. This generally follows the *open-closed principle* by keeping the business logic closed for modification (i.e., support for the cross-cutting concern does not require modification of the business logic) by making the code open for extension (i.e., extending to support one or more cross-cutting concerns). Cross-cutting concerns include things like logging and auditing, but also may include things like error detection and exception handling, input validation, monitoring, caching, etc.

Aspect-oriented programming gets its name from the principle that the cross-cutting concern is separated into its own units or modules, which are then called *aspects*.

Aspect-oriented programming is generally implemented through the use of frameworks. These frameworks take one of two forms. One form is a framework and post-compilation (or sometimes, pre-compilation) environment that performs *weaving* based on attributes, configuration, or conventions. The other form is through the use of an API or library to perform wrapping, decoration, injection, delegation, etc.

There are several tools that do code weaving, such as PostSharp. PostSharp does this through configuration where you tell it which aspect is your audit aspect and configure the project settings to use it.

Decorator Pattern

When you don't have an aspect-oriented framework, you can get some of the same functionality with dependency inversion and the decorator pattern.

As you will see with the dependency inversion principle (Chapter 7), dependencies should be on abstractions (or interfaces). We can define what we want to be decorated by defining an interface. In the context of auditability, let's look at another pattern—the repository pattern. We could use the repository pattern to model data access and create an interface for the repository, for example IBankAccountRepository in Listing 4-1.

Listing 4-1. Using the Repository Pattern to Model Data Access and Create an Interface for the Repository

```
public interface IBankAccountRepository
{
    decimal Deposit(decimal amount);
    decimal Withdraw(decimal amount);
}
```

Suppose another class used an instance of that interface, like BankAccountCompounder shown in Listing 4-2, for example.

Listing 4-2. Another Class Using an Instance of the Preceding Interface

```
using System;

public sealed class BankAccountCompounder
{
    private IBankAccountRepository repository;

    public BankAccountCompounder(IBankAccountRepository repository)
    {
        if(repository == null)
            throw new ArgumentNullException(nameof(repository));
        this.repository = repository;
    }
    //...
}
```

A new class that implements IBankAccountRepository could be created, wrapping the standard repository (like BankAccountRepository) and could be implemented to perform auditing functions. See the example in Listing 4-3.

Listing 4-3. A New Class that Implements IBankAccountRepository

```
using System;

public sealed class AuditingBankAccountRepository : IBankAccountRepository
{
    private IBankAccountRepository repository;
    private IAuditor auditor;

    public AuditingBankAccountRepository(
        IBankAccountRepository repository, IAuditor auditor)
    {
        if (repository == null)
            throw new ArgumentNullException(nameof(repository));
        if (auditor == null)
            throw new ArgumentNullException(nameof(auditor));
        this.repository = repository;
        this.auditor = auditor;
    }

    public decimal Deposit(decimal amount)
    {
        auditor.AuditActionStart(
            Actions.Deposit,
            System.Security.Principal.WindowsIdentity.GetCurrent());
        try
        {
            return repository.Deposit(amount);

        }
        finally
        {
            auditor.AuditActionEnd(
                Actions.Deposit,
                System.Security.Principal.WindowsIdentity.GetCurrent());
        }
    }

    public decimal Withdraw(decimal amount)
    {
        auditor.AuditActionStart(
            Actions.Withdraw,
            System.Security.Principal.WindowsIdentity.GetCurrent());
        try
        {
            return repository.Withdraw(amount);

        }
        finally
        {
            auditor.AuditActionEnd(
                Actions.Withdraw,
```

```
                    System.Security.Principal.WindowsIdentity.GetCurrent());
        }
    }
}
```

Now `AuditingBankAccountRepository` can be passed to the existing `BankAccountCompounder` and auditing will occur when `BankAccountCompounder` is executed without any changes to `BankAccountCompounder`.

Since `AuditingBankAccountRepository` uses the dependency inversion and utilizes an `IBankAccountRepository`, any number of `IBankAccountRepository` implementations could be used to perform more than auditing, including logging, authorization, security, etc.

Availability

Availability is the time a system is running and able to be used. This is sometimes considered uptime. Many systems do not have a 100% availability guarantee, but have a certain percentage of time where availability is guaranteed. This availability is generally above 99% and sometimes called "x 9s" of availability, where x is the number of 9s in the guarantee. For example, if there is a 99.99% availability guarantee, that's four 9s.

Architecting for availability can be very complex. The root of the solution is to be able to provide resources to users almost all the time. For this to occur, you need to know how many users your system will have and know what resources the users will need while using it. In terms of web-based applications, this is generally a number of users per second and knowing how many resources are required to service each user. You also have to take into consideration *spikes*—when an above average number of users simultaneously use the system. Handling average user load can be easier than handling spikes. You can architect a system to always have the resources online to handle the largest expected spike, but that is problematic. This can be very expensive, for one. A spike could take much more resources on average for a small amount of time. If these resources were online all the time, this could cost the organization much more money than necessary.

Practices

Typically, availability is architected so that the system is available 100% of the time; the downtime is a portion of time the system is taken down for servicing or updates. A system can be architected so that it can be serviced or updated *in situ,* or without taking it down. But providing a realistic uptime guarantee that is between 99 and 100% allows for more realistic planning in the cases where the system must be down. It's better to give users the right expectations rather than have surprise downtime.

So, how do you architect for near 100% availability? Well, tomes have been written on the topic. Although it depends on your circumstances, there are basic traits of highly available systems and patterns that can be used to achieve high availability (HA).

For one, highly available systems are *scalable*. Although availability is its own non-functional requirement, let's jump from availability right into scalability to continue addressing availability.

Scalability

Scalable systems respond to extra load by distributing that load across elastically available (or statically available, normally dormant) resources. Scalability requires that the workload be able to be divided among the resources. This means that each item of work is well defined and is independent at some level from all the other work that needs to be performed. There may be dependencies between the items of work, but their execution must be mostly independent. This means that work can be distributed to any number of resources for execution and something manages the collecting of the results of that work into a response or passes it along as another unit of work.

Scalability Patterns

Many patterns for scalability address the ability to manage those items of work independently. All these patterns stem from creating highly-decoupled systems. Let's look at some of those patterns.

Message Orientation

One simple way to break work down into smaller units is to break them into messages. There are a variety of message types to coherently view that work, including commands, queries, events, etc. Each message would be processed independently and thus offers scalability such that more resources can be given to the system to handle extra load without architecturally changing the system. To handle messages, a system must use some form of message queue.

A message queue can be at the heart of the system, or the system can use another technology where a message queue is at the heart of that technology, like buses/brokers, or even simply the use of HTTP (and load balancers, caching, content delivery networks, etc.). In architectures like this one, a process produces messages and another process receives and processes the messages. See Figure 4-1 for a diagram of this concept.

Figure 4-1. *A message queue*

That is not to say that message-oriented systems must send messages across process boundaries. Within a process, messages can be sent to other parts of the process internally. That can be application-specific, where one thread simply checks a queue of some sort (like ConcurrentQueue<T>). Or it may be framework-specific, where the framework being used is message-based. Windows graphical user interface applications are inherently message-based, where interactions with the user interface are processed by the application as messages. In Win32 applications, messages are processed by a main Windows procedure (WndProc) and in other Windows graphical user interface applications, messages are processed as C# events (like Windows Presentation Framework or WinForms).

How does that also affect availability? Well, now that we can have multiple message processor processes, we could have at least one process per availability domain. An application availability can be affected by several things, including upgrading, server type, Ethernet switch, power supply, server rack, data center, etc. If one process was created for each of those domains and was isolated within that domain (e.g., one process per server, one process per Ethernet switch, one process per server rack, one process per data center, and one process per group of computers that will be upgraded at the same time) then availability effectively becomes 100%. As long as you can provide effective process granularity. If you forget to take into account something that could cause your application to fail and don't isolate it from all the other processes (e.g., a database), there is a risk of downtime.

Once a system embraces message-orientation, other patterns could be employed to manage the messaging. Let's look at some of those patterns.

Command-Query Responsibility Segregation

Based on Command-Query Separation (CQS) , which separates write operations (commands) from read operations (queries) when designing methods, Command-Query Responsibility Segregation (CQRS) takes the separation of commands from queries to the architectural level of a system. Although not an architecture in and of itself, the CQRS patterns impact a system's architecture drastically. CQRS suggests that not only should commands (writes) and queries (reads) be separate but they should also be segregated from one another at an architectural level. This means that there are separate components for each. This could be components in different processes or within the same process in different classes (the next level of abstraction above methods) or higher. This also generally means that commands operate on a different view of data than do reads. We call those *write models* and *read models*. The segregation can be taken as far as to have different databases or data stores (one may not be what is conventionally thought of a "database," such as an event store).

At the heart of CQRS is the definition and separation of responsibilities. This is a form of the single responsibility principle in that the architecture decomposes the system into components responsible for one and only one thing. Typically, in a CQRS-influenced system, there are command-focused components and query-focused components. The quintessential CQRS logical design can be seen in Figure 4-2.

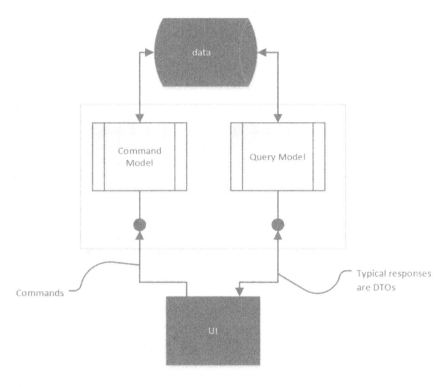

Figure 4-2. *The quintessential CQRS logical design*

In this design, a UI communicates with a component (either in process or out of process), which consists of a command model and a query model. Requests to change state or perform logic are sent as commands to the command model that updates the database. When a query of information is required the query goes to the query model, it responds with objects generally considered DTOs. That is, they are simply shapes or containers of information and do not have logic or behavior. In less simple designs, the command and query models are out-of-process, typically communicated as RESTful services.

That provides a very decoupled system but may not be as scalable as necessary. A more advanced design could further separate concerns by providing domain storage (often stored as events or message representations of how the data changed) and a read model, as seen in Figure 4-3.

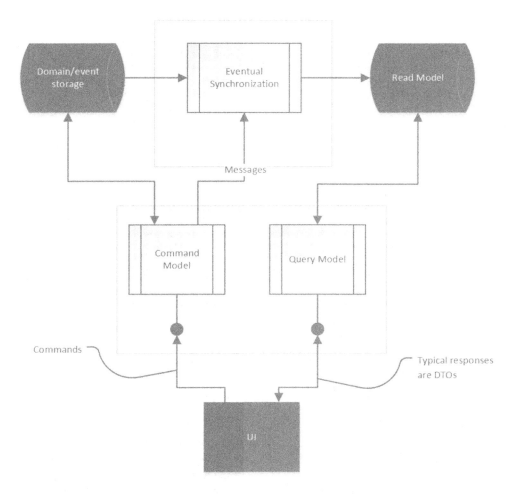

Figure 4-3. *A more advanced design that provides domain storage and a read model*

In this more advanced design, the read model is eventually consistent (not strongly consistent in all operations) and updated through the processing of messages that contain the information about how the data changed (typically the events). This design allows the domain model storage and the read model storage to utilize database technologies geared to their respective usage (write-heavy or read-heavy). Structure of the read model typically mirrors the DTOs being requested of it (or very denormalized) to facilitate rapid and scalable reads.

Systems employing CQRS are typically task-based; they don't simply mirror the data in the database and operations like create, read, update, and delete/archive can be performed on them. These systems are typically focused on how the user performs tasks and arguably take on a more domain-driven design methodology, focusing on data last (as a means to support the tasks).

Unit of Work

What message-orientation and CQRS effectively do is reduce coupling to a unit of work. The unit of work pattern typically involves modeling a database operation transactionally. The unit of work pattern manages all the data involved in the operation and manages a *business transaction* at the application level, abstracting whether or not a database transaction is involved from the rest of the application. It also abstracts the actual data from the rest of the application so that the rest of the application can continue with the data independently.

That abstraction of the business transaction is effectively the same with message orientation and CQRS. The processing of the message becomes the unit of work and the involved data becomes independent from the rest of the application by the message containing a copy of the data.

CQRS specializes message orientation by distinguishing between commands and queries and moves the responsibility to process each into separate processes.

This unit of work separation and the resulting level of decoupling offers a lot of flexibility. The most notable, and the original intent of, unit of work is the abstraction of the data involved with the unit of work from the rest of the application. With the unit of work pattern this allows the actual database operation to be independent from the unit of work interface, allowing the database operation to be executed only when the unit of work deemed it to be necessary. The unit of work would then track all the data involved and determine how that data could be written to the database transactionally. In the case where a database transaction was unable to be employed, the Saga-like pattern could be utilized and could model a transaction by performing the compensating actions in order to perform a "rollback". Of course, with this pattern, true ACID consistency is not possible because data changes are not entirely isolated.

Once we have the level of decoupling (of unit of work and data from the rest of the system), where, when, and in what order that work is performed can vary from situation to situation. With each unit of work being decoupled from other units of work, we can freely perform that work on any number of threads, processes, or computers. This allows our application to scale horizontally with no logical limits. You're clearly limited by the amount of physical hardware and money, but those limits are effectively intangible.

Workflow

This unit-of-work method of decoupling is fine and allows work to be executed concurrently, but what if you want some work to be done sequentially or model work that is dependent on the result of other work?

Fortunately, just because some code processes a message doesn't mean it can't also send messages. This is how we can chain work together to produce a workflow. As one unit of work completes, it sends out a message with the results of the unit of work so that other units can process it.

This method of chaining work means effectively coupling two units of work together because the first unit of work needs to know to send a message requesting work from the other unit. Sometimes even that level of coupling is too limiting. This forces the first unit of work to know how to communicate with the other and that there are a certain number of units of work dependent on its result. If that needs to change, the code needs to change and the system needs to be redeployed.

You can reduce the level of coupling even further through the use of a particular type of message: an event. Rather than the first unit of work *sending* a message to another to perform some work, it can simply *broadcast* a message for any number of listeners to subscribe to and perform any action they see fit. This allows the code and the process that executes it to continue doing what they are doing without modification while other processes can be added in the future to perform necessary processing. The event effectively notifies other listeners that something has happened, or completed, and provides the data involved (e.g., the outputs).

Using events for workflows also allows work to be broken down further, especially if operations can be performed concurrently. For example, let's say that one message processor processes new account information. That processor can simply broadcast an event that a new account has been created. Other event listeners could then receive that event and perform work in parallel. One listener may create an entry in a database and another may send an email to the account holder welcoming them to your services.

Backup Requirements

Non-functional requirements for operability often require some level of fault tolerance that tolerates failure of the data store or the database. This manifests itself as a requirement for backups and restores.

Typically, this non-functional requirement is implemented via features of the database system (DBMS) used to store the data. But sometimes with complex and highly scalable systems, the "database" often spans many different DBMS instances and different database types (it's heterogeneous in that case).

In cases where the data landscape of the system is complex and heterogeneous, the system may need to be designed to perform backup and restore as a functionality, using DBMS functionality where appropriate. For example, simply restoring one database from backup would not leave the system in a coherent state. The invariants of the system may only be known by the system and cannot simply be modeled within the database, otherwise one database and the system must take on the responsibility of ensuring those invariants during restoration.

Extensibility Requirements

Extensibility is not often a non-functional requirement, it's more commonly a functional requirement. The system or application under development needs to be extensible in very specific ways. Applications are specifically extensible in their ability to be programmed—sometimes in scripting ability and sometimes in their support of add-ons or extensions (no big surprise).

The ability of a system to be extensible in other ways can be viewed as a type of decoupling known as the *open-closed principle* (OCP).

The open-closed principle states that software should be open to extension, but closed for modification. What this is saying is that software can be made to do new things (extended) without having to modify existing code.

Without modifying existing code, that existing code can continue to function with a known quality without having that quality affected. This makes for more reliable systems because code is changing less frequently, is good for longer, and is being real-world tested more often.

Operability Requirements

The operability of a system is the system's ability to remain operational. There are many aspects that define operational and these vary from system to system. Basically, operability is the ability of operators to perform the tasks necessary to keep the system operational.

The operability of a system, although its own requirement, often is fulfilled by other non-functional requirements. Typically, these non-functional requirements come into play when addressing operability:

- Scalability

- Performance

- Security

- Recoverability

- Backward compatibility

- Monitorabiliy

There can be many other aspects to what makes a system operational, so be sure to analyze the requirements when considering the operability of your system.

Performance Requirements

Known best algorithms is probably the easiest practice to follow, in theory. While some algorithms are simply known to be the best at the time (like SHA512 as a secure hashing algorithm), what is "best" for any given circumstance may vary.

What is "best" for any given system, or even any particular scenario within a system, may be different. The recommended practice here is to measure and compare and then pick the algorithm that best suits the needs of the system at the moment for any particular scenario.

Recoverability Requirements

The recoverability of your system could be as simple as restoring backups or it could be as complex as restoring connections to multiple third-party services that your applications use. This topic is broad and context-sensitive, but some things to consider when addressing recoverability include the following:

- Dealing with backups.

- Restores (perform simulations or trials to ensure they work).

- Ability to repair hardware (extra parts, ability to move to different hardware, etc.).

- Ability to reinstall dependent software. If your software depends on a specific version of Windows, for example, make sure you can reinstall it to another computer.

- Documentation. Make sure other people know how the system works and how and in what ways they can recover.

- Research, plan, and test recoverability for your circumstances. Chances are, if you've never tried it, it's not going to work. You don't want to find out it doesn't work when you're trying to recover a system.

Reliability Requirements

Reliable systems are dependable and remain functional over a period of time. More reliable systems remain functional longer than systems that are less reliable. A reliable system is one that, in a specific environment with specific inputs, produces expected outputs.

Reliability is measured by testing software. Various testing techniques should be used to measure this reliability. Systems whose reliability does not meet certain criteria should not be put into production. The following is a non-exhaustive list of testing types that can be used to ensure a known level of reliability:

- *Load testing*: This is when a system is tested under load and certain performance metrics are gathered (like transactions per second, latency, etc.).

- *Functional testing*: Probably the most understood type of testing, it tests how the system works and whether inputs produce the correct outputs with no other side-effects.

- *Regression testing:* This is some level of testing (functional, integration, etc.) performed after any bugs have been fixed. It measures whether the fix didn't cause another new bug to appear.

- *Integration testing:* In complex systems that involve more than one component, those components need to be integrated. This can be as simple as performing an install and smoke testing the software or it can be complex and involve many teams to perform many different actions and perform smoke tests to verify that integration was performed correctly.

- *Acceptance testing:* For any given functionality, stakeholders usually have criteria for success or acceptance criteria that defines whether something works or is complete. Acceptance testing is performed (usually by the stakeholders) to ensure that criteria has been met. This usually involves functional testing, but that depends on the stakeholder's criteria and could involve load testing.

- *Smoke/sanity testing:* Smoke or sanity testing is performing a small set of tests to ensure a system is of a minimal reliability to perform further testing. This type of testing could simply be functional testing of features that tend to break, or it could be a short series of checks to ensure all the required connections function properly in integration testing. What is and isn't part of a smoke test is entirely up to the system being tested.

- *Security testing:* Many systems need to verify that they are secure. Security testing ensures that a system is reliable in terms of security. There are many types of security tests; here's a non-exhaustive list:

  - Intrusion testing

  - Confidentiality testing

  - Authorization testing

  - Authentication testing

  - Injection testing

- *Fuzz testing:* Performing testing with invalid, unexpected, or random data. This is usually automated but could be based on other types of testing, like functional or security testing.

Robustness Requirements

We ideally would prefer to design and implement highly-reliable systems. But as we create highly-composable and highly-scalable systems, we introduce different risks for failure. Message-oriented systems, for example, introduce a dependency on a message channel (typically a message queue or a message broker) that can independently fail for reasons out of the control of the rest of the system. Highly-robust systems are systems that remain functional despite the presence of errors or failures.

Let's look at some of the practices involved in making a system robust.

Validation

Any given system has certain operating parameters; these are the scenarios in which the system is guaranteed to work, including what is and isn't valid input. One easy way to make a system robust is to verify that only data that is known to be valid is processed. All other data can be rejected to avoid error and failure.

Retry

With highly composed and distributed systems, components within the system communicate among other components by any number of channels. A *channel* is a means by which information can be transferred between two components and usually performed by third-party software or hardware. That could be another process (like a RESTful interface or a message queue) or could be another piece of equipment that's in a temporary failure state. Maybe a message queue is full or a network component is temporarily unavailable.

This can be compensated for by retrying operations. If a connection to a RESTful interface fails, for example, it can be retried in a couple of seconds with the assumption the problem is temporary and that it may eventually work. It's important to know what operations can be retried and what operations will never magically work no matter how often they are retried. With RESTful interfaces, for example, an HTTP error 503 (service unavailable) is generally temporary (and sometimes the reason and timeframe is included in the response) and retrying the request could work. Error 400, on the other hand, means the request is bad in some way and no matter how many times it is tried, it will still be wrong. There's no point in retrying operations that will never work.

Despite some operations potentially working after retrying, the application may not be able to retry forever or even after a certain amount of time. In cases like that, only a certain number of retries should be performed. Under certain circumstances the *circuit breaker pattern* could be used to avoid the operation in the future until it is deemed to be working again.

Traceability

In many systems, especially distribute systems, the ability to trace an action or the impetus of an action throughout the system is very important.

For example, a client application may ask a system that is proxied through one component to reach another that makes requests of several other components. It may be necessary to trace back from the action of one component to the other components involved upstream in the interaction.

This is most commonly required for detecting the root cause of failure in distributed systems. But this could also be for auditability and security. The action performed in component C may need to be traced back to the actions performed within component A—potentially a front-end interface and the person who performed the action.

Security

Security is a hot topic and an area of much scrutiny and research. Security is an area that has many patterns, too many patterns to discuss in a book focusing on Visual Studio. We can, however, talk about some of the areas that relate to Visual Studio application users.

There are lots of practices and patterns that anyone writing software in Visual Studio could use; let's look at some common areas related to security.

Authentication

If you're developing a Web API, web service, WCF service, or RESTful API, authentication will come up fairly early. If your API is pay-per-use or client-specific, you will quickly need to address authentication. Let's look at some of the typical practices involving authentication.

Let's focus mainly on ASP.NET. If you're reading a book on Visual Studio, you're more than likely using ASP.NET for web-based APIs. There are two types of authentication on the web. The first is intranet authentication.

Intranet authentication is when an application is logged in to a Windows computer that is connected to a private network. When the application connects to an intranet application on the local network, it can pass along a security token to the server that represents that you've been authenticated and who you are. This token can easily be populated by the framework you're using to connect to the API. For example, in .NET:

```
WebClient c = new WebClient
{
        UseDefaultCredentials = true
};
var text = c.DownloadStringAsync(new Uri("http://server/customers"));
```

This token is typically validated before your web app gets the user information, but the existence of this user information signifies that a user has been authenticated.

The other type of authentication is Internet authentication. This can have many flavors. The simplest when talking about an API is a client ID and a client secret. Typically, an administration portal generates the client ID and client secret for a particular application that wants to access the API. The ID and secret are then passed to the API via request headers. Passing them via the request headers ensures that the data is encrypted when using an SSL or TLS channel, unlike within the URL. For example:

```
using (var client = new HttpClient())
using (var request = new HttpRequestMessage(HttpMethod.Get, uri))
{
        request.Headers.Add("client_id", "my_client_id");
        request.Headers.Add("client_secret", "my_client_secrety");
        using (var response = await client.SendAsync(request))
        {
                Console.WriteLine(await response.Content.ReadAsStringAsync());
        }
}
```

Those aren't your only options, they are likely just the most popular or minimal implementations. Depending on your system, you may need much more involved security. Using a client ID and secret can be a bit insecure. Applications don't have to store the secret in the clear, but they can. A more secure route is to send a client certificate that is retrieved from a local certificate store (that presumably can be denied access or cleared). For example:

```
using (WebRequestHandler handler = new WebRequestHandler())
{
    var certificate = GetCertificate();
    handler.ClientCertificates.Add(certificate);
    using (var client = new HttpClient(handler))
    {
        var response = await client.GetAsync("https://example.com/customers");
        // TODO: use response, e.g.
        var responseText = await response.Content.ReadAsStringAsync();
    }
}
```

On the server side when detecting the authentication, this could take one of several forms. For the Internet authentication, it could be as simple as checking the request headers. For example:

```
var hasClient_id = this.Request.Headers.Keys.Cast<string>().Any(e => "my_client_id".
Equals(e));
var hasClient_secret = this.Request.Headers.Keys.Cast<string>().Any(e => "my_client_secret".
Equals(e));
```

Truth be told, you'd rarely do this in your server code; you'd likely be using an API gateway of some sort that does the authentication for you.

For the other methods, you're probably just looking for blanket authorization, whereby you authorize an API to be used by any authenticated user.

Authorization

Once authenticated, the identity of someone can be used to decide their authorization to use certain functionality. Typically, this is done by assigning roles. The identity would contain what roles the identity holds and thus what functionality was available to them.

In terms of generic .NET code, this can be done as follows:

```
var p = (WindowsPrincipal)Thread.CurrentPrincipal;
if(!p.IsInRole("CRM Users")) throw new UnauthorizedAccessException();
```

If you're writing ASP.NET MVC applications or APIs, this is slightly different and simpler. You can simply authorize roles to use specific controllers. For example:

```
[Authorize(Roles="CRM Users")]
public class ValuesController : ApiController
{
    //…
}
```

Protected Information

As detailed earlier, protected information like personally identifiable information needs to be treated differently. It needs to be protected. This type of information, when in the wrong hands, could have negative personal or financial consequences.

This type of information can be handled in one of two ways. You can simply encrypt it when at rest or in transit. This is sufficient to protect the information from anyone who doesn't have the encryption key. Sufficient encryption means that the encrypted data cannot be used to identify a person. One drawback of that is that the encrypted data cannot be used as identification, for example, to search on. For example, let's say I wanted to search for someone based on a phone number. If that information was encrypted, I'd have to decrypt each phone number of each record until I found the one I wanted. In cases like this, information can possibly be kept separate from other information so that it is not personally identifiable. For example, a phone number alone may not be deemed personally identifiable and you can store it alone, in the clear, so that it can be searchable.

The other way to protect the information is to store in-the-clear hashes of information. This allows you to perform searches to a certain extent (exact searches, most of the time) but also provides some flexibility. When hashing, it's best to use a cryptographically secure method to make it reasonably hard to reverse-engineer the information.

Principle of Least Privilege

As you develop solutions and run across situations that require security, authentication, or authorization, there is one principle I find to be very useful in guiding decisions made about these topics. This is the principle of least privilege.

The principle of least privilege details that for any access required, the level of access that is lowest in order to grant access should be used. Someone with Administrator rights will have access to read a user directory, but that's overkill. The particular user rights could be granted to read the directory. Or, if access is not for the owner, a role that grants only read access to the directory could be granted.

Anti-Patterns

Future-Proofing

Future-proofing an application or system is the act of architecting it in such a way as to avoid significant change as requirements or technology changes in the future.

An architecture that is future-proofed attempts to foretell or prophesize what will happen in the future that will impact the software. I've chosen specific verbiage here (foretell, prophesize) on purpose. I could have chosen "forecast" or "anticipate" to make the pattern seem more legitimate. But the process is the same—you are guessing at what might be needed in the future. This is problematic on many fronts.

The most problematic part of future-proofing is that it ignores requirements. The guess that something might be needed in the future *at best* matches a future requirement that has yet to be created. *At worst*, it completely conflicts with a yet-to-be-created requirement.

Guessing what requirements will be needed in the future also means you're guessing at what "success" means.

Symptoms and Consequences

Architectures that are future-proofed have design features that neither map to a specific requirement nor address accepted architectural or design best practices. And although implementing a best practice might seem like a good thing to do, if it's not in response to some form of requirement, it's really just future-proofing.

This is a design that is template-based or that attempts to make a lot of design decisions before even talking to stakeholders. Some of those design decisions may be things like database type/brand, use of caching, mapping (including object-relational mapping), etc.

Use of weakly-typed artifacts in a system is another sign of future proofing. The types are loose to accept future change. This offers flexibility at the cost of reliability; the weak types can allow the system to accept unrealistic values and put the system in an unknown state.

Causes

Future-proofing is a natural response to software. Creating software is largely inventing things that have not been created before. If they haven't been created before, there needs to be a process to analyze and prove the solution to the problem. This is, by definition, an empirical process. It includes testing theories and proving the theory correct or incorrect. The process of proving a theory wrong, creating a new theory, implementing it, and proving it right (or wrong, and repeating) is time consuming. If it's not done correctly, it's also error prone. Naturally we want to avoid needless work and low-quality code. In response, we try to create systems that address a looser definition of "success" to avoid that extra thought and implementation.

Exceptions

There's really no exception to this anti-pattern because you should always be addressing requirements and avoiding accidental complexity. If you address requirements (non-functional or otherwise) in your architecture, then you're not performing future-proofing.

Solution

There are many patterns that address non-functional requirements specifically to avoid many of the problems that result from changing already-implemented code. For example, highly-decoupled architectures, highly-scalable systems, etc.

When an architecture is created that addresses scalability, cohesion, decoupling, maintainability (complexity), etc., it addresses the effects of change. This creates a more agile architecture that can respond to change faster and with better quality and helps reduce the pain-points that come from the inevitable changed or new requirement.

See the section called "Accidental Complexity" for more information.

Monolithic Architecture

A monolithic application or system is built as a single unit. As an application, that generally means one binary entry point that relies on zero or more libraries or assemblies. As a system, that means several binary entry points (or processes) that rely on the execution or presence of one or more other processes. A monolithic system could be based on a client-server or n-tiered architecture such that the processes consist of a front-end user interface, a middleware or business logic tier, and a back-end data tier. An n-tier application like this is "monolithic" when higher-level tiers cannot function without the ability to connect to the lower-level tiers and when all the tiers need to be deployed at once.

Symptoms and Consequences

With *greenfield* systems, the monolithic architecture most closely matches the initial production deployment of the application. The planning of the initial deployment can often near-sightedly influence the architecture of the system. Initially there may be little consequence to this architectural pattern, but over time this architecture can cause friction with maintenance and updates.

Updates to a system may be small or large. With small updates, a monolithic architecture requires the entire system to be updated at once. This has several negative consequences. The major consequence of course is that as the system becomes more complex over time, deployment becomes more and more time-consuming and riskier.

It's highly-coupled. With any software development project, the aspect that causes pain requires that that pain be felt continuously and compensated for in order for that the pain to be addressed. Monolithic architecture accepts and promotes a high degree of coupling. As time moves on, monolithic architectures become more and more resistant to change. Those changes often include change in topology, change in platform, change in resources, etc. The needs and atmosphere of a system change over time. With no need to address coupling as part of the architecture, the monolithic architecture does not view tight coupling as a pain-point, so it is not addressed inherently nor continuously.

Required change often revolves around the use and processing performed by the system. It's not out of the ordinary to see usage of a system go up over time, resulting in the system performing more and more processing. A monolithic architecture is tightly coupled to the hardware resources that it is deployed to. As a system is required to support more and more users (and as a result, more and more processing power), a monolithic architecture consequently limits the degree to which it can scale to support extra processing by limiting vertical scalability. A monolithic system is hard to change to different quantities of hardware resources (horizontal scaling) and scales only by faster and larger resources (vertical scaling). Vertical scaling is limited and costly.

A monolithic system is highly-coupled. Any change to one part of the system often has a far-reaching ripple effect throughout the rest of the system. If a small change cannot be made to a system without having many adverse effects to the rest of the system, it's likely a monolithic system.

Causes

Simplicity. A monolithic system is easy to reason about. Coupling is usually logical or obvious and easy to understand. The resulting system probably has one or very few "moving parts" (components to deploy), making the system easy to deploy.

Anemic requirements. Requirements that lack depth and are narrow of focus can make a project or system appear simpler than it actually is. If the system is viewed too simply, a monolithic architecture may seem like the best solution when it fact the actual complexity would result in it being counterproductive.

Focusing on one platform. Often when a system is implemented in one and only one platform, there is a tendency to put all the components together. This is partially due to the fact that it's possible to put all the components together. The resulting monolith actively prevents the use of other platforms and reduces the system's agility or response to change.

Lack of cohesiveness. Cohesiveness in software development and architecture was defined by Edward Yourdon and Larry Constantine as *the degree to which the elements of a [component] belong together*. Without thought or analysis of cohesive sub-components of a system, the cohesive parts become the whole. The lack of cohesive separation of responsibilities, functionality, data, etc. limits cohesiveness to the entire system, which almost dooms the project to being monolithic.

Exceptions

If all the causes of a monolithic system are explicitly defined as requirements or features of a system, it may be the exception to monolithic architecture as an anti-pattern.

It's counterintuitive to think that a system should have anemic or shallow requirements. So, the exception to monolithic as an anti-pattern really is that the system is simple, needs to be implemented on one platform, and be deployed as a single entity. Examples of this could be a simple console or WPF application.

Solution

The pain and friction points of a monolithic application almost always revolve around the degree and type of coupling. That coupling is often that the entire application is coupled to a single binary, but could also be that *tiers* have a one-to-one coupling. The solution to the monolithic architecture is to introduce decoupling at the binary and process levels. An n-tier application is decoupled at the process level, so that decoupling often means going deeper so that any one-to-one coupling is at a logical level. In effect, the one-to-one coupling becomes a one-to-at-least-one coupling. That decoupling can simply take on the form of an RESTful HTTP request so that the request can be load-balanced to two or more tiers. Or the decoupling could take on a delegation pattern so that a third dependency acts as a broker facilitating communication between the individual components.

As mentioned earlier, one specific solution is decoupling at the process layer and moving communication between code/units/modules to HTTP. One architectural pattern for this is the microservice pattern. The microservice pattern basically suggests decomposing a system into a set of collaborating services communicating via an over-the-wire protocol like HTTP or AMQP. Each component in a microservices architecture implements narrowly related functionality. Although this can technically be viewed as a broker because the decoupling between requestor and responder can have components like load-balancers inserted, we don't view it as a broker. Let's look at brokers more closely.

You can take the interprocess architecture and over-the-wire decoupling to another level by viewing what is communicated over the wire as messages and have a third component to broker that communication of those messages between components. The communication between RESTful HTTP microservices can be viewed as sending and receiving messages, but it's a single type of messaging: request/response. Using messages in a message-oriented architecture takes that communication to another level to support different messaging types, such as point-to-point, request/response, pub/sub, and so on.

Enterprise Architecture

Enterprise architecture, although it's only been around about 20 years, has become a fairly well-defined role within the enterprise. The Federation of Enterprise Architects defines enterprise architecture as:

> *Enterprise Architecture is a well-defined practice for conducting enterprise analysis, design, planning, and implementation, using a holistic approach at all times, for the successful development and execution of strategy. Enterprise Architecture applies architecture principles and practices to guide organizations through the business, information, process, and technology changes necessary to execute their strategies.*

Although there may be other definitions, they do not stray far from this one. Enterprise architecture is a strategic role that leads the enterprise to reach its vision and strategic business goals.

Why Use an Enterprise Architecture?

An enterprise needs to function consistently across its organizations. Lessons learned in one area of the enterprise need to be clear to other areas of the enterprise.

Specific solutions to specific problems focus on the locality of the problem and can ignore the broader picture or ignore higher-level business goals. A role to holistically address problems across the enterprise in a strategic way and account for longer-term strategies is needed.

Enterprise-wide solutions need clearly defined and strategic architectures that address enterprise-wide problems and strategies. This way, specific solutions can address the needs of the enterprise as a whole, now and in the future.

What Is an Enterprise Architect Used For?

An enterprise architect can be called upon to perform many tasks, depending on the context. That context can be reactive or proactive. An enterprise architect may be called upon to analyze existing business problems and provide requirements, guiding principles, and conceptual models so that solution architects can find solutions to business problems. Enterprise architects may be called upon to analyze the current state of the enterprise and work with stakeholders to understand the future state (vision, strategy, etc.) to provide a roadmap so the enterprise can reach its future state.

Regardless of reactive or proactive reasons, enterprise architects often analyze business structure and processes to make decisions and recommendations that address the goals of enterprise architecture. That architecture may not be limited to IT/IS solutions. Those goals are often related to effectiveness, efficiency, agility, and endurance of the enterprise.

Enterprise architecture provides strategies for changes to policies, procedures, and projects to plan for business environment change and support business development.

In addition to strategies, vision, and recommendations, typical architectural information is provided by enterprise architects. This includes information like models that describe business functions, capabilities, roles, structure, relationships, etc. As well, enterprise-wide architecture policies and principles are provided along with standards and procedures and recommended practices.

Solution Architecture

Solution architecture is concerned with the architecture of a distinct solution. That solution may be the definition of a complete system, it may be the definition of one or more new components to a system, or it may be the architectural definition of a change to an existing system.

That sounds pretty straight-forward, but what does "solution" mean? It may seem obvious to some, but let's narrow down that definition. For the purposes of solution architecture, a solution is a cohesive set of specific business functionalities that are relevant and fulfill their requirements.

Solution architecture cannot be performed in isolation. The mere notion of solution mandates that a business problem existed and was communicated by stakeholders (i.e., a relationship with stakeholders exists and conversations and discussions have occurred or are on-going). It should be assumed that for any business domain, there is more than one business problem that needs a solution. Therefore, it should be expected that there will be more than one solution architecture and that there may be more than one solution architect. This means that broader, enterprise-wide principles and constraints need to be taken into account for any given solution (i.e., a relationship with an enterprise architect exists and conversations are on-going).

Why Use a Solution Architecture?

The architecture, design, and implementation of the individual components that comprise the solution to a business problem require orchestration. A bridge is required between the tactical implementation and deployment components and business strategy.

Tactically addressing business problems needs to be performed in a way that aligns with the strategy of the enterprise. The vision of a solution needs to align with the vision of the enterprise, both in terms of business as well as information.

What Is a Solution Architecture Use For?

What a solution architect does is somewhat nebulous. I have been unable to track down a standard or consistent description of the role (and to be fair, I have not been able to track down a standard or consistent description of all but the most menial of roles). Having said that, most can agree that the scope of a solution architect is always a specific business problem requiring a solution.

As with many IS/IT roles, solution architecture is partially an empirical task, not a planned task. When performed empirically it is fundamentally a research task involving making decisions or proving hypotheses based on observation and experimentation.

With any empirical task what is observed and what is learned may not be unique. What is involved in a problem may have been solved in the past. Part of the role of solution architecture is to recognize these circumstances and employ generally accepted patterns and practices to compose at a solution (rather than to discover a solution). Whenever possible, it's best to perform planned tasks that can be defined and repeated with a repeatable level of quality. Part of the role of a solution architect is to recognize these planned tasks and perform them as defined to avoid having to *reinvent the wheel*.

A solution architect is involved during the problem definition, requirements gathering, vision, design, and implementation activities of software development. The solution architect should take over from an enterprise architect to continue establishing the business context and refine the vision and requirements. The solution architect should then be involved in elaborating on the solution or the options and either mentor or evaluate development. A solution architect should also be responsible for communicating and evangelizing the solution-level architecture of the solution to stakeholders.

Solution architecture is a tactical role and should operate with strategic guidance of an enterprise architecture or an enterprise architect.

Application Architecture

Software risks include being unable to support future requirements and being unstable or difficult to manage without proper structure and consistent principles. A structure that does not consider broad constraints and requirements or does not consider enterprise principles may be unable to support future business requirements. If that structure does not change holistically to support those new requirements, constraints, or principles, it will become unstable and very difficult to maintain.

Software architecture mitigates the risk involved in managing software by providing a structure that takes into account overarching constraints and principles and considers broader business requirements.

A software architecture takes into account operational and technical requirements, performance requirements, and security requirements to provide a structure and design to produce more manageable software that's higher quality and easier to maintain.

Summary

With this chapter, you should have a good introduction to architecture. Architecture has a lot to do with defining the structure of a system, building on patterns and practices, and being able to communicate that structure to other team members. Non-functional requirements are the key to building on the broader organizational practices. They lay the foundation for an architecture to provide reliable and maintainable software.

In the next chapter, we will discuss the diagramming architecture and the design of the applications you write in Visual Studio.

CHAPTER 5

Diagramming

Software isn't just about code. Don't get me wrong, it should be about the code as much as possible when it's not about the person using the thing the code produces. After reviewing a bit about the history of diagrams, we go over some of the reasons why we need them. Then we discuss creating, using, and communicating with the diagrams. Let's jump in.

Diagrams, a Brief History

Almost as long as there have been programming languages there have been diagraming techniques to document and analyze the structure and behavior of software systems.

Flowcharts have been around probably longer than software. Flowcharts use a defined series of symbols so that the behavior of a system, subsystem, or algorithm could be diagrammed. They showed interaction between logical or physical components and how they interact. I'm sure if I looked hard enough, I could find a flowchart template I used to use to draw flowcharts with pen and paper. We've come a long way since then, but some of the basics of flowcharts are still used.

Original flowchart symbols included a lot of equipment and technology that we simply don't use anymore. Things like cards, paper, tape, sequential data, and printed documents. These things simply either aren't used any more or are rare enough that we rarely seem them in a diagram. Other aspects like decisions, processes, and data are common in many contemporary diagrams.

As different programming techniques, frameworks, and paradigms evolved, so did diagramming. For example, as object-oriented programming (OOP) entered the industry, different analysis and diagramming standards started to emerge. One of the early and well accepted diagramming techniques was created by Grady Booch, called the *Booch Method*. It expanded on the basic shape, arrow, and flow technique used in flowcharts to include the concepts of classes, instantiations, inheritance, modules, and so on. These types of diagramming techniques turned into analysis and design frameworks or processes. Other visionaries at the time had other diagramming and modeling techniques, such as Ivar Jacobson and James Rumbaugh.

Eventually these three people and their techniques would merge to spawn off the Rational Unified Process (RUP) and eventually the Unified Modeling Language (UML.)

Much of the process definitions that came from these diagramming techniques and their usefulness are disputed based on other initiatives like Agile. But one thing is for sure—they provide a defined way to diagram aspects of software with a common way of communicating those aspects.

P. Ritchie, *Practical Microsoft Visual Studio 2015*, DOI 10.1007/978-1-4842-2313-0_5

Why Do We Need Diagrams?

Software should be about working software over comprehensive documentation. That is true, but this Agile statement does not imply that there should be no documentation. If it should be about working software, then why do we need documentation like diagrams at all?

Producing software is complex. That complexity is compounded by the complexity of the software or by the system under development. To be able to produce software, we enlist teams of people. The number and types of teams can be many: business analysts, software engineers, user-interface designers, enterprise architects, solution architects, software/application architects, quality assurance engineers, documentation writers, deployment engineers, IT administrators, information security, security analysts, and more. Each team and each person on each team needs to communicate enough information to the other team or other person for that other team or person to do what they need to do.

It's probably clear by now that *working software* is used by people, worked on by people, maintained by people, deployed by people, managed by people, and tested by people—have I made my point yet?

All of these people may know nothing yet about the software you're working on. In order to do your job, you have to figure out what the software needs to do and the constraints in which to do it. You also have to figure out how to get the software to do what it needs to do within those constraints. Further, you have to ensure the software does what it should and fix it when it doesn't. Often, you also have to figure out how to make it usable. These are all tall orders, but that's not enough to constitute *working software*.

Okay, maybe we should step back a bit and define what working software *is* first. Agile typically defines working software as software that is fully integrated, tested, and ready to be shipped or deployed to production. That alone should raise some alarms about communicating.

Testing? What does that mean? For an engineer, at a minimum, that should mean unit testing to an acceptable level of code coverage and at least some integration testing with a slant toward proving some of the acceptance criteria. Okay, a small team of engineers may not need a whole lot of communicating to get that done. But that's not only what *testing* means in Agile. Testing also means usability testing, acceptance testing, integration testing, regression testing, functional testing, non-functional testing, load/performance testing, security testing, and potentially many other types of testing, depending on your organization and the environment in which the software is used. It's almost impossible for you or your engineering team to do all of this.

In order for software to be *working*, it involves many people. For those various people to be able to do their job, they need you to *tell* them the information they need to do it. These people need to be able to understand the software and conceptualize the system to be able to cogitate about the system without having to know all of the details right from the start. That involves knowing about the logical components, the physical components, the component dependencies, the system dependencies, the deployment requirements, etc. As software complexity rises, this level of detail also rises. This information could be communicated verbally, but there are lots of people who need to know that information. Verbalizing it over and over again to each person or each set of people (you *have* tried to book a meeting with many people, right?) is not scalable. You could share the information by writing it down, but that could be lengthy and possibly a hard read. Why do all that when a picture is worth a thousand words?

The old adage is true, a picture is worth a thousand words. For people to understand a system, they need to absorb increasingly complex parts of it. For that to be conveyed by a set of words, sentences, and paragraphs is very difficult. All but the most experienced writers can't do it. But you can draw a simple diagram, can't you?

This is where diagramming comes in. You can easily create a diagram that creates a hierarchy of the information, from abstract logical information down to detailed physical information.

Types of Diagrams

There are two basic types of diagrams: architectural and behavioral. All the types of diagrams that Visual Studio 2015 supports fit into one of these two types. Let's first have a quick look at architectural and behavioral diagrams before digging deeper in the diagramming tools supported in Visual Studio 2015.

Architectural Diagrams

Architectural documents communicate the structure of the system and the software within the system. The audience of architecture documents is varied. Enterprise and solution architects may use these diagrams to be assured that the system is abiding by the higher-level architecture or that the system is architected correctly. Other administrative people need to know the structure of the system in order to perform tasks like allocating hardware, granting permissions, deploying files, allocating system resources, and creating or modifying other systems (like monitoring, help desk, change request, etc.).

In order for these other teams to do many of the things they need to do, they need the information in which to do it. Architectural diagrams help to communicate that information in a clear and concise way, either by introducing logical concepts or patterns or reusing existing logical concepts to aid in quicker understanding. A hat tip to domain driven design and the concept of ubiquitous language, even at this high level. Don't create new names and terminology where names and terminology exist and are already understood. Keep it DRY, even at this level.

▪ **Note** Domain-driven design (or DDD) is an approach to building complex software by associating core business concepts directly to the design and implementation.

Behavioral Diagrams

Behavioral diagrams are sometimes optional. They describe or specify how code works or how the system works. Code and the software is the best tool for that. But you may need to use behavior diagrams to communicate what a future system might need to do to people who don't understand code. After the software is "working," there may need to be some behavior diagrams to help communicate intent and flow of the system or the algorithms within the system.

Directed Graph

A *directed graph* is a diagram of vertices (or nodes) connected by edges (or vectors, or arrowed lines). The directed graph that Visual Studio 2015 supports is technically a directed multigraph because it supports having more than one line connected to a node.

Although they are mathematical in nature, directed graphs are great for diagramming dependencies. Dependencies can take many forms and thus directed graphs support a variety of software design and architecture diagrams. The obvious are basic dependency diagrams: architectural structure diagrams. Types of these diagrams include class diagrams, component diagrams, and layer diagrams. Certain types of behavior diagrams are also basic dependency diagrams, for example use case diagrams and activity diagrams. The directed graph doesn't support all the chrome of some diagrams like interface lollipops, UML icons, attributes, operations, etc. They support nodes and lines, along with comments/callouts and grouping.

Node

Any graph contains at least one node. A node can represent anything that needs to show a connection, a dependency, or a relationship to something else.

Edges (Lines)

Dependencies are delineated with arrows. The direction of the arrow is from the dependent to the provider. In the Figure 5-1, the controller depends on the view (and that the view *does not* depend on the controller).

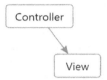

Figure 5-1. *Dependencies delineated with an arrow; the controller depends on the view*

Self-Reference

Dependencies can be circular. For example, if we were modeling a team member, the team member object may link to a team leader, i.e., an instance of a team member. The relationship would appear as shown in Figure 5-2.

Figure 5-2. *A circular dependency*

Bidirectional Edges

Relationships do not need to be unidirectional. For example, to describe that an application sends *and* receives data from a message queue, it would appear as shown in Figure 5-3.

Figure 5-3. *An example of a relationship that is not unidirectional, delineated by bidirectional edges*

Although two nodes can have a bidirectional, or cyclic, relationship, edges are generally unidirectional vectors. When Visual Studio 2015 lays out the entire diagram, it will likely show the relationship with two lines, as illustrated in Figure 5-4.

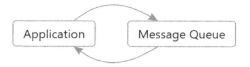

Figure 5-4. *A cyclic, or bidirectional, relationship*

Just something to be aware of when using directed graphs. This can cause a bit of surprise and consternation.

Group

A diagram with just nodes can be difficult to understand. A set of nodes can relate to a single logical or physical thing. We can use groups to convey that information on a diagram. A group is a box that can hold zero or more nodes and their edges. You can group them for any reason (or no reason at all). Depending on what you are trying to communicate with your diagram, you may group by deployment artifact, logical component, physical component, etc. Figure 5-5 shows an example of a group.

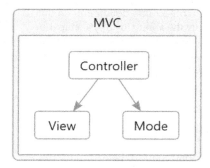

Figure 5-5. *A group of nodes*

Comment

Directed graphs also support annotating a diagram with comments. Comments appear like another node but are colored yellow. Figure 5-6 shows an example.

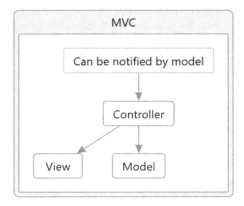

Figure 5-6. *A diagram annotated with a comment (at the top)*

For quick and dirty diagramming, directed graphs are quite handy. They provide an easy and flexible way to create a variety of diagrams. But Visual Studio is not a comprehensive diagramming tool and as such lacks many of the features and finesse of other tools devoted to creating and editing diagrams.

Directed graph diagrams are very flexible and are the base of some other diagrams supported by Visual Studio. In a pinch, directed graphs can be used for a variety of diagramming, from class diagrams, to data flow diagrams, to activity diagrams.

Directed graph diagrams are difficult to share with other team members. There is no directed graph viewer other than Visual Studio. There is also no way to embed them as an object into documents so that they can be updated as the diagram is updated over time. There exists only the ability to copy a snapshot of the diagram as a bitmap to the clipboard. For any diagramming you need to embed or share with non-engineering team members, I recommend using another diagramming tool like Microsoft Visio (which is included with a MSDN license) or, if your documentation is online, something like Gliffy.

Recommendations

- Choose direct graph diagrams in a pinch for quickly drawing diagrams.

- Choose other diagramming tools for sharing diagrams with non-technical team members.

- Choose other diagramming tools for diagrams that will be complex.

UML Diagrams

Visual Studio 2015 also supports a variety of UML diagrams. Some are based on directed graphs, some are not. Visual Studio 2015 supports five UML diagram types: class diagrams, sequence diagrams, use case diagrams, activity diagrams, and component diagrams.

Class Diagrams

Class diagrams are the UML diagrams you've probably come to know and expect. They support attributes (properties/fields) and operations (methods). They also support associations. There are existing association you can add to a class: Association, Composition, Aggregation, Dependency, inheritance, and Connector.

Although you can add an association to a UML class diagram, the specific types of associations like Aggregation, Composition, Inheritance, and Dependency are usually what you'll use on class diagrams. There is also a Connector, but that's not part of a typical UML diagram.

Figure 5-7 shows an example of a composition association.

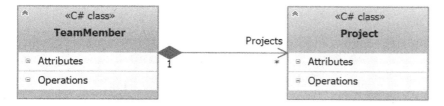

Figure 5-7. *An example of a composition association*

This diagram details that the `TeamMember` class will have an attribute named `Projects` that is a collection of zero or more `Project` instances.

Oddly, you cannot drag-and-drop classes from Solution Explorer (e.g., expand a file to show the classes within), nor can you add a class from the Class View. You can only add classes within a class diagram or within the UML Model Explorer from within a modeling project. The types you define in that modeling project stay within that modeling project and are not accessible to other projects like class libraries or applications. This also means that these types are visible only to other team members who have an Enterprise license of Visual Studio 2015.

Sequence Diagrams

Sequence diagrams, as the name implies, illustrate a sequence of events (or "messages" to use the UML vernacular) that occurs between processes. Although sequence diagrams are often detailed in the context of processes, I find that sequence diagrams are excellent for diagramming the sequence of events (as messages) with any type of physical or logical component, from processes to classes, to team members.

A sequence diagram consists of one or more *lifelines*. Each lifeline represents one component, vertically, in the sequence of events. Events in the diagram are represented as named horizontal arrows. Events can be represented as synchronous events, asynchronous events, and event responses (or replies). Activation boxes on the lifelines represent a process being performed in response to an event. Activation boxes often refer to the scope of the instance of the component being messaged. An event going to the start of an activation box means that event caused the component to be instantiated or to be created to service the request. When dealing with classes, that often means the class represented by the one lifeline created an instance of the type represented by the other lifeline.

The diagram shown in Figure 5-8, created in Visual Studio 2015, details the sequence of events that occur when a user (the first lifeline) makes a purchase and takes delivery of a product that was ordered via the shopping chart of an ecommerce system.

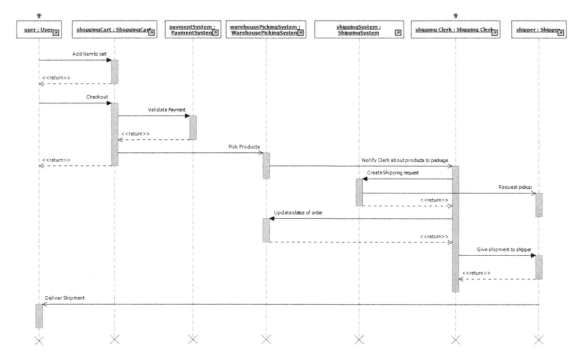

Figure 5-8. *The sequence of events that occur when a user makes a purchase and takes delivery of a product ordered via the shopping chart of an ecommerce system*

The dashed vertical lines are the lifelines, the rectangles on the lifelines are the activation boxes, and the horizontal solid lines the events or messages. Dashed horizontal lines represent responses or replies. Horizontal solid lines with a solid arrowhead represent synchronous events and horizontal solid lines with a wireframe arrowhead represent asynchronous events.

Use Case Diagrams

Use case diagrams were pioneered by the aforementioned Ivar Jacobson and have been incorporated into UML with very little change since they were introduced. Use case diagrams show event steps that are taken by a role (a type of user of the system) to detail the interaction that role has with the system.

Although a sequence diagram could detail much of the same types of information, use case diagrams focus on logical aspects like people and use cases that are more easily understood by non-technical people during requirements-gathering phases. Sequence diagrams generally detail more technical information like *how* the use cases are, or will be, implemented in the system.

Figure 5-9 details three use cases and two roles. It details how the two roles interact with the system for each use case. In this example, a *user* adds a product to the shopping cart and purchases a product or products. The image illustrates how that use cases interacts with another role (Shipping Clerk), and how that role interacts with the user through the Deliver Products use case.

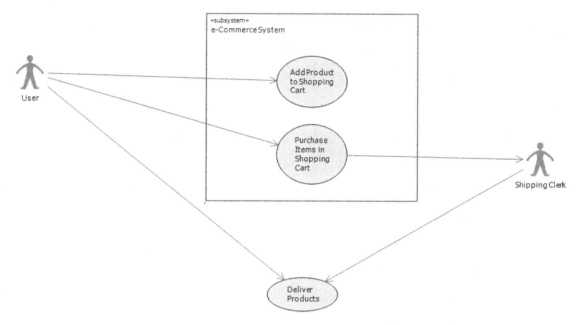

Figure 5-9. *A diagram showing how two roles interact with the system for each use case*

Activity Diagrams

Activity diagrams are probably the closest thing UML has to flowcharts. They detail behavior and flow in a similar way to use case diagrams, but deal at an activity level rather than at a use case level. Activity diagrams detail a workflow and contain activities (rounded rectangles), decisions (diamonds), bars (joining or splitting of concurrent activities), vectors (arrows), and terminators (circles—solid black is the start of the workflow and an encircled solid black circle represents the end of the workflow).

Figure 5-10 shows a simple shopping cart workflow. It shows that the start of the workflow is when a product is added to the shopping cart. If more than one product is desired, the decision shows a recursion to the Choose Product activity. When it's done, the Checkout activity is performed before completing the workflow.

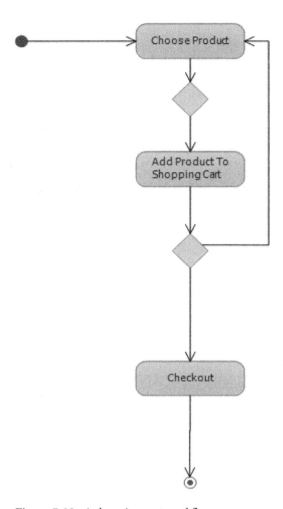

Figure 5-10. *A shopping cart workflow*

Component Diagrams

Component diagrams detail components (like executables, documents, databases, tables, and files) and the interfaces those components require or provide. Components are represented by a rectangle with a blue header bar with a component icon. Components can contain other components and only the header bar of the component (the chevron on the top-left of the component) can be toggled.

Interfaces are detailed with lollipop notation. Provided interfaces are the typical lollipop and required interfaces are similar but are a half-circle or arc.

The component diagram shown in Figure 5-11 details a web site that interacts with a Web API component via a specified interface. The Web API is a composition of two other components that provide an internal interface to add a product, and external interfaces to request a product and make a shipment request, respectively. These two external interfaces are delegated via the Web API component from the Web Site and to an external ShippingProvider component.

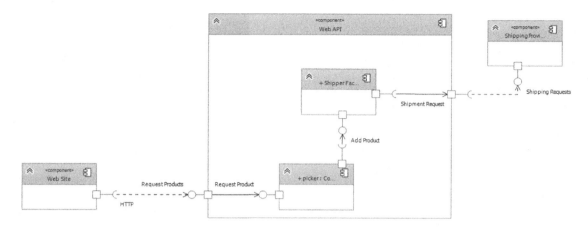

Figure 5-11. *A component diagram showing a web site that interacts with a Web API via specified interface*

As with directed graph diagrams, UML model diagrams are difficult to share with non-technical team members. They cannot represent the state of your project as you can no longer generate any of the diagrams from code. If you need to share any diagrams with other non-technical team members and embed them in documents, I recommend using Microsoft Visio instead, which is included in an MSDN license. If you need to share diagrams with other team members online, Gliffy (`http://gliffy.com`) may be another useful option.

I do not recommend using UML class diagrams for code generation. I think you'll find that it's much easier and faster to write classes in code than it is *create* the code in a class diagram. You can generate code from the diagrams but you cannot update the diagrams from code, so if you update the diagram after you've edited the code, you'll lose all your changes. Also, the code is generated in the modeling project that is accessible only to team members with Enterprise licenses; it's unusable to others.

Recommendations

- Choose simplicity over complexity.

- Use Visual Studio 2015 UML diagrams only when necessary.

- Choose other diagramming tools for sharing diagrams with non-technical team members.

- Avoid generating code from Visual Studio 2015 UML diagrams.

- Consider sharing diagrams securely online instead of within document files.

Layer Diagrams

Layer diagrams are supported in Visual Studio 2015 and are similar to directed graph diagrams, with nodes that have a background and can be resized, and no grouping (see Figure 5-12).

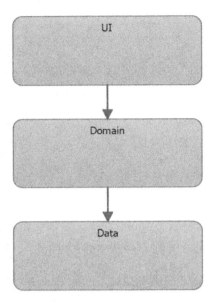

Figure 5-12. *An example of a Layer diagram*

The layer diagram pattern is very clear: layers interact only with adjacent layers and a layer only depends on a layer below it. No layers depend (or use) on the layer above. Layer diagrams in Visual Studio allow you to create diagrams that abide by the layer pattern constraint. But they also allow you to diagram layers that are bidirectionally dependent—i.e., both a dependent of and dependent upon the layer above. This is technically not a layered architecture and should be avoided. Don't use the bidirectional dependency connectors on your layer diagrams.

While layer diagrams allow you to diagram the layers in the architecture of your solution, they also define the layer constraints on your solution. This means that you can validate code that abides by these constraints and doesn't inadvertently violate the layered architecture.

As far as diagramming goes, layer diagrams suffer from the same problems as directed graph and UML diagrams do. They are difficult to share with non-technical team members. When you want to share layer diagrams with other team members, I recommend using another diagramming tool like Microsoft Visio (which is included with MSDN) or, if your documentation is online, something like Gliffy.

Recommendations

- Avoid bidirectional layer dependencies.

- A layer should only depend on the one, lower adjacent layer.

- Use layer diagrams to validate layer constraints of the rest of the system.

- Avoid sharing Visual Studio 2015 layer diagrams with non-technical team members; use another diagramming tool.

Other Diagramming Options

There are a lots of good diagramming options out there. I tend to lump them into the two ways of communicating diagrams: embedded in other documents or within web pages.

Embedded Within Documents

In a more *traditional* environment, documentation about software may live within files that are passed around and read within readers/editors. These document files may be created with things like Microsoft Word or saved/exported as PDF files. In this model, it's recommended that anything not edited directly by Microsoft Word be an embedded link and what is viewed in the viewer (Word, or Acrobat Reader if exported as PDF, etc.) be a graphical view of the last update to the linked document (file/image/diagram). This allows the linked document to be edited natively and its view be updated when needed (without having to manually create an image of the document and then copy/paste it into the other document).

Unfortunately, the diagramming in Visual Studio 2015 does not support linking and embedding. Any software documentation becomes out of date almost as fast as you complete writing it. Documentation needs to be kept up to date constantly (one reason to write it only when you need to). So, using Visual Studio 2015 to do your diagram takes on a level of technical debt that requires you to know which diagram in Visual Studio 2015 was copied into another document as a bitmap and update each manually. Linking and embedding generally requires updating links manually, but you can simply update all links embedded in a document automatically and you don't need to know where the linked document is (if you deleted it, you will, but *don't do that*). So, unless you're doing a quick one-off diagram for something that won't live beyond it being shown once to people, I don't recommend using Visual Studio 2015 for your diagramming needs.

Choosing an external diagramming tool is mostly a matter of choice; some offer a lot of features, some offer just enough. Since most readers will have an MSDN license, I suggest using Microsoft Visio for diagramming. You can use Microsoft Visio to create a vast number of software diagrams that can be linked and embedded into other documents. Those documents can be kept up to date with relative ease.

Embedded Within Web Pages

Unfortunately, typical file-based documentation like Microsoft Word and Adobe Acrobat suffer some of the same problems as using diagramming tools that do not support linking and embedding. File-based documentation is disseminated by means of copying. So, at any given time you may have x number of copies of your document floating around. A greater problem is that you may have as many copies of that document as versions. Each person working from a different version of the document.

More and more, teams are turning to online tools for disseminating documentation. Tools like Microsoft SharePoint or Atlassian Confluence are being used more and more to host documentation. I don't mean simply as a file repository that can manage versions of Word of PDF documents, I mean creating and editing the documentation right in a web page.

The drawback of this is that team members need to have access to the intranet and have access to the page they want to view or read. But, this is the same problem with Word or PDF documents. For those to be accessible by any other team member, they need to be on the network and accessible.

File shares can elevate some of the sharing issues, but that often means the document becomes locked by an editing application and the original author has to force it unlocked or wait in order to edit it (remember the lock-modify-unlock revision control model?). Tools like Confluence and SharePoint provide versioning mechanisms to deal with changes better and take on a more copy-edit-merge model that makes editing the content much more flexible.

Fortunately there are a number of online diagramming tools that have many features supporting creating and editing software diagrams. One that I recommend is Gliffy. Gliffy offers integration into Confluence allowing you to embed Gliffy documents within Confluence pages and edit them from within the page, keeping the entire page and your documentation up to date with very little effort. (The same can be done with Microsoft Word and Microsoft Visio; you can embed a link to a Microsoft Visio diagram, or part of the diagram, and either edit within Word or open Microsoft Visio to edit the linked content and then refresh the Microsoft Word document when it's saved.)

The online model of disseminating documentation resolves many of the issues around disseminating and communicating documentation. Online documentation lives in one place. When you attempt to view the documentation, you're always seeing the latest version. Collaborating on the documentation is much easier as well, with merge and history abilities, all in one place.

Recommendations

- Prefer an online model for software documentation storage and dissemination.

- Prefer tools that support linking and embedding when using an offline documentation model.

What to Diagram

As we've seen, there are multitude of options for diagramming. You could very well diagram everything about your software from the logical structure right down to each line of code. There are times when each of these diagrams may be applicable, but rarely do we always need them all.

Unless you're working on a system by yourself, you're always going to need to interact with other team members. That could include other software engineers, testers, or deployment engineers, at a very minimum.

In any system other team members are always going to need a minimum of information to understand, analyze, use, and test your system. Two aspects of your system will need to be communicated to other team members: structure and behavior.

Structure tries to focus on physical components and how they relate to one another, the outside world, and users of the system. Behavior focuses on the logical and physical components of the system, how they behave in relation to one another, and the type, flow, and constraints of data.

Any sufficiently complex system needs to eventually be deployed or installed. It's common that the task of deploying and/or installing is done by another group of people. That group of people needs to plan the resources and team members that your system will need to use to be functional. For enterprise systems, that usually requires team members to administer the system, hardware to run the system, processes to monitor/maintain/use the system, etc. None of that can be done unless the related requirements of the system are communicated.

One of the reasons we need to communicate via diagrams with non-technical or non-software team members is the difference in vocabulary. Diagrams offer a more common language to communicate with. The very reason that the readers of our diagrams are non-technical or technical in a different way often means that using diverse and broad modeling techniques fails to communicate with these team members because it still effectively a different language to them.

I recommend not using highly-technical diagrams with these types of people and focusing on the basics (effectively flowcharts). When talking about diagrams, it's the diagrams that we use to communicate with team members like this that we almost always need to produce. I rarely recommend *always* creating UML diagrams, I only recommend those diagrams when you need to communicate technical behavior with other technical people in a less formal environment or who aren't proficient in the programming language being used.

The two diagrams that are almost always produced are what I call high-level architecture and low-level design.

High-Level Architecture Diagram

When the structure of a future system needs to be communicated, there is a lot of implied information that is required for the system to function properly. It's best that that implied information be explicit. Much of that information as it relates to the structure of your system can be communicated on a high-level architecture diagram.

High-level architecture diagrams should almost always focus on the physical aspects of the system. This means what the components are, how they relate or depend on one other, where they will live, and what they require. Some of the things that need to be communicated might include:

- Communication technique
- Direction of communication
- Type of data being communicated
- Types of external components
- Names of external resources being communicate with
- Type of components
- Permissions

Some of these things are included in the nodes and lines on the diagram, and some are included in textual annotations. When all of this information is included in a diagram, all the information almost any other team member requires to plan, install/deploy, grant permissions, configure resources, test, and otherwise administer are available in one tidy place.

The high-level architecture diagram should also be a place where you can communicate the ways the system fulfills non-functional requirements of the system. Things like security, testability, scalability, availability, reliability, and to certain extent extensibility, and maintainability.

There are, of course, many more non-functional requirements possible, and each system has a unique set of non-functional requirements (although the above should be very common to all). Diagramming high-level architecture is a good technique to either flesh out non-functional requirements or show that they have in fact been considered and planned for.

Figure 5-13 shows an example of a simple high-level architecture diagram.

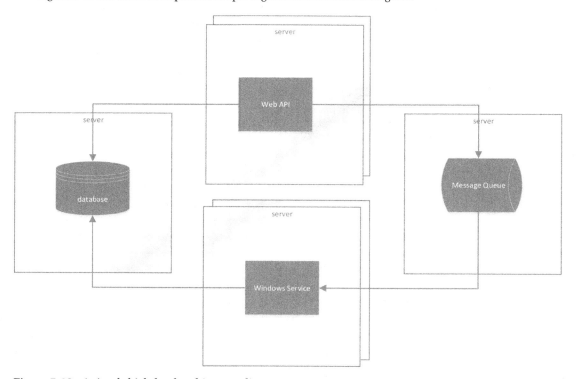

Figure 5-13. *A simple high-level architecture diagram*

It describes a system that has one WebAPI hosted on one or more servers (scalability, availability), and a Windows Service hosted on one or more servers (scalability). The WebAPI uses a message queue to send messages to the Windows service (scalability, extensibility). The Windows service and Web API use a shared database.

There are various things missing from this diagram that could very well be included to communicate other non-functional requirements. For example, a firewall could be added to show that all traffic coming into the WebAPI accounts for security. Additionally, the two types of servers could be expected to be deployed to different zones. For example, the WebAPI could be in the "DMZ" and the Windows service could be in the "production" zone—also added to address security.

■ **Note** Each system has unique non-functional requirements, so be sure to put thought into your system. Do not assume what is detailed here is correct for your system.

Low-Level Design

Other team members will require a different type of information: the behavior of the system. Functional requirements of a system need to be communicated and evaluated by various other team members. Diagramming behavior is essential for communicating the suitability of the system being worked on.

There are many instances where deeper detail needs to be communicated. In complex systems with many components, the seams by which these components are separated need to be communicated so that they can be defined and agreed upon. The communication technique and structure used in these seams needs to be documented so that the different teams involved and communicate in the correct ways to be successful.

A *seam* is a physical means by which to separate components. Think of a seam as where or how components are decoupled. Some systems have seams at communication points, like an HTTP endpoint. Other systems can have seams lower down, especially systems that employ dependency injection or inversion of control. Seams in these systems may be the interfaces defined to facilitate dependency injection or inversion of control.

At any rate, depending on how the tasks involved in implementing your system are delegated, much information about those seams must be communicated so those teams or team members can perform their work in isolation so that work can be done in parallel and integrated at a later date.

Figure 5-14 shows an example of a low-level design document for the system mentioned elsewhere in this chapter.

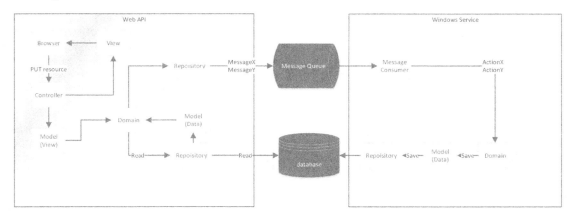

Figure 5-14. An example of a low-level design document

The various seams and behavior are detailed here. For example, there is a resource that the browser PUTs, sends MessageX and MessageY, and has several models to represent external information (either arriving from the HTTP request or departing to the database via the repository). This clearly delineates various seams that can be the interaction points between team members or teams. They can easily be able to communicate needs and progress using this diagram.

I find it useful that when using online diagramming tools, the details about the seam protocol/structures can link to textual information. For example, "PUT resource" could link to the request structures (XML, JSON), the "Model (View)" could link to the view model, "database" could link to the table/document specification, the "MessageX" and "MessageY" could link to the specification of the structure for these messages, etc. This would give other team members or other teams the information needed to work in parallel.

Deployment Diagrams

As the software nears being released and deployed, the diagrams used to describe it become more and more stable and change less and less. These diagrams should and will evolve much up to this point. The diagrams purpose is to communicate information and they should evolve to ensure the least amount of friction in that communication. This discussion should only be a starting point for you and you should adjust it for your audience.

As things start stabilizing and the other two diagrams start changing less, the information in those diagrams is *known* (memorized) by more and more people. That's a good thing, but one of the evolutions that I tend to use a lot at these points is to start using a third type of document—the deployment document—to start containing the deployment details. Those details could live in structural diagrams like the high-level architecture, but changing them at this point could confuse the people who know that document inside and out. It can also make that document busy and hard to follow. If you have a complex architecture, I recommend creating a new diagram that contains that information. Let's call that new diagram the *deployment diagram.*

Now it may seem like the UML component diagram would be good for this. The component diagram is meant to contain some of the information that needs to be obtained and communicated, like interface types and information (server, ports, etc.). But I find that creating component diagrams is time-consuming and busy work. These diagrams are very technical in nature, with UML-specific technicalities. A component diagram *could* have interfaces and connectors to components to show the components and seams in the system, as shown in Figure 5-15.

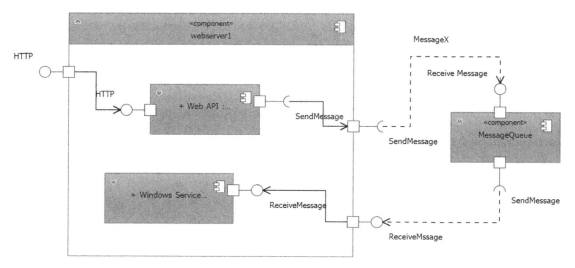

Figure 5-15. *A component diagram with interfaces and connectors to components to show the components and seams*

Other team members can use this diagram to provide information like server names, URIs, quantities, etc. In Visual Studio 2015 component diagrams, the annotations for connectors is limited to a name. So, while some information can be provided, it's difficult to provide all needed information (such as the necessary HTTP endpoints). It *could* be done with comments, as in Figure 5-16.

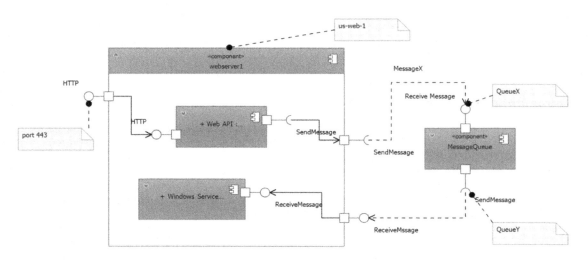

Figure 5-16. *Providing further context to a diagram using comments*

I find that using comments clutters up the diagram and makes it difficult to arrange (there are several instances where Visual Studio 2015 rearranges automatically). Plus, the comments are disconnected from the lines (you can't comment on a line) and could make the necessary information difficult to associate to the right things.

Also, creating the component diagram shown in Figure 5-16 required adding 18 different elements to the diagram. Four components, three provided interfaces, three required interfaces, two delegations, four comments, and two connectors. In other diagram types, that would be six elements (four components and two connectors). In more complex systems, expect the creation of component diagrams to be that much more work.

Rather than spending a lot of time in component diagrams for very little extra value, I recommend just using the simplest diagram possible. Often a flow diagram works just fine. What we want on the deployment diagram are the physical components, the direction of communication (possibly what is being communicated), and the configurable details (server names, queue names, protocols, ports, etc.). All this information can be given to the various team members who need to do something to deploy the software: allocate servers, create queues, route messages, change firewalls, create permissions, etc. A simple flowchart diagram in Microsoft Visio, as shown in Figure 5-17, can accomplish this feat very quickly.

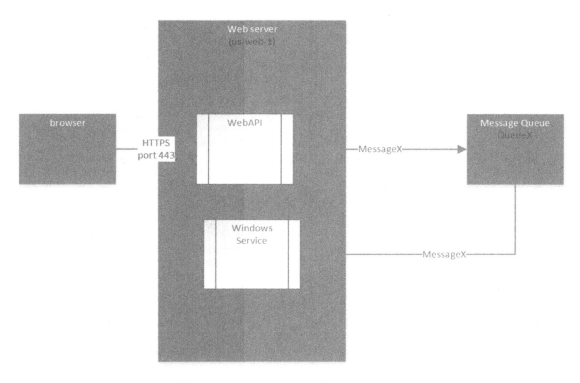

Figure 5-17. *A simple flowchart diagram created in Microsoft Visio*

In the diagram in Figure 5-17, we can easily have much more information at the appropriate places and have it formatted to be more readable.

Transient Diagrams

The other four diagrams that I've already detailed I consider *required diagrams*. Any sufficiently complex system needs to communicate the information contained in those diagrams. Throughout the process of designing and creating software there are many times when technical team members need to communicate and discuss the system that is being built. For the most part, the structure and the behavior detailed in the high-level architecture and low-level design diagrams communicates much of that information. But there are times when the interaction of two or more components is much more complex to put in the low-level design diagram.

This includes the interactions of a user, shopping cart, shipping service, picking service, and shipper, for example. To communicate that and to be able to reason about that process with a group of people, it's best to use a transient diagram. For example, we can create a sequence diagram in Microsoft Visio, like the one shown in Figure 5-18, in order be able to reason about the flow.

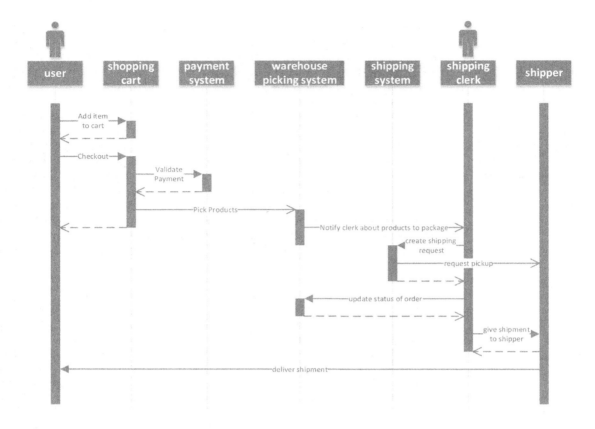

Figure 5-18. *A sequence diagram created in Microsoft Visio*

With more eyes on the sequence as a graphical flow, it's much easier to talk about and reason about. For example, the diagram makes it blatantly obvious that, although the shipping clerk updates the status of the order, that status it not communicated to the user. The diagram can quickly be updated and continue to be used for the discussion (or within Microsoft Visio, projecting on the wall). For example, see Figure 5-19.

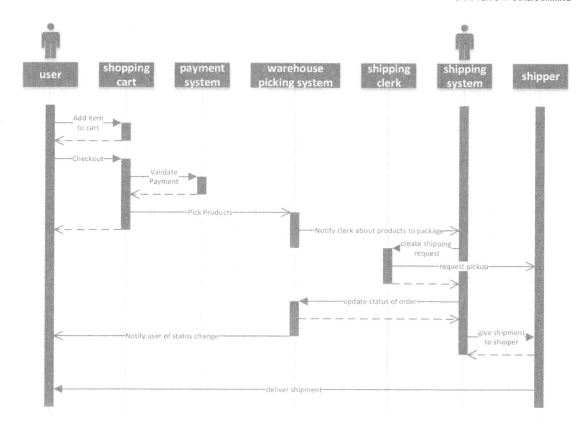

Figure 5-19. *The sequence diagram, updated to reflect feedback from other team members*

When all agree on the changes, they can be implemented and the diagram can be archived or deleted.

Recommendations

- Choose working code over comprehensive documentation.

- Avoid Visual Studio 2015 diagrams when diagrams need to be embedded or when diagrams need to be communicated to non-technical team members.

- Use other tools like Microsoft Visio or Gliffy when communicating with non-technical team members, especially when you need to embed diagrams or communicate online.

- Use UML diagrams only when necessary and only when you know your audience will understand them.

- Use high-level architecture diagrams to detail structure, physical dependencies, and how many non-functional requirements are met.

- Use low-level design diagrams to detail behavior, data structure and requirements, and how some functional requirements are met.

- Use Visual Studio 2015 layer diagrams to document layers and validate code when the solution is not violating that constraint.

- For complex systems, use a deployment diagram to contain all the deployment-related information in one place.

Summary

This chapter has tried to detail the importance of communication among team members within software projects. Team members require a variety of information in order for software to be delivered correctly and in a timely fashion.

Diagrams provide a powerful means of communicating much information about software, its architecture and design, in a small amount of space. We saw how we can use high-level architecture diagrams to communicate structure and low-level design diagrams to communicate behavior. We also saw how to use deployment diagrams as the software project becomes more stable to communicate deployment needs.

As with any documentation, we learned that Agile software projects are about working software rather than comprehensive documentation and that diagrams should be tempered so they're used only when necessary.

Visual Studio 2015 provides a variety of diagramming abilities, some more useful than others. We saw how we can utilize layer diagrams to define and constrain a system to a particular layer architecture and use tools like Microsoft Visio and Gliffy to diagram other aspects of the system when they need to be communicated to other team members.

The next chapter covers some of the day-to-day activities in Visual Studio 2015 that team members frequently need to perform. Information like tips and tricks, practices, etc. will be discussed.

CHAPTER 6

Development: Patterns and Practices

Creating software, as we've seen so far, is much more than simply programming. It's even much more than just knowing the syntax of a language. Despite each language having a specific syntax, the use of that language syntax constitutes semantics. Each language can even have different semantic dialects, sometimes referred to as being *idiomatic*.

Languages can be used in certain recognizable ways, called idioms. Wiktionary defines idiom (in the context of programming) as, "A programming construct or phraseology generally held to be the most efficient or elegant means to achieve a particular result or behavior." While several computer languages share much in the way of syntax, the style of achieving the same thing in each is expected in a certain way or is slightly different.

Some idioms are baked right into the language; C# has IEnumerable<T> that can be iterated via the foreach keyword:

```
foreach(var item in collection)
{
    // do something with item
}
```

Many types that implement IEnumerable<T> are also implementations of fixed-size collections (arrays, vectors, stacks, queues, lists, dictionaries, maps, tables, etc.) and offer the ability to index into the collection by an index value offering the ability to iterate a collection similarly to other languages:

```
for(int i = 0; i < collection.Length; ++i)
{
    var item = collection[i];
    // TODO: do something with item
}
```

But, the *idiom* in C# is to use foreach, which is technically a form of the *iterator pattern*.

Metrics

It's hard to find a principle or practice that isn't measurable. In fact, many patterns and practices are based on improving one or more metrics. SOLID principles (Single Responsibility, Open-Closed, Liskov Substitution, Interface Segregation, and Dependency Inversion), for example, are based on improving the metrics *cohesion* and *coupling* (by increasing cohesion and reducing coupling).

It's worth covering some of the most common metrics to help provide context for upcoming patterns and practices.

Cohesion

Cohesion is the degree to which any logical group of code is related. That group of code is said to have cohesion if it is closely related. We want to write code in groups that are highly cohesive.

Coupling

Coupling is the manner and degree to which software elements are dependent. Any element in any one system is "coupled" to anything else in the system simply because it is a part of a whole. When people talk about "decoupling" they really mean *reduced coupling*, or a more appropriate and flexible manner of coupling.

Afferent Coupling

Depending on the tool that gathers your metrics, you may come across *afferent coupling* metrics. This is a measure of coupling *from* the outside, or incoming coupling. This measure is a quantity: how many outside elements are coupled to the element being measured.

Efferent Coupling

The opposite of afferent coupling is *efferent coupling,* which is the measure of coupling *to* the outside. Or outgoing coupling.

Cyclomatic Complexity

Cyclomatic complexity is the measure of the independent paths through a piece of code (usually method, but some tools aggregate method metrics into class metrics, etc.). This value is effectively the number of branches in code plus one or two (depending on the tool gathering the metric).

Cyclomatic complexity tells you how maintainable a method is. A large number either means the method is lengthy or it is lengthy *and* has many nested branches. In either case, it's probably taken on too much responsibility.

Some object-oriented purists believe that there should be no branches in well-written OO code; the "branches" should be handled by some sort of polymorphism. In other words, the way a shape is drawn isn't based on a flag, it's based on a specialized subtype (subtype polymorphism). Another example is what method to call for a value; that shouldn't be a condition, it should be an overload (ad hoc polymorphism).

Essential Complexity

Fred Brooks described two types of complexity in software: essential and accidental. *Essential* complexity is the complexity required to solve a specific problem with software.

Essential complexity is what goes into creating the features, from the gathering and managing of requirements, to the deployment and maintenance of the software. These tasks must be performed in order for the software to be used: this is essential complexity.

The complexity in software has several adverse side-effects, which are too numerous to detail here. Some include communicability, maintainability, verifiability, and ability to estimate. Reducing any complexity increases the success that the software can be delivered on time, on budget, with expected quality, and the expected features. Essential complexity cannot be reduced and sustain all of these attributes; features must be removed to reduce essential complexity.

Another way of looking at essential complexity, I believe, is to look at what Aristotle described as essential properties. An *essential property* is a feature of something that is fundamental to its meaning.

Although a measure of code complexity, I'm not aware of any calculated metrics around essential complexity—this is more of a judgment.

Accidental Complexity

The inverse to essential complexity is *accidental complexity*. Accidental complexity is introduced to support the essential complexity. Complexity that doesn't directly solve the problem that the software solves is accidental. Things like technical debt, not automating repeatable/defined tasks, duplicate code, etc. are accidental complexity.

Reducing accidental complexity and the processes that create accidental complexity can help increase the likelihood that software can be delivered on time, on budget, with expected quality and expected features.

From requirements to implementation, when you focus on the essential properties of something, you focus on the essential complexities and avoid accidental complexities.

Although a measure of code complexity, I'm not aware of any calculated metrics around accidental complexity—this is more of a judgment.

Code Coverage

Code coverage is the calculation of the percentage of code that is executed when unit tests run. I find that guidance is required on this metric because invariably there will be someone who takes it upon themselves to decide that 100% coverage should be the goal of the unit tests.

Let me be clear, 100% coverage is where your coverage should be *heading*. That makes it sound like a *goal*, but it's really an *ideal*. Your coverage goals should be to always be approaching 100% and not going backward (yes that might include stalling). Coverage is like an exponential function. As you approach 100% coverage, the effort increases exponentially, as shown in Figure 6-1.

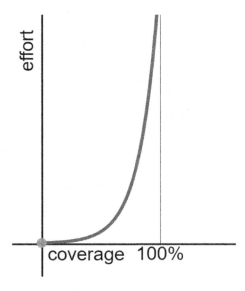

Figure 6-1. *Effort expended in relation to coverage*

Patterns

Software languages provides syntax and some idioms in order to implement software. That language offers a limited ability to communicate intent. With the correct naming and structure, you can possibly communicate intent but the reader may not see it or may see intent that was not intended. Also, that communication is very language-specific. In order to address some of those issues and provide a language-agnostic way of describing common design techniques or artifacts, *design patterns* were created.

A design pattern is described by Christopher Alexander as, "Each pattern describes a problem which occurs over and over again in our environment, and then describes the core of the solution to that problem, in such a way that you can use this solution a million times over, without ever doing it the same way twice". Typically, what this has resulted in is a set of required information to describe a pattern. Obviously, that includes the problem and the solution; we often include a context in the problem, the specific consequences of the solution, as well as meta-like information about the pattern like a name. You, of course, can provide a much richer set of information about the pattern if it is required, for example: applicability, known uses, also known as, related patterns, collaborations, participants, sample code, etc.

Patterns also help the software effort in a very important way, by facilitating the ability to add defined process to what is effectively an empirical process.

An *empirical process* is one where the next step depends on observations made in the previous or current step. This means it's hard to plan very far ahead. When we can take chunks of work in our empirical process and effectively plan ahead, we can take some of the uncertainty out of the empirical process. Patterns allow us to make those empirical observations and use something more repeatable, where possible.

There's all sorts of already-documented patterns (which we'll look at shortly). A taxonomy of patterns has already been devised. Some of the common classifications of patterns include creational, structural, and behavioral.

I find that when implementing patterns that I include the name of the pattern in whatever module I'm using to contain the solution (class, filename, module name, process name, etc.).

Let's look at some important patterns.

Dependency Injection

Almost every class has at least one dependency. When the class takes on the responsibility of knowing how to, and creating those dependencies it is very tightly coupled to those exact implementations. This makes the class hard to maintain in terms of its ability to be reused or modified. It's also very hard to unit test the class independent of those dependencies (think of testing business logic over testing database access).

As an alternative to having a class know how to create its own dependencies, the principle of dependency inversion can be used to invert those dependencies. Rather than the class depending on details (like another concrete class and how to instantiate it), it should depend on abstractions. This means that something outside the class knows how to create those dependencies and pass those instances on to the other classes that need them.

There are two main types of dependency injection: constructor injection and property injection. Let's first discuss constructor injection.

Constructor Injection

One way to pass along all of the objects that a class needs to perform its responsibilities is to pass them along in the construction of that object. This is useful in creating an instance of class in a known state (or otherwise would fail construction) so that it is less likely to fail, invoking any of its behavior. This assumes you have some level of knowledge about the type of the dependency at compile time in order to write the code that invoked the constructor.

Let's say, for example, that I want to create a pedantic instance of a Car class. Let's also say that that Car instance can't function without an engine, some tires, a chassis, a console, an exhaust system, and a transmission. (Did I mention this was pedantic?) Listing 6-1 shows how you can enforce those requirements in a constructor.

Listing 6-1. Enforcing Requirements in a Constructor

```
public Car(IEngine engine, IChassis chassis, IConsole console,
    ITransmission transmission, IExhaustSystem exhaustSystem,
    IEnumerable<ITire> tires)
{
    if (engine == null)
        throw new ArgumentNullException(nameof(engine));
    if (chassis == null)
        throw new ArgumentNullException(nameof(chassis));
    if (console == null)
        throw new ArgumentNullException(nameof(console));
    if (transmission == null)
        throw new ArgumentNullException(
            nameof(transmission));
    if (exhaustSystem == null)
        throw new ArgumentNullException(
            nameof(exhaustSystem));
    if (tires == null)
        throw new ArgumentNullException(
            nameof(tires));
    _engine = engine;
    _chassis = chassis;
    _console = console;
    _transmission = transmission;
    _exhaustSystem = exhaustSystem;
    _tires = tires;
}
```

Now performing constructor injection is a simple matter of constructing a Car instance, as shown in Listing 6-2.

Listing 6-2. Constructor Injection

```
var v8Engine = new V8Engine();
var standardChassis = new StandardChassis();
var standardConsole = new StandardConsole();
var automaticTransmission = new AutomaticTransmission();
var standardExhaustSystem = new StandardExhaustSystem();
var allSeasonRadialTires = new AllSeasonRadialTire[4];
var car = new Car(v8Engine, standardChassis,
    standardConsole, automaticTransmission,
    standardExhaustSystem,allSeasonRadialTires);
```

Constructor injection mandates that interface-based programming be used because the purpose of constructor injection is to accomplish dependency inversion so that the class we are constructing depends solely on abstractions, not concretions. So, in Listing 6-1 you'll notice all the arguments are interface types and obviously that each of the instances passed as parameters to the constructor implement a least one interface.

Constructor injection also assumes that the dependencies don't change for the life of the dependent. If that's the case, property injection might be a better dependency injection technique for those dependencies.

Property Injection

I find this injection technique to be problematic because a) the object is in an unknown state (its invariants are violated) up to the point of invoking the setter on the property or properties. And b) the responsibility of knowing the semantic order in which to pass along the dependencies lies in the user of the object (unlike constructor injection, in which the language verifies the "order" of passing along the dependencies by verifying arguments passed to the constructor at compile time).

That's not to say you can't create working code by using property injection, but dependencies become implicit rather than explicit and compile-time verification is avoided, allowing the potential for putting the object in an unknown state.

I believe this leads to more fragile code, as it could easily be modified to remain syntactically correct, but semantically incorrect and fail occasionally at runtime.

Composite Root

Composite root is a dependency injection pattern described by Mark Seemann. It explains that the composition of required objects and their dependencies (the object graph) should be done in one place, as close to the application entry point as possible.

This recognizes the responsibility of composing the required object and it groups code with that responsibility together, thereby making it easy to be explicit and maintainable.

In .NET, this can simply be `Program.Main` in console or Windows-based applications. In ASP.NET, this is often done in `Global.Application_Start` or `Startup.ConfigureServices` (or potentially the `Startup` constructor) in the ASP.NET Core.

Abstract Factory

To put it simply, an *abstract factory* knows how to provide abstract objects while retaining the implementation detail of which concrete type to instantiate.

This is implemented by creating an abstract class to represent the abstract factory and then implementing concrete classes to contain the implementation detail of creation. Clients would use the abstract class and would request the factory instances of the abstract class they require.

This keeps the client of the abstract factory loosely coupled from the implementation details (the concrete classes) that it uses.

Listing 6-3 shows an example of an abstract car factory type.

Listing 6-3. An Example of an Abstract Factory Type

```
public abstract class CarFactory
{
    public abstract ICar Create();
}
```

This provides the interface for client code that requires a car to create one. Listing 6-4 shows a couple of concrete implementations of the abstract car factory.

Listing 6-4. Implementations of the Abstract Car Factory

```
public class CorvetteFactory : CarFactory
{
    public override ICar Create()
    {
        var engine = new Ls7Engine();
        var chassis = new Corvette2015Chassis();
        var console = new Corvette2015Console();
        var transmission = new AutomaticTransmission();
        var exhaustSystem = new Corvette2015ExhaustSystem();
        var tires = new AllSeasonRadialTire[4];
        return new Corvette(engine, chassis,
            console, transmission,
            exhaustSystem, tires);
    }
}

public class AudiA7Factory : CarFactory
{
    public override ICar Create()
    {
        var engine = new Audi30V8Engine();
        var chassis = new AudiA72015Chassis();
        var console = new AudiA72015Console();
        var transmission = new AutomaticTransmission();
        var exhaustSystem = new AudiA72015ExhaustSystem();
        var tires = new AllSeasonRadialTire[4];
        return new AudiA7(engine, chassis,
            console, transmission,
            exhaustSystem, tires);
    }
}
```

One of the concrete factories would be passed along to the client as a type of the abstract factory. For example, if we had an `AutomobileCompany` class, we may pass along in the constructor a factory that would create cars as needed. See Listing 6-5 for an example `AutomobileCompany` class constructor.

Listing 6-5. An Example of Passing Along a Factory in a Constructor

```
public class AutomobileCompany
{
    CarFactory carFactory;

    public AutomobileCompany(CarFactory carFactory)
    {
        this.carFactory = carFactory;
    }
    //...
}
```

Adapter

The adapter pattern is a type of wrapper that wraps a single interface and presents a new, presumably easier to use, interface to clients.

The adapter pattern is different than a façade in that an adapter wraps one interface or one instance of one type of object, whereas a façade would provide a new interface to pass through to several instances of several types.

The adapter pattern can be implemented in many ways. One way is to implement a simple container that completely wraps an instance of the type you want to adapt. Another implementation is to use subtype polymorphism (inheritance) to extend or replace the interface of another type.

C# offers another, unique, way of implementing an adapter: extension methods. The class that contains the extension method is essentially an adapter that provides a new or polymorphic method. The extension method is an adapter because the method performs only what is necessary to adapt an instance of the existing type.

Circuit Breaker

The circuit breaker pattern detects and prevents reoccurring failures. It acts in much the same as a real-world electrical circuit breaker that detects a specific type of fault in a circuit and stops the flow of electricity until someone manually closes the circuit.

Listing 6-6 shows an example of an implementation of the circuit breaker pattern.

Listing 6-6. An Example of an Implementation of the Circuit Breaker Pattern

```
public class CircuitBreaker
{
    private int exceptionRaisedQuantity;
    private DateTime lastOpenDateTime;
    private Exception lastException;
    public bool IsOpen { get; private set; }
```

```
public void Execute(Action action)
{
    if (IsOpen)
    {
        // the policy
        if ((DateTime.UtcNow - lastOpenDateTime)
            .TotalMinutes > 5)
        {
            IsOpen = false;
            exceptionRaisedQuantity = 0;
        }
        else
        {
            throw new CircuitBreakerOpenException(
                lastException);
        }
    }
    try
    {
        action();
    }
    catch (Exception ex)
    {
        exceptionRaisedQuantity++;
        if (exceptionRaisedQuantity > 3)
        {
            lastException = ex;
            IsOpen = true;
            lastOpenDateTime = DateTime.UtcNow;
        }
        throw;
    }
}
}
```

In this example, we have a reference type that has an Execute method to mediate the execution of some code represented by an Action delegate. The class contains the policy around how many times code can throw an exception before the "circuit" breaks and we simply stop allowing execution. In this case, we have a hard-coded policy that closes the circuit after a five-minute delay. This is an arbitrary amount of time and is hard-coded. Typically, you're going to want that policy to be configurable.

In addition, this example simply shows the structure of a circuit breaker implementation. In almost all cases where you want to perform this type of thing, you probably want to inform someone there was a problem. And in some cases, you don't want to close the circuit without some sort of manual interaction (the example in Listing 6-6 is an *automatic* circuit breaker). In such cases, you'll need to persist information (to database) so that the fact that the circuit is open can be stored and can be changed to closed. Information about the exception and the quantity would probably also be stored. Policy information would also be configurable, so the number of exceptions before opening or the timeout duration would be loaded from config or database. For the sake of clarity, that sort of thing is not shown here.

I find the need and usefulness of this pattern to be increasing over time as we are developing more complex and more distributed systems.

Bridge

The bridge pattern can seem like a façade or an adapter, but it is different. It is a *type* of adapter whose purpose is to abstract and encapsulate an implementation. This is typically done to decouple client code from the type of the implementation. It would be the adapter pattern if it were not for the fact that the wrapper depends on an abstraction and not directly on the implementation (i.e., two layers of abstraction). It is an alternative to an abstract class implementing an interface and the varying implementations subclassing that abstract class. It is an implementation of composition over inheritance.

A bridge pattern implementation includes an abstract interface that clients depend on and an implementation of that interface that wraps the implementation details being bridged to.

The difficulty with this pattern is that it is initially implemented as the bridge pattern but if the implementation evolves, it can become an adapter pattern implementation because it is now adapting one interface to another rather than passing through.

This pattern is known in platforms that support pointers as Pimpl (or pointer-to-implementation).

IoC Container

An IoC (or Inversion of Control) container is a framework to facilitate dependency inversion. It provides the ability for code to depend at compile-time almost entirely on abstractions and leave building up instances of the concrete types to the framework. It's called an inversion of control container because you configure the container to call back into your code (or someone else's code, but outside the IoC container code) to perform the building up of the required instances. That is control flow is *inverted* from typical control flow from the framework back into client code.

IoC containers should be used with caution. They should be used for a specific need other than simply dependency inversion. Dependency inversion can be accomplished simply by dependency injection. IoC containers should be used when simple dependency injection cannot be performed. While it's a bad example (see my caveat following), I could use an IoC container to build up the Car object that I described in constructor injection. Listing 6-7 shows using the NInject container to configure it to be able to instantiate a Car object with specific parts.

Listing 6-7. Using an IoC Container to Build Up the Car Object Described in the Constructor Injection

```
var kernel = new Ninject.StandardKernel();
kernel.Bind<IEngine>().To<V8Engine>();
kernel.Bind<IChassis>().To<StandardChassis>();
kernel.Bind<IConsole>().To<StandardConsole>();
kernel.Bind<ITransmission>().To<AutomaticTransmission>();
kernel.Bind<IExhaustSystem>().To<StandardExhaustSystem>();
kernel.Bind<IEnumerable<ITire>>().ToMethod(_ =>
    new AllSeasonRadialTire[4]);
var car = kernel.Get<Car>();
```

Using IoC containers are like service locators and singletons, in that they add a new dependency and accidental complexity (potentially a lot of it), as the semantics to using that specific container can be complex. You end up being very tightly coupled to one type of container due to the distinct semantics of that container.

If used improperly, I would call an IoC container an anti-pattern.

Command

There are a couple types of command patterns. One has to do with messaging and the other has to do with a behavior. They are similar in that they encapsulate a copy of the data required to fulfill a request. But the behavior pattern also models executing the command. The command message would be a specific (over-the-wire) type of parameter object. See Chapter 4 for more details on command messages.

Basically, the command object encapsulates all the data required to invoke a request without having the requestor know anything about the particular data. The requestor would know about a command object (maybe a specific type, maybe a generic type) and whether to execute it. Think of a Start Car command. You don't want to know how electricity works to cause a motor to rotate to cycle an engine and spark the cylinders, you just want to start the car. The command pattern allows you to encapsulate details like that.

Typically, the command pattern is implemented as an implementation of a generic class or interface that implements one Execute method. Anything that uses a command object would simply invoke the Execute method when it needed to. The rest of the work would be performed by the command implementation.

You can see this pattern used with Windows Presentation Foundation (WPF), which expands the pattern slightly to include members like CanExecute and CanExecuteChanged.

Decorator

The decorator pattern is probably one of the most powerful patterns that facilities decoupling and composability. The decorator pattern is named because it "decorates" or adds to existing functionality. In order for the decorator pattern to work, we must first start with an abstraction. The decorator then implements that abstraction and wraps another implementation of the same abstraction and calls through to wrapped implementation. Although the decorator pattern is also a wrapper like the adapter pattern, a decorator is not an adapter because it performs no adaption to publish a different interface. (See the section called "Liskov Substitution Principle" for more information.).

The power of the decorator pattern is that if you implement a highly decoupled system and follow principles like the dependency inversion principle or the interface segregation principle, you likely have everything you need to utilize the decorator pattern.

What can be decorations? Well, pretty much anything. The key thing is that they are *additions* to existing data/behavior. Ensure you follow the Liskov substitution principle so that you're not changing the behavior-wrapped instance (such as changing inputs to make it behave differently). Often what decorations mean are quality attributes (or non-functional requirements): logging, authorization, auditing, etc. But don't let that limit what you can do with decorators; the canonical example is to provide scrolling ability to an existing window class.

A couple of the open source projects I work on are a set of messaging primitives and a set of messaging implementations. One of the primitives is a bus modeled as the interface IBus. The implementations include an implementation of IBus that facilitates connections of messages to message handlers. I could easily decorate an IBus implementation to provide logging. Listing 6-8 shows how the Handle method could be decorated to log the start of sending a message, the message, when the send completed, and the time it took to send the message.

Listing 6-8. Decorating the Handle Method to Log the Start of Sending a Message

```
public void Handle(IMessage message)
{
    traceListener.WriteLine(
        $"Message sent at {clock.Now}. "+
        "Message details: {message}");
    var stopwatch = Stopwatch.StartNew();
```

```
        wrappedBus.Handle(message);
        traceListener.WriteLine($"Message processing completed "+
            "at {clock.Now}. Duration: {stopwatch.Elapsed}");
    }
```

Listing 6-9 shows a complete LoggingBus class. More details on IBus can be found at http://bit.ly/1RINTyi.

Listing 6-9. A Complete LoggingBus Class

```
public class LoggingBus : IBus
{
    private readonly IBus wrappedBus;
    private readonly TraceListener traceListener;
    private readonly IClock clock;

    public LoggingBus(IBus wrappedBus, TraceListener traceListener,
        IClock clock)
    {
        if (wrappedBus == null)
            throw new ArgumentNullException(nameof(wrappedBus));
        if (traceListener == null)
            throw new ArgumentNullException(nameof(traceListener));
        if (clock == null)
            throw new ArgumentNullException(nameof(clock));
        this.wrappedBus = wrappedBus;
        this.traceListener = traceListener;
        this.clock = clock;
    }

    public void Handle(IMessage message)
    {
        traceListener.WriteLine($"Message sent at {clock.Now}. "+
            "Message details: {message}");
        var stopwatch = Stopwatch.StartNew();
        wrappedBus.Handle(message);
        traceListener.WriteLine($"Message processing completed at "+
            "{clock.Now}. Duration: {stopwatch.Elapsed}");
    }

    public void AddTranslator<TIn, TOut>(IPipe<TIn, TOut> pipe)
        where TIn : IMessage where TOut : IMessage
    {
        traceListener.WriteLine($"Translator added to translate "+
            "{typeof(TIn)} to {typeof(TOut)} at {clock.Now}");
        wrappedBus.AddTranslator(pipe);
    }
```

```csharp
    public void AddHandler<TIn>(IConsumer<TIn> consumer) where TIn : IMessage
    {
        traceListener.WriteLine($"Handler added to consume "+
            "{typeof(TIn)} at {clock.Now}");
        wrappedBus.AddHandler(consumer);
    }

    public void RemoveHandler<TMessage>(IConsumer<TMessage> consumer)
        where TMessage : IMessage
    {
        traceListener.WriteLine($"Handler of message "+
            "{typeof(TMessage)} removed at {clock.Now}");
        wrappedBus.RemoveHandler(consumer);
    }
}
```

One side-effect of the decorator pattern is that you can more closely satisfy the single responsibility principle where the wrapped instance sticks to one responsibility and each decorator another responsibly.

Façade

In many systems, there is a number of complex classes that might perform complex things (maybe legacy, maybe they're just complex). Regardless of why they're complex, you may find that certain usage scenarios use a consistent subset of several instances of classes. This is where the façade pattern comes to your rescue.

The façade pattern provides a new, simplified interface over another set of interfaces (a façade). This differs from mediator pattern in the façade does not provide new functionality, it just passes through to a contained or aggregated set of objects.

I've successfully used patterns like façade to implement transitional architectures where the FAÇADE was the ideal interface to reach in the future. Things would use the façade while the implementation behind the façade evolved to the new, desired state. Code that used the façade never needed to change while the implementation evolved.

Factory Method

The factory method pattern is an inversion of control implementation typically used with subtyping. An abstract class will define an abstract method that will be called to create an instance of a type (typically an instance of an implementation of another abstract type or interface). Subtypes of this class then implement this abstract factory method (not to be confused with abstract factory) to implement whatever means necessary for that scenario to create an instance of the required type.

Listing 6-10 shows an example of a factory method that implements an abstract method.

Listing 6-10. An Example of a Factory Method that Implements an Abstract Method

```csharp
public abstract class FileSystem
{
    public abstract Stream OpenFile(string name);
    //...
}
```

```
public class LocalFileSystem : FileSystem
{
    private string root = ".";
    public override Stream OpenFile(string name)
    {
        return File.OpenWrite(Path.Combine(root, name));
    }
    //...
}
```

In this example, we have an abstract FileSystem that we will use to model using files in a variety of file systems. We then model a specialized file system, LocalFileSystem, to model a local file system. We then implement a factory method called OpenFile that is responsible for creating a Stream object that can be used by any FileSystem code or anything using a FileSystem, to process data in that file system.

Iterator

The iterator pattern facilitates iterating collections without knowing the implementation of the collection (i.e., that it's an array, a list, a stack, etc.). I won't go too much into detail about this pattern because it's baked into the language in .NET via IEnumerable<T> (more languages like Java have followed suit).

The canonical pattern is defining an Iterator class/interface that provides methods like First, Next, IsDone, and CurrentItem to navigate the collection and get and item out of the collection. The collection itself would have a method like CreateIterator that would create a concrete Iterator instance for that collection.

This pattern is slightly different in .NET in that there is an IEnumerator<T> class (the equivalent of Iterator) that provides three members: Reset() (the equivalent of First), MoveNext() (the equivalent of Next), and the Current property (the equivalent of CurrentItem). Something like IsDone is implemented as the return value of MoveNext() (false if at the end of the collection or true otherwise). Collections would implement IEnumerable<T>, which provides the GetEnumerator method (the equivalent of CreateIterator).

Layers

The layer pattern is probably one of the most commonly used patterns. Unfortunately, it's also one of the most misused patterns. Let's first define what the layer pattern is. The layer pattern models a real-world pattern: layers. A layer in the real world is something that is adjacent to one or two other layers (bottom and top layers would have only one adjacent layer) and don't touch any other layers. With software design layers, we include one other constraint: that lower layers cannot depend on the higher adjacent layer. We can see an example of layered dependencies in Figure 6-2.

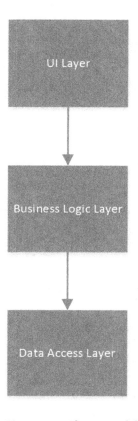

Figure 6-2. *Three-tiered design*

Here we see the typical three-tiered design (which isn't tiered, but that's another book) where the UI layer uses the business logic layer and the business logic layer uses the data access layer. But layering rules (and non-circular-dependencies common sense) detail that the UI layer does not use the data access layer; the business Logic Layer does not use the UI layer; and the data access layer does not use UI layer. But on almost every project I've seen this used, at least one layer pattern violation occurred. Typically, this was due to shared models, where the shared model lived in a data layer and the UI layer ended up needing a reference to the data layer. The models lived in the business logic layer and the data Layer needed a circular dependence, etc.

There's nothing wrong with the layers pattern, just be sure to use it correctly so it doesn't introduce technical debt where it's supposed to solve it.

Mediator

In many domains you can model business logic within individual classes (called domain classes). Each one has a single responsibility. But domain classes are never used in isolation; they are used in a system in groups. You may have a `Customer` entity that's used along with an `Invoice` entity to handle invoicing. Neither entity may interact directly with the other, and the behavior being modeled isn't part of the modeled entity. (I typically use the example of an office chair, as it can move, be delivered, etc., but that's not the responsibility of the chair. Something else performs that behavior on the chair. Other entities like `Invoice` seem to be more commonly thought of having non-real-world behaviors like `Print`. But, I digress.) An invoice may use a `Customer` entity and a user may need to print an `Invoice`, but it's something else that prints the invoice.

The mediator is the something else that would print the invoice (maybe an InvoicePrinter class). Its responsibility would be to know about the invoice and maybe the Customer and know what needed to be interacted with to print the invoice. It's different from the façade pattern in that it provides extra functionality.

The mediator pattern is useful for supporting the single responsibility principle and keeping domain logic separate from infrastructure or support/service logic.

Memento

Have you ever wanted to provide the ability to go from one state to a past state? The memento pattern details an abstraction for that. Typically, this is used to perform functionality like undo/redo, but think of anything that needs to go back to a previous state (like rollback). Memento provides the ability to provide a consistent interface regardless of the implementation (undo, rollback, etc.).

Effectively, the class that owns the state that needs to change will provide an ability to save and restore state (this class is considered the *originator*), that state will be requested of the originator (the class that asks is considered the *caretaker*), and the encapsulation that stores the state is called the *memento*.

The caretaker requests the current state (or a memento) from the originator and when state needs to return back to that state in the future, the caretaker sends the state back to the originator to return to that state. The originator is responsible for doing everything it needs to do to return to that state. In the simplest case, that would just be setting fields/properties; in a more complex state that could involve a transaction or compensating actions that need to be performed to return to that state.

Listing 6-11 shows a simple originator and memento implementation that provides an undo ability.

Listing 6-11. An Originator and Memento Implementation that Provides an Undo Ability

```
public class Document
{
    private List<string> lines = new List<string>();
    public class Memento
    {
        internal Memento(Document document)
        {
            Lines = new List<string>(document.lines);
        }

        public List<string> Lines { get; private set; }
    }

    public void AddLine(string line)
    {
        lines.Add(line);
    }

    public Memento GetMemento()
    {
        return new Memento(this);
    }

    public void Undo(Memento memento)
    {
        lines = new List<string>(memento.Lines);
    }
```

```
public IEnumerable<string> GetLines()
{
    return lines;
}
//...
}
```

Listing 6-12 shows sample caretaker code that works with Document and its memento pattern to perform an Undo function.

Listing 6-12. A Sample Caretaker Code that Works with Document and its Memento Pattern to Perform an Undo Function

```
var document = new Document();
document.AddLine("first");
var memento = document.GetMemento();
document.AddLine("third");
Debug.Assert(
    document.GetLines().Aggregate((c,n)=>c+n) == "firstthird");
document.Undo(memento);
Debug.Assert(
    document.GetLines().Aggregate((c, n) => c + n) == "first");
document.AddLine("second");
//...
```

In .NET, it's possible to make type serializable. With types like this the memento becomes that serialized state and the caretaker simply serializes the type to a caretaker-specific place to deserialize the state that needs to be restored. In other words, you don't have to implement a method on the originator to save/restore the memento.

Model

This is typically part of other patterns like model-view-controller (MVC) or model-view-presenter (MVP), but I've chosen to treat it independently (along with view) because this pattern is not unique to user interface design and offers benefits in many other places.

In the model/view/* patterns, model takes on one of two distinct responsibilities (probably one reason this pattern sometimes takes a while to master). The first is typically a logical/nebulous "model" that represents a "domain" or some "business logic". The second is an abstraction of data (sometimes via a data access layer).

In either case, what model/view/* is trying to facilitate is a layered architecture where the model is a lower-level layer to the UI (the view). This means that the model *cannot* depend on the view; the view can only use the model (not vice versa). In the domain version of the model, the view simply uses a bunch of domain class instances that model business behavior and data encapsulations. This is typically used in monolithic-type applications where a "layer" becomes a bit muddied.

The data-centric model begins to arise when you have strict layers or a tiered architecture where the model lives in another layer from the view and the view should depend on abstractions (i.e., interfaces) rather than concretions (like a specific repository type). In order to maintain the strict layering dependency directions, model classes either end up living in the data layer and become nothing but data containers (no logic) to maintain being abstractions, or live outside of both the UI layer and the data layer. The important part here is the model classes simply become data containers to easily maintain that separation.

With model/view/controller, the controller has the responsibility of interacting with the "user" via the web requests. With model/view/presenter, it is the view that interacts with the "user," typically via GUI elements. In either case, if we're looking for some consistency of "model" across these two types of patterns, the common denominator is that model is data-centric. Software with any level of complexity often begins to have issues with monolithic architectures, so I generally favor the model being data-centric. But this offers up some great pattern reuse when we start to recognize the view as being much more than just a user interface metaphor.

As we've seen with either MVP and MVC is that a "view" of the data is presented. In MVC, that view is more API-based (via HTTP requests and HTML responses) than MVP, where the view is stateful and has its own logic. It's when we start to recognize that any over-the-wire-/API-based presentation of data can benefit from a model/view pattern in that the model can provide the abstraction for the view of data so that our domain or business logic can remain decoupled from APIs (including front-ends). That is, the API is the view.

From the standpoint of how you would organize that in your Visual Studio projects, I've been advocating that the model classes live within the same project as the classes that populate the members of the model classes, or otherwise what implements the API. This can make it more apparent when the model classes have become part of a circular dependence. This also means that each API has a distinct set of model classes to ensure no cross-dependence and ensure single responsibility in each API. For example, in Figure 6-3 if the API projects shared a models project, one API project can influence the development of the other API project. If I change how the RESTful API responds and I change a model, the .NET API now has two reasons to change, which violates the single responsibility principle.

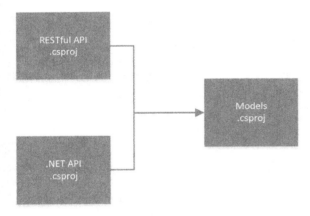

Figure 6-3. *Shared model*

In this simple example, that may seem fairly benign, but your reason to change the model for a particular API may be at odds with the other in many ways. Take, for example, serialization of a model. Let's say that our RESTful API needs to support XML and JSON serialization. You often have to use attributes to provide the metadata to serialization engines to serialize correctly. If we then look at the other API that may need to serialize as binary data like Protobuf, you quickly run into competing attributes. If two serializers use `DataContractAttribute` but need to use them in two different ways, you've just reached an insurmountable problem with a shared model project. This becomes even more apparent if you look at how RESTful implements versioning compared to Protobuf (where one has different versions of a Model and one versions members of one Model). It's just easier to recognize the single responsibility principle and have the model dependencies detailed in Figure 6-4.

 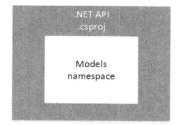

Figure 6-4. *Embedded models*

Retry

I include a pattern for retry because it's an often forgotten cross-cutting concern that is very prevalent with complex systems that rely on network communications, when they make network requests (and remember that many occur outside of using `HttpClient/WebRequest`) with database access, message queue access, e-mail access, etc.

The intent of this pattern is to encapsulate the policy (or polices) around retry logic and the action of retrying from the particular action or request that need to potentially retry. This is very similar to circuit breaker.

Making a request to a RESTful API can fail for a variety of reasons. Some of those reasons are "fatal," and some of those reasons are *transient*. A transient error is a temporary error so that even though this request might have failed, doing it again in the future may work fine. An ability to pause for a certain amount of time before retrying an operation could allow a larger process flow to continue eventually without completely failing.

As already noted, this can easily apply to raw HTTP communications. This pattern can be applied to any situation where transient errors can occur. Over-the-wire type communication is one of the best examples because intermittent network errors can and often do happen. This type of pattern would not necessarily be useful when there is a direct interaction with a user, in which case the user interface can simply inform the user what is happening and leave it up to them to decide what to do next.

Listing 6-13 is an example of a simple class to encapsulate retry policies and logic.

Listing 6-13. A Simple Class to Encapsulate Retry Policies and Logic

```
public class RetryExecutor
{
    readonly Action action;
    private readonly int maxTryCount;
    private readonly TimeSpan interTryDelay;
    private int tryCount;

    public RetryExecutor(Action action, int maxTryCount, TimeSpan interTryDelay)
    {
        if (action == null) throw new ArgumentNullException(nameof(action));
        this.action = action;
        this.maxTryCount = maxTryCount;
        this.interTryDelay = interTryDelay;
    }
```

```
public void Execute()
{
    do
    {
        tryCount++;
        try
        {
            action();
            return;
        }
        catch (Exception)
        {
            if (tryCount >= maxTryCount)
            {
                throw;
            }
        }
        Thread.Sleep(interTryDelay);
    } while (tryCount < maxTryCount);
}

}
```

This, of course, is overly simplistic and uses hard-coded values but gets the idea across. A true implementation will need to consider where the policies are stored (config, etc.) and the other types of delegates that you may need to execute (like Func<T> or asynchronous code).

With the act of retrying you may eventually find the need to give up. Under those circumstances you may want to work with the circuit breaker pattern to stop all similar requests until the problem is resolved. With transient errors that could mean simply waiting longer than what is programmatically configured, with other types of errors, interaction with a service provider may be required. In either case, the circuit breaker would be closed when those types of operations are expected to succeed again.

View

The view pattern has been closely aligned with MV* patterns like model view controller and model view presenter. But, as I detailed in the model pattern, those are really only two ways to interpret view with respect to a model.

In the traditional MVC pattern, the view is content that is communicated back to a browser and then displayed out-of-band from the application logic. Which is different from the MVP pattern, where the view directly interacts with the user (through UI controls) and with application logic (the presenter). MVP hasn't really been adopted in the .NET community, so we won't get into any more detail on it.

The often-overlooked applicability of view is really anywhere software provides a data-only response. In MVC, the model comes into play in both the *inputs* to the controller and the *outputs* of the controller (that feed into the view). But, as we detailed in the model pattern, that's exactly like a Web API. This use of the view pattern and the model pattern can also be used anywhere we have an API. The logic that the API performs decouples itself from clients of the API by using model classes at seams and mapping them to internal structures before performing any logic. This use of view and models is very similar to what the bridge pattern accomplishes, only at the seams. Effectively bridging the outward facing API (view) from the implementation.

Anti-Patterns

Service Locator

The service locator pattern is a type that locates dependencies. Similar in side-effect to a factory, but the service locator will *locate or create* dependencies if they don't exist, whereas a factory should always *create* the dependency. It's akin to a static factory that allows injection of service instances to be located. You could also view it as an IoC container. It is used like an IoC container, but an IoC container has the ability to build a complete dependency graph based on configuration/settings. You can use an IoC container like a service locator, but that is not symmetric equality: A service locator is not an IoC container.

This *sounds* like a great idea (especially when you view it simply as a static factory or an IoC container), but what it's really doing is only *adding* a dependency. Sure, it's releasing the responsibility of knowing how to create the real dependency, but at what cost? The real dependency is *still* a dependency and despite not having the responsibility of knowing how to create the real dependency, it is now also dependent on a *service locator*.

Wherever possible, a composite root should be preferred for injecting dependencies (via constructors) into the instances that need them. That is an ideal design and often designs evolve to a point of greater knowledge and may have technical debt, making it really hard to get to that ideal state. In those cases, an IoC container is the next best choice to offload the creation *and* injection of the dependencies.

Singleton

The singleton pattern is defined as something to "ensure a class only has one instance, and provide a global point of access to it." Your anti-pattern senses should be tingling with the use of the world global. What a singleton really is a glorified global variable and is likely introduced because the language in questions disallows global variables for very specific reasons.

It might be worth reviewing the issues of global variables. Because globals are global, you can't easily see the scope to which they apply, how your code affects that scope, nor how that scope affects your code. Additionally, you effectively have infinite coupling to everything else because you have no control over what accesses that global. That introduces problems with concurrency (and your ability to support it), memory, ownership, and testing.

Sure, singleton provides another level of abstraction. But that extra level of abstract is another dependency. As with service locator, we don't really change dependencies, we introduce a new dependency, which suffers all the same problems as service locator. In addition, it adds the responsibility of knowing that the dependency should only be one global instance by knowing it needs to use the singleton. Most classes only use one instance (maybe many references to the one instance), and if the class handles dependency injection, then it never knows how to create an instance either. In that case, it doesn't matter that there may be one global instance.

Singleton is a sign of technical debt. It's likely being used in response to a design issue. It's better to try to pay down that technical debt and remove the use of a singleton by correcting the design.

Static Factory

The static factory pattern is a static class that provides factory functionality. The static factory sounds like it would provide much of the same benefit as the abstract factory, but as with service locator, we're really just adding a new dependency, and a static one at that.

The new problem that a static factory introduces is the static dependencies. A static factory can encapsulate complex creation logic in the same way as an abstract factory does, but it usually creates a Gordian knot of dependencies to other static factories. For example, if ClassA requires an instance of ClassB then a ClassA static factory must know about that and couple to a ClassA static factory. This really creates a great big ball of factory mud. This is what Mark Seemann calls a *volatile dependency*. We don't want to take dependencies on things that are volatile like this because we don't want to take on that volatility. Plus, we should be depending on abstractions rather than concretions by following the dependency inversion principle. And what dependency inversion is attempting to accomplish is decoupling from the volatility of concrete implementations.

Practices

Wiktionary defines practice as, "Actual operation or experiment, in contrast to theory." That is, actually *performing* an operation. We use it to generally mean defined practices or processes that can be reused and applied to multiple situations over time in much the same way.

Practices are our way of taking repeatable or defined tasks and systematizing them. The ability to repeat a task the same way each time it is performed reduces rediscovery and human error. We define and apply practices so that we can perform our craft more reliably and in less time.

Principles

The application of generally accepted principles is probably one of the most common practices on teams that produce software. There are many definitions of principle; the one that's applicable here is having to do with a rule used to provide a solution to a problem.

Single Responsibility Principle

The single responsibility principle (SRP) was first defined by Robert C. Martin in the context of object-oriented programming. He defined it as, "A class should have one, and only one, reason to change."

Known as the "S" in "SOLID," this principle, of course, can be applied to more than just object-oriented classes. It can be applied to the lowest-level programming construct (a method or a function) and to the highest-level software architecture construct (a module), as well as anything in between.

What the principle has come to mean is something should only do one thing. Sometimes "...and do it well" is included to that meaning, but that seems somewhat obvious. But, the principle applies to how cohesive something is, in that it has cohesion in responsibility.

The tricky part of single responsibility and what often lets people be myopic about applying this principle is the meaning of *responsibility*. How little something has in terms of responsibility has to do with the granularity of that responsibility. In the context of a class, we could have one class that is responsible for the domain concept of an invoice repository. That's a fairly clear responsibility. With the repository pattern we say that we define one class to handle the storage of data related to an entity. But when we start to talk about things like CQRS (see Chapter 4), we start to talk about a different granularity of responsibility, one where one class is responsible for the *writing* of entity data and another is responsible for the *reading* of entity data.

Both granularities are correct, of course; it just depends on your circumstances. If you can increase the granularity of responsibilities, maintain/increase readability/understanding, and maintain/increase maintainability, you reduce coupling. When you reduce coupling, you reduce the level of coupling between things in a software system and thus reduce the impact of change.

Open/Closed Principle

Another principle attributed to Robert C. Martin and the "O" in "SOLID," is the open/closed principle (OCP). Open/closed principles state that "software entities should be open for extension, but closed for modification."

What this principle is really saying is that you should be able to change or extend something without directly modifying it. Again originally in the object-oriented context (specifically C++), this principle deals primarily with abstraction. The more things depend on abstractions the easier they are to extend.

In the original C++ context, this was realized with inheritance (and code that depended on an abstract Shape rather than specific shape implementations). This principle can be applied in a number of ways and at a number of levels. There are many patterns that are implementations of this principle (strategy, decorator, and façade, for example). The principle can be implemented with a variety of technologies (interfaces, inheritance, and composition, for example). The principle is also inherent to other principles and practices (dependency inversion principle, inversion of control, and dependency injection are some examples).

Liskov Substitution Principle

The Liskov substitution principle (LSP), and the "L" in "SOLID," basically state that whatever is provable about a base type should be provable about any subtype implementation. Or to say it differently: any subtype should be usable where the base type is expected without any adverse side-effects.

This principle was devised in the context of object-oriented design, but I think it applies, or is observable, to a wider context. The easiest context to imagine is with interfaces. Any implementation of an interface should be acceptable where any implementation of that interface is required. You may say that's obvious, but there are many instances where interfaces are defined as a set of possible members to use and, depending on some circumstance that need be known outside of the interface implementation, the interface is used differently. Stream is one example of this, where you can pass along a Stream to other types that need to do stream-based IO but any number of members may throw an exception (like Seek throwing NotSupportedException on non-seekable streams, or Write throwing NotSupportedException on read-only streams).

The canonical example is an abstract Rectangle type and a Square implementation. Although a Square is a type of Rectangle, it acts differently than a Rectangle: if you change its width, its height changes, for example.

We can view this principle in a wider context still to basically say that for any contract we define in whatever way we define it, we abide by that contract. It doesn't matter whether that contract is a subtype, an interface, other types of polymorphism, HTTP endpoints, etc.

Interface Segregation Principle

One of the things we described in the section on the Liskov substitution principle was how Stream's interface sometimes doesn't work depending on some sort of internal state of the stream. This is an excellent segue into the interface segregation principle (SRP).

The interface segregation principle is another of the SOLID principles (the "L" in "SOLID") and first described by Robert Martin as, "Clients should not be forced to depend upon interfaces that they do not use." In the Stream example, clients that use a read-only stream must depend on the existence of a Write method (as well as know not to use it, even if implicitly) through their dependence on Stream.

With the interface segregation principle, Stream would be broken into multiple interfaces like ISeekableStream and IWriteableStream, and those clients could depend on *those* interfaces instead of having to depend on the whole gamut of potential Stream members. That, of course, doesn't stop there being one implementation of multiple interfaces. Listing 6-14 shows an example of having a single implementation with three interfaces.

Listing 6-14. A Single Implementation of Multiple Interfaces

```
public class FileStream : IWritableStream, IReadableStream, ISeekableStream
{
    public void Write(byte[] buffer, int offset, int count)
    {
        //…
    }

    public int Read(byte[] buffer, int offset, int count)
    {
        //…
    }

    public long Seek(int offset, SeekOrigin origin)
    {
        //…
    }
}
```

This allows clients to depend on only one or two of the interfaces implemented and be more decoupled from any particular implementation. Be wary of this particular example though. It's easy to understand and gets the point across but introduces other problems. For example, what about all the different types of streams, such as file, memory, buffered, encrypted, etc.? Interfaces like this may put too much onus on the framework author (which may be why we have the Stream abstract class).

When analyzing requirements like this, remember to think of the bridge pattern because it's meant to provide a refined interface and bridge to an implementation. That may be a better option for a stream-like framework.

Interface-Based Programming

Interface-based programming is a form of design in which interfaces over implementations are used when making API calls.

Interface-based programming is a form of the dependency inversion principle, ensuring that dependencies are abstractions. The abstractions are specifically interfaces in this principle.

Dependency Inversion Principle

The dependency inversion principle is another of Robert Martin's principles that make up SOLID (the "D") and states that, "A: high-level modules should not depend on low-level modules. Both should depend on abstractions. B: Abstractions should not depend on details. Details should depend on abstractions."

A basically details layering. And B details that dependencies should be upon abstractions only. B reinforces A's detail about depending on abstractions.

To implement layering appropriately, a higher-level layer *uses* a lower-level layer through abstractions only. It should not know about any concrete types within the lower level.

You have to know about concrete types in order to instantiate something to get at it via an abstraction. This can lead code down a very circular dependent cycle. A way to manage this is to use dependency injection effectively. Despite having a program know about a concrete type in some way for the rest of the application to use the abstraction, the concrete type can be used in only one place (or by a framework) so that the rest of the code can maintain dependency inversion. (See the inversion of control section as well.)

Listing 6-15 shows an example of depending on a concretion.

Listing 6-15. Using Dependency Injection

```
public void Dump(List<string> items)
{
    foreach (var item in items)
    {
        Trace.WriteLine(item);
    }
}
```

The Dump method accepts a list of strings in order to dump to trace. Seems benign, but what if I wanted to change my code to use an array instead of a list? Or what if I wanted to support dumping of other types of collections? If we depend on an interface, we can continue using the Dump method as-is and anything that wants to use Dump will provide something that implements that interface. Luckily, with our example, we can use one of the framework interfaces like IEnumerable<T>. Listing 6-16 shows use of an interface instead.

Listing 6-16. Depending on an Interface to Continue Using the Dump Method

```
public void Dump(IEnumerable<string> items)
{
    foreach (var item in items)
    {
        Trace.WriteLine(item);
    }
}
```

The body of the method didn't need to change, but now we're not coupled to a particular implementation.

Inversion of Control

Besides the obvious meaning of the words within the principle, the inversion of control principle (IoC) details that the invocation direction be inverted from the tradition control. Traditional control is from client code to framework code (or higher-level code to lower-level code). Inversion of control inverts that so that framework code or lower-level code invokes client or higher-level code.

In order to avoid a circular dependency and chicken-and-egg situations, this means that those dependencies must be strictly abstract. Take the case of a framework. In order for someone to provide a framework to a future customer, they must first develop and test that framework. They then sell that framework to someone *and then* that customer writes code for the framework. Without abstractions, the customer would first have to write the code the framework would invoke. An impossible chicken-and-egg scenario. This means that the framework must own the abstractions.

Frameworks that provide dependency injection abilities are often called IoC containers (although sometimes referred to as DI containers). They're named in this way because the container becomes the responsible party for building up instances of objects based on configured rules. That is, they *invoke your constructors* to instantiate the objects in an appropriate order to be able to inject into other instances they need to create.

Composite Reuse Principle

Also known as composition over inheritance, this principle advocates the use of delegation over inheritance to implement reuse or to abide by DRY (don't repeat yourself).

A typical example (and typically pedantic) is the modeling of a team member and a team leader. A team leader is a team member who has leadership responsibility. A typical instinct is to model that with inheritance: a team leader is a type of team member. But that could be modeled through composition rather than inheritance and behavior delegated to other classes.

Listing 6-17 compares the two described implementations of a TeamLeader.

Listing 6-17. Comparing the Two Described Implementations of a TeamLeader

```
public abstract class TeamMember
{
    public string GivenName { get; private set; }
    public string FamilyName {get; private set; }
    public abstract void PerformWork();
    //...
}

public abstract class TeamLeader : TeamMember
{
    protected TeamLeader()
    {
    }

    public override void PerformWork()
    {
        //...
    }
}

public abstract class TeamLeader : TeamMember
{
    readonly TeamMember teamMember;

    protected TeamLeader(TeamMember teamMember)
    {
        if (teamMember == null)
            throw new ArgumentNullException(
                nameof(teamMember));
        this.teamMember = teamMember;
    }

    public override void PerformWork()
    {
        teamMember.PerformWork();
    }
}
```

```
    public void Lead()
    {
        // …
    }
}
```

Many patterns are designs of this principle. For example, façade, mediator, etc.

Don't Repeat Yourself

Also known as DRY, don't repeat yourself is about the clearest principle there is—don't repeat yourself (see what I did there?). While some associate this with reuse, that's a bit shallow. I prefer to view DRY as a principle for being explicit. If you look simply at reuse, you're addressing the side-effect of not repeating yourself. You can easily create things to reuse and miss out on the benefits of focusing on explicitness. For example, I can easily replace two lines of identical code invoked in two different places by a one method named Stuff (or a new class and a method named Utility.Stuff) and achieve reuse. But, have I added *more* or *less* value?

I'd argue in that example I've added less, much less. Clearly a pedantic example, but the degree to which de-duplicating adds value is more than just the ability to reuse. When we focus on making the implicit explicit, we get the value of that self-documenting code and the *side-effect* of reuse.

The uncontrolled quest for reuse has led many a team (and in some instances, whole language communities) astray and into an explosion of complexity and ambiguous naming.

Principle of Least Knowledge

The Principle of Least Knowledge is also sometimes called the Law of Demeter (LoD). The Law of Demeter is summarized as, "Only talk to your immediate friends". This principle is about the degree of coupling of code. Traditionally thought of at a method level, it means that of the objects that code has access to, it should only access instances (and the members on those instances) that the code has direct access to. This is often detailed as the class containing the method, the parameters given to the method, any object instantiated within the method, and the class's component objects (i.e., any classes the class has been given or has instantiated). Some definitions include "…and global variables," but we know better, right?

What confuses most people is what the code has access to. Code does, of course, have access to the members of the members of the objects it has access to, but the Principle of Least Knowledge suggests those shouldn't be accessed and the information must be provided by another means.

The canonical example is a paper boy. If you want a refund from a paper boy, you ask him for it, you don't reach into his wallet and pull out the money to get your refund. We could model this interaction in code, as shown in Listing 6-18.

Listing 6-18. The Principle of Least Knowledge Expressed as a Model Interaction

```
paperBoy.Wallet.Total -= refundAmout;
this.Wallet.Total += refundAmount;
```

Notice the number of dots when using paperBoy.

This isn't necessarily a hard and fast rule of counting dots; you need to use you own judgment as it applies to your design. For example, invoice.Customer.GivenName may be perfectly reasonable despite reaching beyond the object that the method was given. One thing to help you determine whether code could be improved is whether you're reaching in a changing state and whether what you're attempting to do is something else's responsibility.

This principle is trying to scope just how coupled any piece of code is. By reaching out beyond what it is given, a method becomes much more tightly coupled to implementation details outside of its control. This also limits how what it is coupled to is able to evolve.

I find that we can expand the meaning of Principle of Least Knowledge beyond the Law of Demeter to help us design less coupled code and achieve something more flexible and agile. The Dependency Inversion Principle of depending on abstractions instead of concretions is, I believe, a type of least knowledge. We know less about implementation details and are free to evolve with a greater degree of flexibility.

We can see an example of this application of Principle in Least Knowledge in the Dump method we detailed in dependency inversion. Clients of the Dump method were able to evolve differently and use different types of collections to suit their needs because the Dump method uses an abstraction (interface) instead of a specific type.

Principle of Least Astonishment

The Principle of Least Astonishment is very useful in programming and design. Basically it explains that you should do the most obvious thing. In the extreme, that could mean that you should not name a method that reads data Write, but it's usually subtler than that.

I find this principle the most useful when building interfaces and frameworks that other people will use. Often we let our implementation details leak into our interface because it is easier to implement. When designing interfaces, though, we should think about how the client would use it, not how it may be implemented. This is called creating task-based interfaces.

Task-based interfaces are similar to task-centered user interface design where you don't provide an interface to implementation, you provide an interface to perform tasks. For example, a bank account user interface could provide the ability to view and edit a balance. That's bad for a variety of reasons. Instead, a bank account user interface would typically provide the ability to perform various tasks on that bank account, like withdraw, deposit, etc.

That metaphor translates almost exactly to a BankAccount class. You would not provide a read/write Balance property, you'd provide a Withdraw and Deposit method.

That way, withdraw and deposit functionality is performed consistently and the ability to update a balance however the client code sees fit doesn't provide astonishing side-effects.

Postel's Law

Postel's Law is also known as the robustness principle. It states, "Be conservative in what you do; be liberal in what you accept from others". Sometimes it is described as "Be conservative in what you send, liberal in what you accept."

What this tells us when designing software and interfaces is to be broad about what you accept and be specific about what you send. So, I may write an interface to accept a string for a number, but may use an integer to send or respond with a number.

Summary

In this chapter, we delved into the realm of reusability through concepts and deliberate action. With patterns we define a way of communicating concepts that are applicable at a variety of levels and are generally language-agnostic.

Practices allow us to define repeatable, definable actions that are not empirical. By defining and repeating these processes, we can improve them over time so that the margin of error is minimal and innovation focuses on new value.

CHAPTER 7

Deployment: Patterns and Practices

Any software that needs to run needs to be deployed. Deployment is an important but often neglected part of developing and delivering software. Many times deployment doesn't get much attention until right before the software needs to be deployed. Often, that's way too late. Deployment needs to be planned, designed, and sometimes architected.

This chapter covers deployment involving two essential types of software development: application development and enterprise development. Both types of software development produce software, but the deployment needs can be drastically different.

Deployment of software is crucial to attain correctly functioning software. The most perfectly architected, perfectly designed, perfectly written, and perfectly tested software won't function properly if it isn't deployed correctly. Let's have a look at deployment with these types of software development.

Application Development

If you're developing a stand-alone application, your deployment needs will be quite a bit different than an enterprise application, which is typically a web application.

Application Development Practices

Stand-alone applications on Windows have some very distinct requirements and can benefit from some practices. Let's look at some practices around deploying stand-alone applications.

ClickOnce Versus Windows Installer

Aside from manually installing software, there are two technologies used to install software on Windows: Windows Installer (MSI) and ClickOnce.

Windows Installer (or Microsoft Installer or MSI) is an installer technology and API for the installation and maintenance of application and its components. Windows installer supports installing software that ranges from system-level software to simple applications and components. Windows Installer creates installation packages that integrate into control panel programs and includes support changing, repairing, and uninstalling. It recognizes that some of the resources a piece of software depends on must be installed or configured with administrative access. It allows a user not in administrative mode to install software. This is done through the user of system-level components and services included in Windows.

© Peter Ritchie 2016
P. Ritchie, *Practical Microsoft Visual Studio 2015*, DOI 10.1007/978-1-4842-2313-0_7

Windows Installer directly supports almost all aspects of integrating applications into Windows, including:

- Registry keys

- Desktop icons

- Start menu folders/icons/shortcuts

- Files

- Folders/directories

- COM components

- Shared components

- Per-user or all-user installations

Windows Installer also supports various installation features:

- Installation on demand

- Reinstall

- Add/remove features

- Roll back failed installations

- Merge modules

- Customer actions

You may not want to choose Windows Installer if you need any of the following:

- Automatic updates

- Non-administrative access/privilege

ClickOnce is an installer technology for Windows (from Microsoft) that will install Windows Forms or Windows Presentation Foundation (WPF) applications without requiring administrative access. ClickOnce applications are installed per-user and use only isolated user storage. Each ClickOnce installed application is isolated from other applications. ClickOnce also offers web-based installation and is self-updating.

Do not choose ClickOnce if your application requires any of the following:

- Installation of COM components

- Registering of components

- Installation of a Windows service

- Installation to a specific directory or to the Global Assembly Cache (GAC)

- Conditionally installed components

- User input

- Configuration of system-level resources

- The application to write to files or the Registry

That is not to say that you can't write an installer with Windows Installer and install components via ClickOnce. In fact, this is an excellent means of adding the ability to update components of your software. The Windows Installer could be used for the top-level installation and would create or change any system-level resources required by your software. Then ClickOnce would be used to deploy the software components. Using this technique results in the best of both worlds. It assumes any level of administrative access during top-level install, but that administrative access requirement would be minimized to initial install.

Migrate from Visual Studio Installer Projects

Visual Studio .NET 2002 introduced Installer Projects. These projects provided a limited, although comprehensive, ability to create Windows Installer packages. After Visual Studio 2010, support for Visual Studio Installer projects was removed. It was not until Visual Studio 2013 that limited support for these projects returned. But the support is via an extension. Although the extension is developed by Microsoft, support is limited (that is, not included in the Visual Studio or MSDN support options).

Given the limited support of installer projects, it is recommended that if you are upgrading from Visual Studio 2010 or are otherwise considering using Visual Studio 2013 or Visual Studio 2015 installer project extensions, you should consider alternatives.

There are several alternatives for Visual Studio Installer projects. One, of course, is the use ClickOnce technology if it fulfils your needs. Visual Studio includes InstallShield LE. LE Stands for Limited Edition, so it's *limited*. Some of the limitations of InstallShield LE include:

- Custom dialogs are not supported.

- Custom actions are not fully supported.

- Only files/folders defined in the solution/projects are supported.

Out of the box there is Windows Installer XML (WiX). Despite the name, WiX is a framework and toolbox that can integrate into Visual Studio to aid in creating Windows Installer packages. WiX is open source and, while it technically has little support, the community is active and development on the software is also active. I believe there is an option for paid support, should that be necessary.

Clean Test Environment

Tracking down the root cause of defects can be a difficult problem. Finding defects in software is essentially searching for things we do not know are there. Once we find a defect, searching for the root cause is another wild goose chase. Adding variables that can impact the behavior of the software we're testing and impact our search for those defects or their root cause makes finding defects and their root cause that much harder.

It is recommended that the software be installed to a *clean* environment at the start of each test. I use the word *clean* to mean an environment where the OS is freshly installed, but really that means a *known-good* environment. It can be very time-consuming to set up a clean environment. Reformatting a hard drive and reinstalling Windows can take a long time.

Fortunately, virtual machines can be created to be used as a location to perform the testing. A single image can be created and used to recreate clean virtual machines on demand. This can be done very quickly, making it easy to have a clean environment to install new versions of the software for testing.

Another way of having a clean test environment with virtual machines is to snapshot the virtual machine after creation so that you can restore to the snapshot before installing the software you want to test. VMWare and Oracle VirtualBox both support snapshots.

Continuous Delivery/Integration

I believe it was Adrian Cockroft who said, "Do painful things more frequently". That's been frequently paraphrased as "If it hurts, do it more often".

Things that are difficult to do are generally difficult because we're not good at doing them. Doing them more often makes us more skilled at doing them. Doing the hard things more frequently often enlightens us to ways of automating the processes. If we can completely automate a difficult process, it gets easier.

Continuous integration is a practice of merging all code changes, performing a build, and running automated tests several times a day.

Continuous delivery is an approach to software development where working software is produced in short iterations or cycles.

Continuous integration and continuous delivery help us embrace the pain-points and resolve them as soon as possible. The automation of the resolutions helps avoid the pain while also ensuring the pain is addressed quickly, often, and as close to the cause as possible. This helps ensure the resolution is as unencumbered as possible

It is recommended to approach the pain of building, integrating, and deploying software through the automated processes that continuous integration and continuous deployment recommend.

Enterprise Development

Deployment Strategies

With enterprise development it's very rare that there is one environment to deploy to. At the very least, there could be a development and a production environment. Preproduction activities like development, testing, user acceptance, etc. could be done in development and production would be reserved for day-to-day use of the system. Alternatively user acceptance could be done in a production environment. Limiting it to two environments can introduce some dependencies and have some adverse side-effects. A testing, staging, and sometimes a user acceptance environment go a long way to alleviating those side-effects. We'll get more into those environmental patterns and practices, but what this means is the potential for deploying code with two different strategies: promotion or build-per-environment.

Build-Per-Environment

The first option I'll detail is the build-per-environment option. What this means is that for each environment, a build is executed and the results of the build are deployed to the one target environment.

There are several perceived advantages to this strategy. Work can be done independently for each environment and each environment can be a branch in source code control.

Caveats

With any choice there are often caveats: side-effects that may not have been apparent when the choice was made. Choosing a build-per-environment strategy comes with some caveats. Build-per-environment obviously comes with some way of tracking the code for each environment: environment branches.

Now that you have one branch per environment, what happens to work for features or bugs? Typically those are also handled by branches but you could end up with many branches to manage and merging them backward and forward. There are some practices that can help guide how we handled bug and feature branches, discussed in the next sections.

Merges Flow in One Direction

With branches for environments, merging should happen in only one direction: *to* the environment branch. This means changes always start in a development branch and work their way through to an environment branch. Nothing ever gets changed in testing, integration testing, staging, or production and is merged back into a prior environment. Anything found in an environment like testing is fixed in development first then merged forward.

The Master Is Stable

With merging only going into environment branches and bugs and features being independent branches, we really need one *stable* branch for all branches. Given the convention of using a "master" branch, this branch would be the source for the build process. This follows fairly well the source code control flows we detailed earlier.

Feature and bug branches can still be used, they would simply be branches from the master (maybe via development branch which should also be branch off of the master) and any changes that need to be deployed would first be merged into the master.

Promotion

One of the caveats of the build-per-environment strategy is that your source code control ends up being read-only branches that contain the code that may be currently deployed to the corresponding environment. Typically you'd only merge into the environment branch for the sole purpose of performing a deployment, but there's no way to guarantee that. So, as some astute readers may have deduced, this ends up being no different than having a *main* (master) branch and *tagging*. By going down the tagging route, you invariably end up on the promotion strategy of managing deployments with the addition of many branches to managed, with little value.

To a certain degree, the strategy you go with is affected by your deployment tools. Visual Studio and Release Management have typically supported the promotion strategy so it's easy to get going with this strategy. Just because the workflow in Release Management assumes "promotion" from environment to environment, it still allows the execution of generic tasks at each stage. So, a build-per-environment strategy could still be performed with Release Management.

Environments

To some degree, the choice of deployment environment follows Conway's Law. For sufficiently complex systems: if you have a team of developers, you'll likely find great value in a Development environment; if you have a discernable Quality Assurance role, you'll likely find great value in a Testing environment; and if you perform User Acceptance testing, you'll likely find great value in a User Acceptance environment.

Needless to say, knowing the value of each type of environment when planning your deployment environments and applying them to the needs of your team goes a long way toward implementing environments that add great value (as well as not implementing those that do not provide much value).

The quantity and types of environments you choose to create and deploy not only depend on the roles you may have that depend on them, but also the degree to which you want those roles to perform their tasks independently. You could, of course, have one non-production environment that a version of the system can be deployed to that is shared amongst all the roles. While developers are designing and developing, they use the environment; while testers test, they use the environment; while integration is being tested, the environment is used for that; while users perform user acceptance, then use the environment. To some degree this may seem logical; after all, developers produce software that testers test and, once tested, users use. Unfortunately, we've learned from Agile (or prior to Agile) that Waterfall development is a myth and software is best developed iteratively. This means that it's quite likely that developers are on to new work while testers are testing and testers are testing new systems while user acceptance is being performed. So, it's highly unlikely that a single non-production environment will be sufficient. Let's have a look at the common environments.

155

Local

Although I detail a Local environment here, there really isn't a local environment, per se. I say that because it's not an environment that someone sets out to build for a particular system. It's an individual developer's computer and any external resources that they have access to. So, on a team, there are many local, disparate, environments.

The disparity of local environments from developer to developer really underscores the need for the environments we're about to describe.

With the differences in these Local environments, if one developer encounters a problem, it's indeterminate that it can't be due to the haphazard setup of *that* environment. Comparing it to another developer's environment may or may not shed some light on the problem. Inherently comparing execution in two local environments is still indeterminate. It's a recommended practice to use non-local, independent, environments for various levels of testing.

Experimental

The creation and setup of any one environment for any system really depends on knowing a fair amount of information about a system. For example, an environment requires one or more computers, each computer having certain resources pertaining to RAM, CPU, and disk. Network connections between computers may need specific configuration involving speed, firewall, etc. Not to mention all the external resources and their types (databases, queues, caches, etc.)

All of these elements of an environment (or environments) require they be known in order for an environment to be built. This leaves a bit of a dilemma—how can we accurately discover what environmental requirements our system has without an environment?

This is where an experimental environment comes in. This environment, sometimes called a *sandbox*, is an environment with access to various resources and the ability to be configured/reconfigured rapidly. This environment allows developers to deploy, redeploy, configure, and reconfigure, until they can prove, through a series of tests, that a particular environmental configuration suits the system that needs to be deployed.

Development

Sometimes a Development environment is considered the same way as the local environment. For simple systems this may be sufficient. A local environment *could* have local resources like multiple local running services, local database, local queues, etc.

In more complex systems, or systems where the dependent resources simply can't exist on local, developer computers, a development environment is a necessity.

A development environment allows developers to deploy software to a system that has some of the same attributes of a production environment (multiple servers, remote queues, remote databases, etc.). The environment can be controlled by developers at a reasonably low level, allowing them to reconfigure the environment to help debug issues without affecting other environments (like testing and testers, or even worse production and users). Developers need to be free to install debugging tools to help them find the root causes of issues (that might not have been discovered in a Development environment).

Integration

An optional environment is an Integration environment. For the most part, if a team has a Development environment, they probably have all the resources they need to do comprehensive integration testing.

Integration testing can be done manually by checking various metrics or attributes through a manual test. An Integration environment provides an independent environment to perform those tests. But it's recommended practice to automate anything that is done more than twice. Integration tests are a perfect example of something that should be automated whenever possible.

Despite having a Development environment an Integration environment is useful as a Continuous Integration (CI) target environment. Continuous Integration tools help to automate much of the deployment and testing process. A Continuous Integration tool can detect source code control commits and start a process of build-deploy-test to verify source code changes. Sometimes this is a build server, but if the continuous integration tool supports other non-unit tests, a separate Integration environment goes a long way to supporting continuous integration.

Testing

As you'll see in Chapter 8, there is more to testing than unit testing and integration testing. We've mentioned in passing load, performance testing, and user acceptance, but there is also QA-typical testing such as functional and regression.

Staging

Staging is a pre-production environment. Staging must be independent from Production but must closely, if not exactly, resemble production. Staging's main purpose is to verify that the software's deployment will work in Production without affecting Production.

Since Staging closely matches Production, any number of types of tests should be verified in Staging. In scenarios where there are no other environments (except maybe Development), then most of the testing described in the other environments should be carried out in Staging. This is because we want to find any issues related to the software being deployed before reaching Production as much as possible. We have means by which to limit the impact of a bad deployment in Production (rollback), but that still affects the availability of production and thus the productivity of its users.

If an integration environment is not in use, one of the main purposes of Staging is to verify integration of the deployed components. See Integration for more detail. But being the non-Production environment that most closely resembles Production, this environment should be used for other types of tests. Staging should be the environment where performance and load testing should be performed. Staging allows these types of testing to occur in isolation without affecting Production and at the same time not *being affected* by Production.

Deployment scripts to deploy to Staging should also closely resemble those (or be identical except for inputs). If Staging deployment scripts are drastically different from the Production deployment scripts, an important opportunity to avoid deployment issues in Production has been missed.

If user acceptance and testing environments are not used, Staging could be used to perform user acceptance testing. Depending on the types of changes being deployed, user acceptance testing may not be performed on each and every deployment. But it is recommended that user acceptance testing be performed on features and functionality before they reach Production. Even though user acceptance testing can be performed in Production, anything that fails user acceptance testing technically isn't acceptable for Production and results in a causality dilemma (a chicken-and-egg scenario). Whether your team performs user acceptance in Production is up to the team; just be aware of the consequences.

Depending on the setup of your environments and the technology used for deployment, Staging may actually become your Production environment. Staging can be the passive Production environment and will be swapped into production assuming all tests are verified.

User Acceptance Testing

User acceptance testing is a somewhat broad statement. At face value, it's whatever testing is required for users (or a representative of the users) to accept the system as it is. This acceptance ushers it on to the Production environment.

Of course it is whatever the users deem acceptable that needs to be tested. This can be functional criteria or non-functional criteria. User acceptance testing must evaluate all the criteria that the users have deemed important.

As with a Staging environment, the User Acceptance Testing environment will likely be very close to that of the production environment. Accurate numbers about non-functional or quality attributes of the system need to be gathered to compare to a baseline or minimum criteria. Although user acceptance might involve load and/or performance testing, the User Acceptance Testing environment shouldn't be deemed the sole environment for load/performance testing. The main reason to have multiple environments is to maintain independence. As soon as the need for load/performance metrics is tied to one environment, that independence is lost. Plan a User Acceptance Testing environment to support accurate load/performance (or other quality attributes), but don't depend on it being the only environment for such tests.

Production

Production is the final, most important environment. It's the environment your customers use and it needs to be as rock solid as possible. Deploying to this environment may mean a number of things depending on the topology of your environment. A deployment may simply a configuration change. A deployment may be deploying some code. A deployment may be deploying everything (all code and all configuration). Whether you can have some of these types of deployments depends on your topology. If you have active/passive servers, you may only be able to deploy everything. Your passive servers will be at least one deployment out of date from the active ones, which makes it difficult to deploy just a delta. Or, if your passive servers are recreated on the fly, you may have to deploy everything because there is no "delta" that can be deployed (unless you consider a difference to nothing a "delta").

If you're working in a scalable environment, you may have multiple instances of your servers. It's unlikely that you want to take them all down for a deployment (otherwise, what's the point of reaching that level of scalability), so you may deploy to groups of servers at a time. This effectively results in a hot-swapping ability, allowing a deployment to Production with no downtime or no interruption of service.

Production is the *live* system. It contains all the real customer data. For the most part, this environment shouldn't be used for various testing. What data would you test with? If you're not using customer data, what are you actually testing? If you *are* using customer data, well, *you'd be using customer data*!

Despite that, you still need to know whether a deployment is successful or not. A series of smoke tests can be run to ensure everything is functioning properly. Each component should perform its own smoke testing upon startup and on demand. If any of those tests fail, you should have it notify you immediately. Ideally the pass/fail state of those tests can be monitored and your deployment script can detect that and give you some sort of pass/fail at the end of the script (or before a rollback is started).

Component smoke tests are limited to just testing integration. If all the components can communicate with each other in the way they need to, and if the software has no bugs, things should run smoothly. Unfortunately that assumes those tests are perfect and that all other variables are perfect. We know that's not always true. So, there may be some testing data added to the system to perform functional smoke tests. These tests are often manual but should be scripted/automatic whenever possible. Anything that is scripted can be run as part of the deployment process and that process can detect failure and automatically start a rollback. This limits the amount of time a bad deployment is accessible by the users of your system. If it's a passive environment, that may have no impact. If it's not, there's impact to the users. Deploying early in the morning or late at night limits that impact, but it still exists.

Active and Passive Environments

We detailed with the Staging environment earlier and alluded to the fact that Staging can sometimes be used as a passive environment. What are passive and active environments?

More and more systems are expected to available all the time. Such systems are considered highly available. Traditionally (or out of necessity or for lack of better resources) deployment to Production may have involved effectively disabling Production while it is being upgraded or reinstalled. This involves a certain amount of downtime (planned or otherwise) while the system is in an "unstable" state. Passive environments are environments where the creation, setup, configuration, and installation is performed and then swapped into the *active* environment. The active environment then becomes the Production environment. The downtime then becomes the amount of time it takes to *swap* the passive environment for the active environment.

Swapping environments could be viewed as updating a DNS record. Unfortunately, you don't have any control over what has cached that DNS entry value. Other computers may resolve your DNS record to an IP address and use that IP address for a period of time. A time-to-live (TTL) can be set on the record so that those computers will requery the record every once in a while, but there will always be some period of time that the old servers' IPs will be used after the DNS records have been updated. It's not recommended to swap active/passive servers this way. It's recommended that the load balancer be reconfigured to use the new IPs, not the old ones. Swapping may also involve updating configuration to point to non-swapped resources like databases or queues. The degree and scope of such swapping is outside the scope of this book.

This technique can be used along with active/active environments so that passive environments are swapped in, one by one, into multiple active environments so that there is never any downtime.

Using active/passive environments is also a technique for mitigating the side-effects of failure. If any resource within Production (active) fails, it can simply be swapped out and replaced by a redundant executing system.

Practices

Composable Systems

Composable systems are systems whose dependencies are not all compile-time dependencies. Some dependencies happen at runtime and can be composed differently during deployment. Deployments of non-composable systems must be deployed in one way. How composable systems are composed is part of the deployment process.

This comes with benefits and drawbacks.

On the plus side, you can't have an outwardly scalable system without it being composable. You can't scale outward if every component in a system is dependent in only one way. Scalable systems offer the ability to introduce more instances of a component or service so that the system can handle more load. If a system must be deployed in the one way (component A to server A that takes to component B on server B; there's no way for that system to handle more load), it cannot scale outward.

As a drawback, the deployment of a composable system be deployed so that the system is composed incorrectly. This isn't unique to composable systems. Any non-composable system can, of course, be deployed incorrectly. But with non-composable systems it's easier to know which ways are wrong.

For the most part, it's best to create systems that are composable in some way or form. The deployment can be catered to composing systems in various ways to support various scenarios without changing the architecture or design, or changing the code.

Health Monitoring

What the attributes are of a healthy system are very diverse. Some are consistent across systems or even types of systems. Whether a server is up and running, whether a server has enough disk space, whether a server has enough RAM—these are all examples of metrics that can be monitored in almost every system. But what is "healthy" varies from system to system.

What a system defines as "healthy" for it must also be monitored. Some of what a system defined as healthy overlaps with other health monitoring. For example, a system may access server EastDB1 and if that server is down or the database service is not running, are health attributes of the server and the database respectively. But if a system cannot access EastDB1 for whatever reason, the *service* needs to report itself as unhealthy. It may be more than just access to the server or the database. The system maybe technically unhealthy if a database table does not exist or the system does not have the correct access to the database table. In order for that health (or lack of health) to be actionable, the system itself must detect and report it.

One of the important aspects of health monitoring beyond the comprehensiveness of what is monitored is the action-ability of the metrics. This becomes very important during deployment as a way to gauge whether the deployment is a pass or fail. If all the health metrics are not actionable, you really can't tell if a deployment is successful until a problem is reported by a user. That's far too late for detecting deployment failures. Ideally a deployment failure should be detected as it is happening and the deployment stopped (if into a passive environment) and rolled back (if deployed to a live environment). The sooner a failed deployment is made inaccessible, the less likely there will be corrupt data and angry customers, and the more likely the problem can be resolved quickly.

Quality Attributes

The strategy as to how a system is deployed is never random. Its strategy and how it is deployed address several quality attributes (non-functional requirements). Let's look at some of those attributes and discuss how a deployment strategy and thus deployment method can address that attribute.

Availability

Availability is the degree to which a system is in a functioning condition. This is somewhat ambiguous description because "functioning" can mean different things. For example, a system may be functional in that it responds to requests and responds with the correct data. But it may not be considered "available" because responding to requests takes several minutes instead of only a second or two.

Deployment applies to availability in that the system being deployed is deployed in a way that makes it highly available. The availability of the architecture certainly affects whether a deployment results in an available system. But a highly-available architecture can be deployed such that the system is not highly-available.

A deployment needs to take into account how a system is deployed and the availability requirements of the system it is deploying. If the system is highly available when it deploys four instances of a component to two different data centers and to two different fault domains then the deployment has to fulfill that. Despite an architecture that handles that particular composition (deployment), the deployment is responsible for making that happen. That means an available architecture is a design attribute and a deployment is the realization of that attribute.

Scalability

Scalability is a lot like availability. In fact, one may depend on another. A system may have high availability because it is very horizontally scalable. But a system is scalable in reality because of how it is deployed.

The deployment is the realization of that scalability. A system is scalable because its architecture allows or supports certain aspects of deployment. For example, one way of being scalable is to have stateless services and those services existing behind a load balancer that balances load to a varying number of services. But those services must be deployed behind the load balancer and the load balancer must be configured to know about those services and how to load balance to them.

That is, the deployment ensures that the scalability attribute of the system is realized.

Performance

A system is performant because of its architecture. An architecture is performant because it is deployed correctly.

A deployment ensures a certain performance attribute of a system by deploying the components of a system to the right places and in the right way. A deployment of a system may be *functional* in that one component can accept requests and perform other requests on other components, but if those requests go through the wrong load balancer or the load balancer is configured to inadvertently go through another load balancer, the performance of the system will suffer and the performance attribute of the system will not be met.

The correct deployment of the system results in the correct performance of the system.

Reliability/Robustness/Resiliency

Reliability is the attribute of system to continue operating as expected over time. Robustness is the attribute of a system to continue to work as expected in light of error or failure. How the system is deployed is partially determined by reliability. Any one node of a system could be faulting. But because a system may be deployed to multiple nodes, those healthy nodes can take up the slack to maintain a reliable system.

High Availability

High availability is often solved through some sort of cluster environment. By the loosest definition, a cluster is a set of two or more computers (nodes) that work together in some way.

High availability is partially about compensating for failure in that one or more nodes take the place of, or do some of the work of, failed computers. Failure is just one reason a computer may not be usable in the system, but there are several cluster models that can be used as deployment targets to satisfy high availability.

Active-Active Clusters

In this cluster model, the fact that there is more than one active node in the cluster is enough to compensate for one of them being unavailable. This assumes that each node is configured identically; otherwise, the loss of one node compared to another would have different availability.

The quantity of nodes must be at least two, but a number greater than two would have be determined by the team supporting the system. If nodes exist for scalability that would also have to be taken into account. Metrics on the average throughput of each node and any Service Level Agreement (SLA) should be used to determine a more exact number of nodes for any given system.

This type of model, of course, affects deployment because software or updates need to be deployed to each of the nodes. In an active-active model, the only criteria is that each node be updated/configured.

Active-Passive Clusters

The active-passive model means there is one inactive node (and fully updated/configured) for each active node.

This type of model affects deployment in a couple of potential ways. As we detailed earlier, this type of model can be used so that the deployment process deploys first to the passive nodes then, if successful, the load balancer is configured to point to the passive nodes and away from the active nodes. For failover, the non-passive nodes would then need to be updated. This, of course, leaves a period of time where there is no valid passive environment. If a failure occurred during that period, that would normally mean swapping active for passive, and the nodes would be out of date. This can be solved by having two passive environments: both would be updated before swapping one out to be active. Once swapped, the nodes in the old active environment could be recycled.

N+1 Clusters

The N+1 model can be viewed as a variation of the active-passive model, but instead of providing a one-to-one passive-to-active failover node, only one extra passive node is available to be swapped in as an active node.

This assumes that all nodes in the cluster have all the same software installed and swapping in as active is seamless. Alternatively, if each node has all the same software but is configured to be not running, the act of swapping could configure the passive node to execute the necessary software running on the failed active node before swapping it out. This is uncommon because of the complexity involved. It's likely easier to just have an active-passive environment unless you have some sort of platform to manage the extra node in some way.

Deployment is affected because an extra node needs to have software deployed to it. Potentially the configuration of the node needs to be unique during deployment, but from a deployment standpoint it is normally just another node. This model doesn't help specifically for availability during a deployment, but could be handled with updated fault domains.

N+M Clusters

The N+M model is an extension of the N+1 model. It's effectively the same as N+1, but instead of one extra node, there are M extra nodes.

Deployment would be affected very similarly to N+1 in that the software would have to be deployed to all nodes during deployment.

N-to-1 Clusters

In the prior models, passive/offline nodes would be swapped in to replace an active/online node and would simply remain that way. Presumably a new node would replace the failed one, be configured, and become a passive/active node. N-to-1 model assumes the passive/offline nodes will replace an active node only temporarily and be swapped out with the previously active node when the failure is fixed.

N-to-1 is effectively the same as N+1 in that there is only one extra node the event of failure.

In much the same as the other models, this means that the extra clusters need to be deployed to like any other clusters. What is and isn't active/online or passive/offline might not be determined during deployment.

N-to-N Clusters

The N-to-N model is similar to a combination of active-active and N+M. All nodes in the cluster are active and have identical software installed. Each node would be configured so only some of the software was active. The number of nodes in the cluster would have to be enough to compensate for the extra load that would occur on each node in the event of one or more failures.

This model is tricky to implement without some sort of platform to know what should and should not be turned on in each node when a failure occurs.

Deployment would likely be affected identically to the N+M model.

Failure Reasons

A node failure in a cluster is one type of failure. We've also seen that upgrades/updates are another way for a node to be unavailable or partially available. But there are others that are worth noting, even if they may not affect deployment.

There are major types of hardware that contribute to the availability of computers, above the actual computer. That computer is connected to other nodes and clients via a network device (hub, switch, router, etc.). That computer is also powered by a power strip or some extension-strip like device. In a data center these two devices are often grouped with several computers into a rack. Because the power device or the hub/switch on the rack can fail, we generally group these together in a rack fault domain and ensure software in our systems is installed in at least two different computers on two different racks. We made a point that the power to the computer could fail. By the same token the power to the data center could also go out. While we could back that up with alternate power sources (or even feeds from different electrical suppliers), we generally group that within a data center fault domain and try to ensure that our system will be deployed to two different fault domains within the data center fault domain in case power to an entire data center is lost. (There are other reasons for data center availability to be lost but the solution is the same.) In addition, any other shared resource could require separation by fault domain (within another fault domain). Storage, for example, is shared among systems, nodes, or clusters. Generally, storage may be deployed in another fault domain (like rack or data center), but it may not.

Delineating these fault domains allows us to ensure that one or more nodes in a cluster live independently of all other fault domains. So, if we delineate fault domains like rack, update/upgrade, data center, storage, region, etc. then we need to deploy our system, or parts thereof, to at least one node in each of these domains. (Yes, that means five or more nodes just for availability.) At a minimum, updates/upgrades should only occur in one update fault domain at a time so that, should a deployment failure happen, it won't take down the system. By the same token, you may need to phase in the deployments to other types of fault domains in case there is a problem with them while deploying.

Creating Environments

It's pretty rare now-a-days for a system to have devoted hardware. Usually systems use virtual machines. Alternatively, systems can use a pool of bare-metal hardware. I've found that virtual machines are more common.

When it comes to creating the environments for our systems, it's important to reduce the amount of repeated work. This should be done at an almost obsessive-compulsive level. Any repeated work introduces the possibility of errors and delays. Anything repeated is a manual step, a step that can get interrupted, delayed, etc. Although the allocation of hardware to the underlying hosting system may be hard to completely automate, any work with the hosting system should be 100% scripted. The creation of the VMs, the deployment of the operating system (that should also be done once in a virtual machine template or image) do the deployment of supporting software like databases.

If an environment cannot be created entirely by script, it is very likely that the creation of that environment will be a bottleneck to the deployment of the system. Keep in mind that in an era of continuous deployment and write-once servers, the creation of an environment could occur several times a day as deployments occur through continuous integration systems that spin up deployments on every source code control commit.

Write-Once Servers

Installing (aka deploying) software is notoriously problematic. Deploying complex systems has a huge number of variables just in dependencies alone. Deploying to *used* servers just increases those variables. E.g. deploying to a brand-new server (or virtual machine image) is a different set of actions compared to deploying an update to a server (or virtual machine image). If you're really dealing with two different acts, how do you manage when one of them runs into a problem?

Figure 7-1 shows three "death star" diagrams of the use of microservices in three different organizations and the degree of dependencies between them. As you can imagine, the added complexity of "updating" servers could introduce a huge aggregated amount of complexity in these systems.

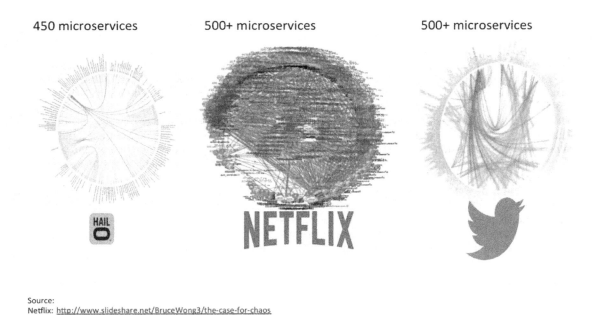

Figure 7-1. *Using microservices in three different organizations, and the degree of dependencies between them*

Some organizations have simply eliminated that second set of unknowns altogether to reduce the complexity of their deployments. They use what I call write-once servers. That is, they deploy only once to a server. In an era of virtual machines, it's easy to simply remove a virtual machine and allow its resources to be returned to a pool and reused by a new virtual machine. With the ability to script the creation of a virtual machine and those virtual machines to be based on images or templates, the act of creating a new VM takes seconds. To replace the unknowns of updating a server, replacing existing software with new software, with a few seconds of VM creation to reduce the possibility of spending hours tracking down update problems is a huge gain.

Environment Flow

With the various environments, there is a recommended flow. This assumes a promotion model of "moving" binaries or build artifacts from one environment to another. First of all, the flow of deployment moves from one environment to another in one direction. Nothing is ever deployed to one environment without having been deployed to the previous, or lower, environment.

Experimental, integration, and user acceptance testing work slightly differently than the other environments, that is you may not always deploy to these environments as part of the flow. Experimental is where the details of what the other environments might need result from observation of experiments. So you work in Local/Experimental for a while, move on to Local/Development, and possibly never return to Experimental. Integration is a bit of the same, you may use it to work out the kinks of integrating external resources in an environment similar to production, but once that's worked out, you may only use Integration occasionally. And user acceptance testing is along the same lines—you may not perform user acceptance testing on every change that you deploy.

Figure 7-2 shows the flow from environment to environment.

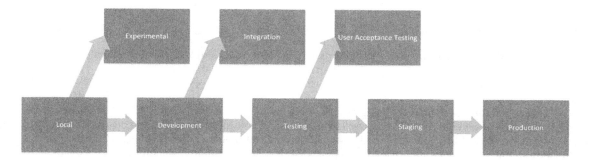

Figure 7-2. *The flow from environment to environment*

Promotion Over Per-Environment

We presented the two types of deployment strategies: promotion (one build of binaries or artifacts) and per-environment (unique binaries per environment). In reality, the generally accepted pattern is to use promotion.

With per-environment binaries, we really have to start from scratch with each environment. We are unable to inherit any level of quality from a prior environment. There are too many variables per environment to treat them in any other way than completely independently.

Try to choose promotion over per-environment so quality builds up from prior environments and you have a greater sense of stability over time. That's not to say you can reduce the amount of testing in each higher environment, but you can have a greater sense of assurance in higher environments.

Parallelize

We have a great number of resources available to use during deployment. If we use only one resource at a time, deployment can take much longer than it needs to. Wherever possible, parallelize actions so that more than one unrelated thing can be done at the same time.

This could be done on the action level or at the work flow level. You may choose to define logical workflows that contain related or dependent actions. Then you can parallelize workflows rather than individual actions.

Know what is independent and what is not. Do not choose to parallelize deployment actions until you know they are independent. Verification or testing, for example, simply cannot be done until all binaries are copied to the environment and the configuration/provisioning/registration of the binaries is complete and successful. Something like deploying a database and deploying an application binary can be done in parallel.

Verify Prior to Production

It may seem obvious to some readers, but it's worth pointing out. Deployment to production needs to be verified, but the verification of the logic and the design should not be done in production.

We've detailed that production has live customer data, and working with customer data in any way that the customer did not initiate is very problematic. Using "test" data in production is also problematic—it's really just the same as using non-customer data in another environment. So, just use another environment to verify logic, design, and architecture in a non-production environment.

But sure that the environment is similar to the production one, to avoid dealing with issues later.

Similar Environments

We have talked about a few practices and patterns to help reduce the complexity of deployments. Many kinds of patterns or practices build up to or end up being dependent on this pattern.

In order to reduce the complexity of deployments, other patterns depend somewhat on each environment being very similar.

This depends on a deployment being a process that happens to create an environment and that, once deployed, an environment does not change. There are cases where an environment can be a process in and of itself. Microservices are SOA services that can be "deployed" throughout an environment in response to monitor-able metrics like load. The "process" or "platform" in play would then deploy new instances of microservices in response to the metrics (and deactivate or uninstall them when not needed). In cases like this, "environment" becomes ambiguous. But, in cases like this, "deployment" becomes more a matter of providing binaries and configuration (metadata) to a runtime platform. In effect, the platform becomes the environment, but you can still have similar "environments".

Similar Deployments

While the process of deploying to each environment must be performed independently, each process should be similar.

As with anything in software, we can choose to do things in a structured or even object-oriented manner (depending on the deployment framework). Similar actions can be reused through libraries, functions, methods, subroutines, classes, etc. At a bare minimum, the control flow can be separated from the "variables" (and from constants or literals in code that can't be reused) to create functions, methods, or subroutines. Those variables can then be inputs to the functions. These functions can then be reused by changing the variables.

A deployment can then be built up from these functions. As deployments to new environments are required it can simply be a matter of changing the inputs to the functions rather than rewriting or recreating any code. Thus, the logic of deploying will be reused and deployments to each environment will be done *in the same way*.

This reduces the amount of work. The logic performed in each environment is built on something tried and true from the prior environment, reducing the number of variables from deployment to deployment and reducing the possibilities of what can go wrong (and thus the possibilities of what needs to be fixed in case something does go wrong). Your sanity will thank you.

Continuous Delivery

Deployment Pipeline

Figure 7-3 shows the automatic flow of changes into the various environments.

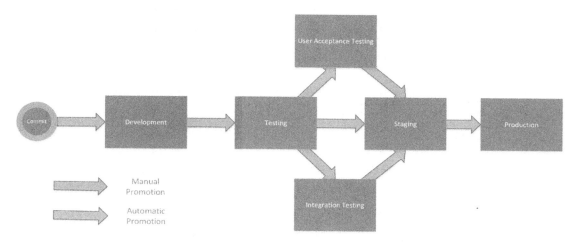

Figure 7-3. *The automatic flow of changes into various environments*

Obviously promotion to each environment would be gated by some sort of criteria. When needed, promotion to user acceptance testing or integration testing would be manually promoted. In a more rigorous environment, possibly promotion to user acceptance testing may be automatic.

This is a common pipeline flow; it's vital to customize this flow to suit your needs.

Smoke Testing

"Failure to plan is a plan to fail" is an adage that has guided many a great practice. Having a plan does not eliminate the possibly of failure, though. So a corollary to this adage could simply be the shortening of the adage to "plan to fail".

The systems we design and implement are complex and as much as we try not to fail, sometimes it happens. Despite our best efforts to avoid failure, we end up having to deal with it. It's not the fact that a failure occurred, it's how damaging the failure is (or was) that matters. To that end, it's important to be able to detect a failure as soon as it occurs so that remedial actions can be taken as quickly as possible to limit the damage. You plan for failure, its detection, and metrics (information) to help compensate for it.

To that end I have found that systems that automatically check for some semblance of correctness go a long way to detecting failure as soon as possible. That semblance of correctness can be viewed as an acid test, or smoke test. A smoke test is a non-exhaustive set of tests that perform a high-level of verification.

What is and isn't part of a smoke test can be somewhat subjective. I have found that at a minimum, a smoke test should verify integration points. Verifying integration points is verification of difficult-to-detect faults, for example.

So, a smoke test should try to detect difficult-to-detect problems and make noise about them as soon as they have failed.

It's difficult to detail a list of things to perform in a smoke test because no two systems are the same and no two organizations monitor their systems in the same way. What may be difficult to detect in one organization may be quickly detected and notified in another.

Here are some things I've found value in smoke testing:

- The ability to communicate to server

- The ability to communicate to web API

- The ability to successfully invoke an API

- The ability to communicate to database

- The ability to read from database

- The ability to write to database

- The ability to receive from queue

- The ability to send to queue

- The ability to communicate with cache

- The ability to write to cache

- The ability to read from cache

Summary

As you've seen, deployment is an important aspect of software development. It is the practice of realizing an architecture. Deploying is the act of putting certain quality attributes into place.

Deployments are complex and that complexity can lead to problems without planning ahead and approaching deployment with established or well-thought-out practices.

This chapter detailed some of those practices that help make deployments smooth and avoid the complexity becoming pain-points. It also provides a good reference to ensure that when you're approaching deployment, you can approach it in a planned way and not as an afterthought (that would allow the complexity to cause pain-points).

CHAPTER 8

Testing

In every industry that produces a *product*, there exists some level of verification that what is produced meets some level of quality. In some industries, that check isn't done on every product produced, but a sample of a batch of products (e.g., the food industry takes one product from a batch to test various qualities against an expected range). Other industries may use jigs or templates to ensure or verify quality. But, it's uncommon for zero checks to be made on products before they are available to customers.

Software is no different. What software developers produce should be verified in much the same way. Although we sometimes like to focus on the coding or even on the design aspects of software development, ensuring that our end product is not flawed is a vital responsibility of software developers and designers. Let's look at some principles and practices that can help us do that more effectively within Visual Studio 2015.

This chapter focuses on how software can be verified, or tested, to ensure it does what it is supposed to do with no adverse side-effects. For the most part, this chapter describes the abilities within Visual Studio for automated testing using MS Test.

Tests

The term "test" is broad and could mean testing a system via the user interface or could mean testing the system via the code or by an API. This chapter focuses only on automated testing via code or by an API. There are several types of tests, and only a handful generally applies to automated testing. For the most part automated testing is also called *unit testing*, so I'll typically refer to automated testing as unit testing, partially because the testing frameworks use that terminology.

Unit Testing

Unit testing is one of the types of test that we can use to verify an application's code. Unit testing is the act of testing the smallest unit of code: a method. There are many unit testing frameworks that facilitate unit testing, but they are really just automated testing frameworks. They provide no restriction on the depth of what is tested, only that zero or more methods from the system being tested are invoked during a test. Code coverage tools can be used in conjunction with the unit test frameworks to monitor and track the depth of what is tested. So the type of automated test could be a unit test, an integration test, a functional test, a user acceptance test, etc. And there are other frameworks to facilitate those other types of tests (like the ability of a test to interact with the user interface).

© Peter Ritchie 2016

P. Ritchie, *Practical Microsoft Visual Studio 2015*, DOI 10.1007/978-1-4842-2313-0_8

Unit Test Patterns

Test Doubles

A *test double* is simply something that takes the place or acts in the place of something else.

The term *mock* is often used in place of *test double*. *Mocking* is a general term for the act of using test doubles to isolate test code. A *mock* is something that takes the place of something else and acts in very specific ways (it mocks something else) so that interactions occur with the mock and code being tested can be isolated. Known side-effects come from the mock so the unknowns are kept within the system being tested and can be asserted in isolation. The mock is then used to verify that it was used in an expected way by the system being tested.

For example, Listing 8-1 shows a CSV parser class. This class uses an IFileSystem interface detailed in Listing 8-2. An example implementation of IFileSystem, called LocalFileSystem, is shown in Listing 8-3.

Listing 8-1. A CSV Parser Class

```
public class CsvParser
{
    IFileSystem fileSystem;

    public CsvParser(IFileSystem fileSystem)
    {
        this.fileSystem = fileSystem;
    }

    public IEnumerable<IEnumerable<string>> Parse(string filename)
    {
        var stream = fileSystem.OpenFile(filename);
        using (var reader = new StreamReader(stream, Encoding.Unicode))
        {
            string line;
            do
            {
                line = reader.ReadLine();
                if (line != null) yield return line.Split(',');
            } while (line != null);
        }
    }
}
```

Listing 8-2. An IFileSystem Interface

```
public interface IFileSystem
{
    Stream OpenFile(string name);
}
```

Listing 8-3. An IFileSystem Implementation

```
public class LocalFileSystem : IFileSystem
{
    private string root = ".";

    public Stream OpenFile(string name)
    {
        return File.OpenWrite(Path.Combine(root, name));
    }
}
```

We could create a mock IFileSystem implementation (MockFileSystem detailed in Listing 8-5) that we could use with CsvParser to verify how the IFileSystem object was used. For example, if we wanted to verify that CsvParser correctly opens a file when it parses, Listing 8-4 shows an example test that we might write to assert that.

Listing 8-4. Asserting a Mock File System

```
[TestMethod]
public void ParsingCsvOpensFile()
{
    var  mockFileSystem = new MockFileSystem("1,2,3\n4,5,6");
    var sut = new CsvParser(mockFileSystem);
    var data = sut.Parse("test");
    var lineCount = data.Count();

    Assert.IsTrue(mockFileSystem.VerifyFileOpened());
}
```

Listing 8-5. An IFileSystem Mock

```
public class MockFileSystem : IFileSystem
{
    private bool openFileCalled;
    public Stream Stream { get; private set; }

    public MockFileSystem(string fileData)
    {
        Stream = new MemoryStream(Encoding.Unicode.GetBytes(fileData));
    }

    public MockFileSystem(Stream stream)
    {
        Stream = stream;
    }

    public Stream OpenFile(string name)
    {
        openFileCalled = true;
        return Stream;
    }
```

```
    public bool VerifyFileOpened()
    {
        return openFileCalled;
    }
}
```

A stub is a test double that provides inputs to the system being tested. It is a test double that the system being tested invokes (calls methods, invokes property getters or setters), etc. and the stub responds in very specific, predetermined ways such that the only unknowns are how the system being tested interacts with the stub. Testing a system in isolation and with only stubs that respond in predetermined ways ensures that the test isolates only the testing system to assert it operates as expected.

A *spy* is a test double that observes the output of the system being tested. You typically use a spy when you want to verify the interaction of the system being tested with a dependent object. Similar to Listing 8-4, we could create a test that verifies CsvParser. But, instead of verifying that the IFileSystem.FileOpen is called, we could verify that Stream.Read was called. A test that would do that might be similar to Listing 8-6.

Listing 8-6. Verifying Stream.Read Is Called

```
[TestMethod]
public void ParsingCsvReadsFile()
{
    var spyStream = new SpyStream(Encoding.Unicode.GetBytes("1,2,3\n4,5,6"));
    var mockFileSystem = new MockFileSystem(spyStream);
    var sut = new CsvParser(mockFileSystem);
    var data = sut.Parse("test");
    var lineCount = data.Count();

    Assert.IsTrue(spyStream.ReadCalled);
}
```

You'll notice that we're now injecting a new type of stream into our MockFileSystem, called SpyStream. This class acts like a Stream, but allows us to spy on the inputs given to it by our system being tested. The SpyStream implementation is in Listing 8-7.

Listing 8-7. SpyStream Implementation

```
public class SpyStream : Stream
{
    private byte[] streamData;

    public SpyStream(byte[] streamData)
    {
        this.streamData = streamData;
    }

    public bool FlushCalled { get; private set; }
    public long Offset { get; private set; }
    public bool SeekCalled { get; private set; }
```

```csharp
public override void Flush()
{
    FlushCalled = true;
}

public bool SetLengthCalled { get; set; }
public bool ReadCalled { get; private set; }

public override long Seek(long offset, SeekOrigin origin)
{
    SeekCalled = true;
    switch (origin)
    {
        case SeekOrigin.Begin:
            Offset = Math.Min(streamData.Length, offset);
            break;
        case SeekOrigin.Current:
            Offset = Math.Min(streamData.Length,
                Offset + offset);
            break;
        case SeekOrigin.End:
            Offset = Math.Min(streamData.Length,
                Offset - offset);
            break;
        default:
            throw new ArgumentOutOfRangeException(nameof(origin), origin, null);
    }
    return Offset;
}

public override void SetLength(long value)
{
    SetLengthCalled = true;
    if (value < 0)
        throw new ArgumentOutOfRangeException(nameof(value));
    if (value > int.MaxValue)
        throw new ArgumentOutOfRangeException(nameof(value));

    Array.Resize(ref streamData, (int) value);
}

public override int Read(byte[] buffer, int offset, int count)
{
    ReadCalled = true;
    int bytesToCopy = (int) Math.Min(count,
        streamData.Length - Offset);
    Array.Copy(streamData, Offset, buffer, offset, bytesToCopy);
    Offset += bytesToCopy;
    return bytesToCopy;
}
```

```
public override void Write(byte[] buffer, int offset, int count)
{
    var bytesToCopy = Math.Min(count, buffer.Length - offset);
    if(Offset + bytesToCopy > streamData.Length)
        Array.Resize(ref streamData, (int) (Offset + bytesToCopy));
    Array.Copy(buffer, offset, streamData, Offset, bytesToCopy);
}

public override bool CanRead => true;
public override bool CanSeek => true;
public override bool CanWrite => true;
public override long Length => streamData.Length;

public override long Position
{
    get
    {
        return Offset;
    }
    set
    {
        Offset = value;
        if (Offset > streamData.Length)
        {
            Array.Resize(ref streamData, (int)Offset);
        }
    }
}
}
}
```

A *dummy* is a test double that is used as a value to either the system being tested or something the system being tested requires. The dummy value is only used because a value is required; nothing about the dummy is verified. A null is often used for a dummy value (like a dummy parameter). A dummy is sometimes a type of stub (see the section about fakes) because the system being tested may need to act upon it, but it is used like a dummy because nothing about the stub's inputs is verified.

A fake is almost identical to a stub except that it is not given any predetermined state (other than default instance state). The system being tested interacts with the fake in the same way as a stub and would result in consistent inputs to the system being tested, assuming the interaction with the fake is consistent. A fake is similar to a dummy, and in some contexts it's considered a dummy.

Arrange Act Assert

There are a couple of ways to organize unit tests. Probably the most common is known as *arrange act assert*. Arrange act assert is a mnemonic for organizing a test such that the start of the test method is devoted to arranging the system under test (SUT), the next part is devoted to invoking the code being tested (acting upon it), and the last part is devoted to asserting the conditions that prove the test passed. In other words, "*Arrange* all the necessary preconditions and inputs. *Act* on the object or method being tested. *Assert* that the expected results have occurred." Each section within (or "paragraph" within) the unit test code is separated by a blank line.

Arrange

The arrange section is the setup of the test. Arranging a test is generally a matter of creating any object needed to be acted upon or used with the objects being acted upon. The arrange/act/assert organizational technique really makes each test method the entire test, leaving little for the class to contain other than to be a grouping (like a namespace) of test methods.

Act

The act is the section that actually does something with or to the system being tested. This could be as little as one line of code, or many lines. Typically, you want to focus a test to be one assert (i.e., verify one thing), so the amount of code to act on the system being tested should be limited. If you find that there is lots of code in the act section, it might be a code smell and a refactoring may be in order.

Assert

As detailed in act, you typically want each test to assert one thing. We do that because we want granular feedback about what isn't working (plus it means individual tests run faster, what goes in to a fix affects less code, etc.). Also, when you assert on one thing, it's easier to name the test. If you assert that MethodX doesn't throw an exception, it's easy to name MethodXDoesNotThrow.

Putting the arrange act assert all together, you can see how it looks in Listing 8-8.

Listing 8-8. Arrange Act Assert Test

```
[TestMethod]
public void CalculatingAgeOfMajorityOnBirthdayWorksCorrectly()
{
    var dateCalculator = new DateCalculator();
    var policyCalculator = new PolicyCalculator(dateCalculator);

    var isAgeOfMajority = policyCalculator.IsAgeOfMajority(
        DateTime.Now.Subtract(TimeSpan.FromDays(365 * 25)),
        new RegionInfo("US"), "MS")

    Assert.IsTrue(isAgeOfMajority);
}
```

Benefits

The arrange act assert technique is simple. It is simple to understand and everything related to a test is in one place. It also clearly separates what is being tested from the setup and verification code.

Drawbacks

The drawback of the arrange act assert technique is that it ignores the power the unit test frameworks. Each test is self-contained within one test method which ignores the test flow of a test class or fixture. For example, MS Test has a TestInitialize attribute to attribute a method to call before every TestMethod to "initialize" the class instance's state. There's also a ClassInitialize attribute that is called before the first test is run to initialize the state of the class instance. With arrange being part of each test method, TestInitialize and ClassInitialize get completely ignored. All the arranging is supposed to occur within the test method so there's no need for static or instance fields.

As each method is an independent test, a test class can easily become unorganized. There's nothing (syntactically, e.g., by the compiler) keeping the test methods cohesive in the class due to the high degree of independence. This can lead to cluttered classes and poorly named classes (even to the point where the names are `TestClass1`) because incohesive classes are hard to succinctly name. With poorly named test classes, there's little to group tests to make test results easier to read.

Incohesive classes have no reason to stay small, so another drawback is that test classes can become huge.

Given When Then

Another organizational technique from behavior-driven design (BDD) is called given, when, then. Given, when, then is based on a human-readable method of describing pre-conditions and acceptance criteria. The format is much like a user story in that the human-readable form is *given* a precondition, *when* something is performed, *then* a post condition is true. For example:

Given the account is in credit,

When the customer requests cash,

Then ensure the account is debited.

This style, much like user stories, should be gathered from or completely written by business stakeholders. This is why it is in English prose. It effectively details acceptance criteria.

Each statement could have multiple parts to it, separated by and, such as given the account is in credit, and the card is valid…

Given

Given details the initial context of the test. For any number of tests there may be many that share particular initial contexts. Given is effectively the same as arrange in Arrange Act Assert.

I find that using the test to contain the context is very useful. Many tests can have the same given context, so grouping all (or a subset) of tests that apply to that given context helps organize your test classes. It also helps with naming them (naming being one of the three hard software development problems). For instance, in the previous given, when, then example we could name our test class `AccountInCredit` (I tend to not add a given prefix because all these would have them and make it extraneous). Given contexts may have multiple parts, in which case we could have different classes for each unique context.

When

When details the action that occurs in the given context. This can be associated with the act in arrange act assert. This is effectively what will happen in the test method (not including the assert). I find that the when statement is useful for naming the test method. So, in the previous example we might name our test method `CustomerRequestsCash`. Typically when statements don't have multiple parts because we want to focus on one single thing, which is the action being performed.

Then

Then details the expected outcome. Then can have multiple parts separated by *and* as does given. In these cases, I tend to have multiple tests and include each *and* statement in the name of the test. So, if I had a then such as "…Then ensure the account is debited, and ensure cash is dispensed" I would have two test methods in the `AccountInCredit` class: `CustomerRequestsCashAccountDebited` and `CustomerRequestsCashDispensed`. This allows us to have a single assert per test method instead of several so it's easier to track what may need to be fixed.

Benefits

I find this method of designing and organizing tests to have several benefits. The most important benefit is that it's based on business stakeholder acceptance criteria. The more acceptance criteria you get, the better quality your application will have in the eyes of the user. I also find that what given, when, then offers for naming and grouping of tests to be very helpful. I've been on many projects where test naming was confusing at best. This adds easy structure to tests and test classes with little thought (other than getting the given, when, then stories).

This technique also pulls shared context and state out of the methods and into the class. This makes better use of testing frameworks and makes that context sharable. That context could even be in a base class if you split a given context across multiple classes. So, it offers more object-oriented tests.

For more technical, developer-related tests, developers can easily put themselves in a stakeholder role and know what the context and the acceptance criteria are for any action. They should easily be able to write given, when, then for lower-level tests.

Given, when, then focuses on functional acceptance criteria so it facilitates writing unit tests that verify functionality.

Drawbacks

If you don't have access to business stakeholders, it may be hard to get given, when, then stories for anything but low-level code. This could lead to developers trying to make it up themselves. (I'm not a big fan of developers acting as stakeholders because of the hint of conflict of interest; they have a bias or two.) So, if you don't have access to business stakeholders, test class and method naming could be equally as problematic with given, when, then.

Depending on your point of view, these test are very functional rather than interaction based. If you're looking to verify interactions, given, when then might not be a good choice.

Record, Replay

There is a third style of organizing a test method. It's less common and dependent (or driven) by a subset of mocking frameworks. I only mention it here because you might encounter it in the wild (especially if you use Rhino mocks). I see it less and less due to the fact that most mocking frameworks support arrange act assert in some fashion.

The idea with record, replay is that the mocking framework "records" the use of the mock (or mocks) and verifies by "replaying" the recorded actions.

Benefits

This style or model really stems from the fact that mocks are being used. Recall that a mock is a test double that performs the verification. So, a record, replay model can make a little more sense in that paradigm because the "recording" by the mock, which is what is acted upon, is different than arranging or acting (and maybe record, replay stems from problems with ambiguity of arrange, act, assert). Having said that though, the use of a mock and its "recording" of actions can easily be viewed as part of arrange and/or act in the arrange, act, assert model.

Drawbacks

The model is mock specific, so it can deviate from the style of other tests that may not have or need mocks.

In general, mock frameworks tend to support an arrange, act, assert style, so record, replay is not forced on developers. It's worth noting that it may become "verify" over "assert" at the end of the unit test with certain mock frameworks.

I also find that this style of test method organization is geared toward verifying interactions rather than side-effects or final state. Personally, I've found more value in asserting final state or side-effects and, if that's how you may approach your tests, the record, replay style may seem unnatural.

Test Naming

I feel test naming is one of the most neglected parts of unit/automated testing. Part of it comes from the style we choose to organize our tests and maybe some of it comes from the default class/method names that Visual Studio creates. Listing 8-9 is the default test method generated by Visual Studio when adding a test project. Whatever the cause, developers aren't doing themselves any favors with unclear names.

Listing 8-9. Default Test Class Generated by Visual Studio

```
namespace UnitTestProject1
{
    [TestClass]
    public class UnitTest1
    {
        [TestMethod]
        public void TestMethod1()
        {
        }
    }
}
```

When we execute the test from Listing 8-1 and view Test Explorer (see Figure 8-1), we can see that we don't see anything about the class names, we only see the test name. Imagine if we just increased the number on the method name; imagine how little information we'd get from Test Explorer?

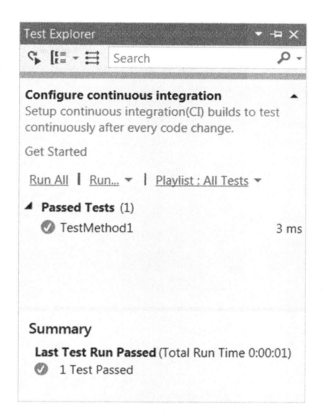

Figure 8-1. *Test Explorer displaying the test from Listing 8-1*

Unfortunately, Test Explorer offers little option for making the results clearer. By default, you can group test method names by outcome (passed, skipped, failed, and not run). You could change that to by grouping by class, duration, traits (category), or by project. All the other groupings include the status of the test (passed, failed, skipped, and not run). So, I find that grouping by outcome to be the least useful grouping because it duplicates information and ignores other, important, information. I personally prefer to group by class because I get that extra metadata from the class name in the results while still retaining pass/fail/skip/not-run. For example, let's say we had poorly named test methods (e.g., duplicate names across classes) and we accept the default grouping in Test Explorer. We could end up with a display, as shown in Figure 8-2.

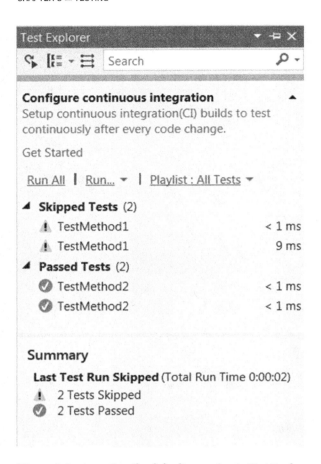

Figure 8-2. *Accepting the default grouping in Test Explorer*

Ignore for a moment the sheer uselessness of the names and look only at the fact that despite there being two passed tests and two skipped tests, it appears that within each grouping, the same test is listed twice. If we group these same results by class, as seen in Figure 8-3, we can get a clearer picture of the results.

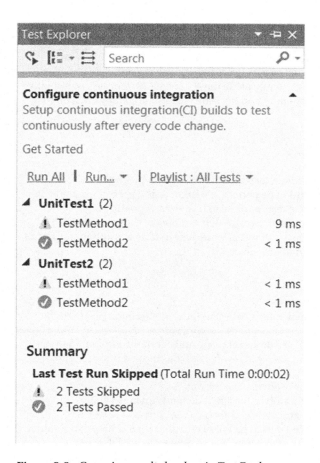

Figure 8-3. *Grouping results by class in Test Explorer*

We still see what is passed, skipped, failed, and not run, but now it's clearer that there are actually four tests, not two. As you add clearer class names and test names, you can get a structured view of your results.

As you can see, although test names are the same, you can see which test class each test method applies to, making it easier to see the current state.

Although any coherent test class can be well named, each of the organizational techniques offers some unique naming abilities. We'll dig a little deeper into those now.

Arrange Act Assert

There's really nothing that can be used to analyze whether act/arrange/assert test classes are or have remained well named. Each method is completely independent and there's nothing shared among the methods. With nothing shared among the methods' cohesiveness, metrics are very low to nothing so they cannot be used to gauge whether the test class has remained cohesive.

This lack of cohesiveness means it very difficult to name the test classes. In some cases, they end up being TestClass1, etc. Naming can be made clearer with a different way of organizing the tests and test classes.

Given, When, Then

With the given, when, then organizational technique, the given preconditions become the class state rather than method state. Cohesiveness metrics then act as a gauge as to how well the test class is named. If cohesiveness is low (i.e., the test methods aren't consistently using the shared state), the class is probably not named well. If it is high, all the test methods are operating on the same class state so they must be well related, assuming the name is clear.

Mocking

As was detailed earlier, a unit test is a test of a single *unit*. A test that tests more than one unit is actually testing the integration of many units. Although it's hard to be perfect in writing tests, especially if you're testing code with design issues, mocking helps us make tests as close to unit tests as possible.

There are many mocking frameworks (or isolation frameworks) that do some of the heavy lifting of creating test doubles. These frameworks allow building up of test doubles within tests at runtime so that full-blown test double classes don't have to be written and maintained.

Microsoft Fakes

One isolation framework that is included right in Visual Studio 2015 (the Enterprise edition) is *Microsoft Fakes*.

I find the terminology used in Microsoft Fakes to be a little confusing and certainly different than the rest of the community. For example, the framework is called Microsoft Fakes but it currently only supports isolation via *stubs* and *shims*.

It's not entirely clear, but I believe the term *fake* is used just like *test double*.

A stub in Microsoft Fakes does in fact seem to be a stub (although it depends on how you use it, as detailed previously). Typically stubs are used with application code (i.e., the code you write). It is recommended that generally-accepted loosely-coupled design be followed rather than simply using shims to test in isolation with types that would otherwise be unmockable (e.g., a tightly coupled design).

The way Microsoft Fakes works is that you have to add a Microsoft Fakes assembly for a given referenced assembly. For example, if I'm writing a test to verify a type within a project and stub-out another type in that same assembly (e.g., `ConsoleApplication1`), I would expand the references for the test project, right-click the `ConsoleApplication1` assembly, and click Add Fakes Assembly (this works only in the Universal edition), as seen in Figure 8-4.

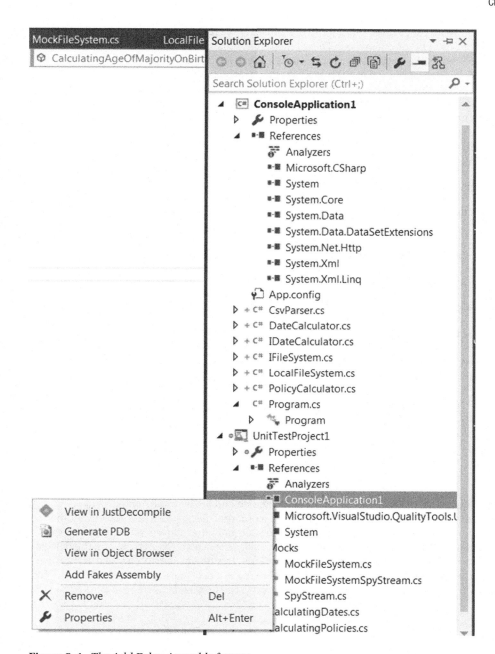

Figure 8-4. *The Add Fakes Assembly feature*

Once this fakes assembly is added, a couple of things are now available to the test code. In the context of stubs, there will be a Fakes namespace within the namespace(s) within the original assembly that add fakes assembly was performed on. In the previous example, we would now have access to a ConsoleApplication1.Fakes namespace. This new namespace will contain new generated stub types that are stubs of the types within the original assembly.

Let's say we had an IDateCalculated interface in our ConsoleApplication1 project that defined various date calculations used by another type in ConsoleApplication1, called PolicyCalculate (which calculates policies). We could fake PolicyCalculator with a Microsoft Fakes stub instead of manually creating a class to do this. The way Microsoft Fakes works is that it creates stubs for all types in the original assembly within the Fakes namespace and prefixes the name with Stub. So, for IDateCalculator, we would now have a type called StubIDateCalculator in the Fakes namespace. The IDateCalculator has a method AgeInYears that calculates the number of years between two dates (age). Listing 8-10 shows IDateCalculator.

Listing 8-10. IDateCalculator Interface

```
public interface IDateCalculator
{
    int AgeInYears(DateTime dateOfBirth);
}
```

For completeness, an implementation of IDateCalculator might look like Listing 8-11.

Listing 8-11. An IDateCalculator Implementation

```
public class DateCalculator : IDateCalculator
{
    public int AgeInYears(DateTime dateOfBirth)
    {
        DateTime today = DateTime.Today;
        int age = today.Year - dateOfBirth.Year;

        if (dateOfBirth > today.AddYears(-age))
            age--;

        return age;
    }
}
```

The way these stubs are used is that they are simply instantiated and the necessary behavior is injected into the stub or default behavior is used (like a fake or a dummy). Each stub type is effectively an implementation of the interface and a series of Func and Action delegates that allow behavior to be injected into the stub. The naming of these delegate fields follows a methodNameParameterType format. So, the delegate for our AgeInYears property would be named AgeInYearsDateTime. To stub out AgeInYears so that it always returns a consistent value (say 44), we'd set the AgeInYearsDateTime to a delegate that always returns 44. This, along with a complete test of PolicyCalculator.IsAgeOfMajority, can be seen in Listing 8-12.

Listing 8-12. A Stub of AgeInYears Property

```
[TestMethod]
public void CalculatingAgeOfMajorityOnBirthdayWorksCorrectly()
{
    IDateCalculator dateCalculator =
        new ConsoleApplication1.Fakes.StubIDateCalculator
        {
            AgeInYearsDateTime = _ => 44
        };
```

```
var policyCalculator = new PolicyCalculator(dateCalculator);
Assert.IsTrue(policyCalculator.IsAgeOfMajority(
    new DateTime(1968, 11, 05), new RegionInfo("US"), "MS"));
}
```

A shim is a new type of test double that Microsoft Fakes introduces. A shim is effectively a stub, but it is a generated object that diverts calls to types typically incapable of being mocked. The call diversion happens at runtime. In the same way we add the ability to stub our own types, we can add shims for third-party types by also adding a fakes assembly. For example, if I want to test a type that uses System.DateTime, I would expand the references of my test project, right-click System, and click Add Fakes Assembly, as seen in Figure 8-5.

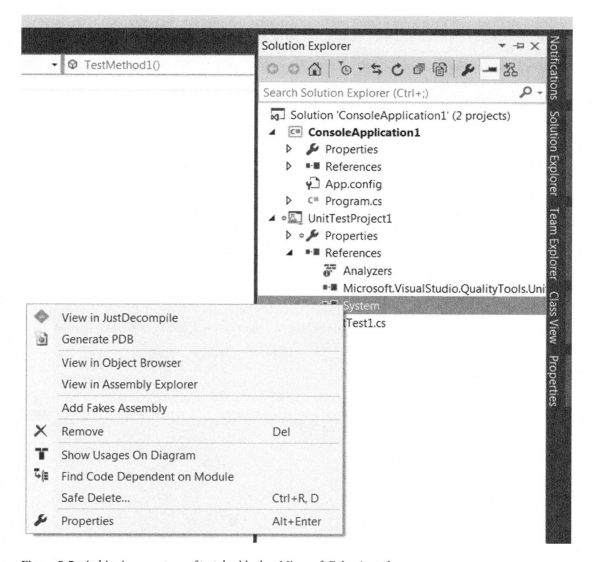

Figure 8-5. *A shim is a new type of test double that Microsoft Fakes introduces*

Along the same lines with stubs, adding a fakes assembly for a third-party assembly introduces a Fakes namespace within the namespaces of that original assembly. In our System.DateTime example, we'd now have access to a System.Fakes namespace. The shims within that namespace would follow a similar naming format as stubs, only with Shim as the prefix. So, with System.DateTime, there would now be a fully qualified type System.Fakes.ShimDateTime that we could use in our tests. Shims work much like stubs in that an instance contains several delegate fields that we can inject behavior with, but the shims are singletons and thus we cannot instantiate new ones.

You might be questioning how that would work if you wanted to use the same type of shim across tests. If they are singletons, wouldn't the behavior injected in one test leak out into another test? The way fakes handle that is by creating contexts in which the behavior is kept. As each context is disposed of, the behavior associated with the shim is lost, keeping behavior from leaking between tests. That context is created with ShimsContext.Create() and is a disposable and "freed" when it is disposed (i.e., at the end of a using block). Listing 8-13 shows the creation of such a context, the injection of 11-Nov-1968 as the value that DateTime.Today returns, and a test for DateCalculator.AgeInYears. The underlying nature of how shims work (by effectively diverting calls from one place to another) is probably why shims don't operate as instances, only as singletons.

Listing 8-13. A Shim Context Example

```
[TestMethod]
public void CalculatingAgeOnBirthdayWorksCorrectly()
{
    using (ShimsContext.Create())
    {
        System.Fakes.ShimDateTime.TodayGet =
                () => new DateTime(2012, 11, 05);
        var calculator = new DateCalculator();

        var age = calculator.AgeInYears(new DateTime(1968, 11, 05));

        Assert.AreEqual(44, age);
    }
}
```

There are a few other types of tests that help us focus on effectively unit testing our code. Let's look at those now.

Moq

Typical mock frameworks, like Moq, allow for fairly painless record, replay whitebox testing. Moq does this by verifying in the recorded actions that a method was invoked. Listing 8-14 shows a test that verifies that our CsvParser.Parse method ends up calling Stream.Read.

Listing 8-14. Record, Replay with Moq

```
[TestMethod]
public void ParsingCsvInvokesStreamRead()
{
    var mockStream = new Mock<Stream>();          ❶
    mockStream
        .SetupGet(m => m.CanRead)
        .Returns(true);
```

```
    var mockFileSystem = new MockFileSystem(mockStream.Object);      ❷
    var sut = new CsvParser(mockFileSystem);
    var data = sut.Parse("test");
    var lineCount = data.Count();
    mockStream.Verify(m => m.Read(It.IsAny<byte[]>(),               ❸
        It.IsAny<int>(), It.IsAny<int>()));
}
```

At ❶, we construct and set up our mock. SetupGet(m=>mCanRead) says that we want to set up how Stream.CanRead responds. In this case, we want to set it up so it always returns true (that is, the Stream is readable).

At ❷, we pass along an instance of the mock Stream object to the MockFileSystem constructor and perform the test on CsvParser.

At ❸, we ask the mock to verify that Read was called with any type of byte[] for the buffer, and any integer value for count and offset.

We aren't forced to use third-party frameworks to perform this type of whitebox testing. As we saw earlier with spies, we use a special kind of test double—a spy—to spy on how a double is used. Listing 8-15 shows the code that uses a spy to perform whitebox testing.

Listing 8-15. Whitebox Testing with a Spy

```
[TestMethod]
public void ParsingCsvReadsFile()
{
    var spyStream = new SpyStream(Encoding.Unicode.GetBytes("1,2,3\n4,5,6"));
    var mockFileSystem = new MockFileSystem(spyStream);
    var sut = new CsvParser(mockFileSystem);
    var data = sut.Parse("test");
    var lineCount = data.Count();

    Assert.IsTrue(spyStream.ReadCalled);
}
```

This, of course, requires that we create a spy type to record the actions to spy on. Technically you could also do that with Microsoft Fakes and a stub. You simply create a stub of Stream that keeps track of whether Read was called (and, of course, perform the other responsibilities of Read). Listing 8-16 is an example of a test that performs whitebox testing by leveraging Microsoft Fakes.

Listing 8-16. Whitebox Test with Microsoft Fakes

```
[TestMethod]
public void ParsingCsvInvokesStreamReadViaShim()
{
    bool readWasCalled = false;                                     ❶
    int position = 0;
    var stream = new System.IO.Fakes.StubStream
    {
        CanReadGet = () => true,
        ReadByteArrayInt32Int32 = (buffer, offset, count) =>
        {
```

```
                readWasCalled = true;
                var bytes = Encoding.Unicode.GetBytes("1,2,3\n4,5,6");
                var bytesToCopy = Math.Min(count, bytes.Length) - position;
                Array.Copy(bytes, 0, buffer, offset, bytesToCopy);
                position += bytesToCopy;
                return bytesToCopy;
            }
        };
        var fileSystem = new ConsoleApplication1.Fakes.StubIFileSystem      ❷
        {
            OpenFileString = name => stream
        };
        var sut = new CsvParser(fileSystem);
        var data = sut.Parse("test");
        var lineCount = data.Count();
        Assert.IsTrue(readWasCalled);                              ❸
}
```

At ❶, we start the setup of the Stream stub. It needs to double for Stream.Read, so we need to keep track of the position in the stream and we want to whitebox test so we need to know if Read was called.

At ❷, we create an IFileSystem stub that just returns the stub Stream when OpenFile is called.

Up until ❸, it's just acting on our system being tested. After we act on the system being tested, we simply verify that our readWasCalled variable was set to true, signifying that CsvParser.Parse called Stream.Read.

While this type of testing is doable with Microsoft Fakes, I find it much easier and more concise to do it with other mocking frameworks like Moq.

Whitebox Testing

We talked about mocking and record, replay and how they effectively test interactions rather than side-effects or functionality. That's effectively what whitebox testing is.

Whitebox testing is knowing the internal workings of what you're testing (the box) and testing it based on that knowledge. Mocks can be used to verify that certain methods are called or properties are accessed.

Whitebox testing in unit tests can verify that code is *executed* as expected.

Blackbox Testing

Blackbox testing is more the typical type of unit test. A blackbox test only tests "the box" via a public or published interface. It doesn't know anything about the internals or implementation detail that can't be inferred from the interface (and a good abstraction shouldn't leak out much in the way of implementation details).

In the context of unit tests, this really gets down to testing the functionality of the system.

As explained earlier, this functional testing is basically the setup of preconditions, performing the test, and verifying the outputs (or state change). See the sections arrange act assert and given, when, then.

Fuzz Testing

Fuzz testing is testing an interface with invalid or unexpected data. Sometimes random data is mentioned with fuzz testing, but that's difficult to reproduce with unit testing. The randomness of the test often comes down to the lack of knowledge of what is *invalid* or *unexpected* based on a published or known interface.

For example, if we have a method called DoSomething(int value), we can't know that a value like 314569 causes a problem based solely on the interface. We could do boundary or off-by-one testing by passing in 0, -1, 2147483647, or 2147483648 simply because those are the boundaries of int and off-by-one from the boundary. The randomness of the values helps us discover these non-boundary invalid/unexpected data. But, as a unit test, it's not something that we can arrange and specifically assert. That is, it's not deterministic.

I mention fuzz testing because it is an attempt at negative testing.

DETERMINISTIC TESTS

One very important aspect of writing tests is that they perform deterministically. Something that is *deterministic* has no randomness. Tests that involve randomness execute differently each time, making them impossible to verify or assert. It's important that tests don't have this randomness. We've shown some ways to mock or shim out non-deterministic inputs.

Another area to be mindful about when making tests deterministic is the shared state. We've detailed that states can be *shared* within the test class among all the tests within the class. Be very careful that the state is reset to the correct precondition for each test. If that's not done, adding a test could cause the order of test executing to change and an unmodified test to start to fail because of new side-effects you didn't know your test was dependent on.

Negative Testing

The easiest unit tests validate that a unit works. But that's not always what happens, and it's certainly not always what is documented of the system being tested. Methods throw exceptions, have bugs, etc. Negative testing ensures that methods act a specific way (are deterministic) when given bad or unexpected preconditions.

I consider regression tests a type of negative test because you're really testing to make sure that a bug doesn't reoccur.

One technique of ensuring bugs are fixed is to first write a failing test (possibly only once enough detail about the bug is known) that will pass when the bug is fixed. It's useful to keep this type of negative test within the unit tests to ensure there wasn't a regression: or a return to a less favorable state.

I consider negative blackbox testing the minimum negative testing that should be performed in the unit tests. The known published interface (the blackbox) should be tested as a minimum, and this includes the known failures (or exceptions).

Parameter validation is typical for methods; negative tests should be written, for example, to verify that contract exists and is maintained. Listing 8-17 is example of a negative test that verifies that invalid parameters cause an exception.

Listing 8-17. A Negative Test

```
[TestMethod, ExpectedException(typeof(ArgumentNullException))]
public void CreatingCsvParserWithNullStreamThrows()
{
    var sut = new CsvParser(null);
}
```

As you may notice, with ExpectedExceptionAttribute, the verification (or Assert) part of the test is yanked out of the body of the test such that if we wanted to follow arrange act assert, we'd have no assert. We could separate the act from the arrange, as shown in Listing 8-18, but I find little value in doing that simply to get a separation of arrange and act, especially with no assert section.

Listing 8-18. Separation of Arrange and Assert

```
[TestMethod, ExpectedException(typeof(ArgumentNullException))]
public void CreatingCsvParserWithNullStreamThrows()
{
    CsvParser sut;

    sut = new CsvParser(null);
}
```

To a certain extent, this often leads me to other testing frameworks. NUnit, for example, recognizes this violation of arrange act assert and offers an alternative with Assert.Throws. Listing 8-19 shows an example of the same test with NUnit.

Listing 8-19. NUnit Unit Test

```
[Test]
public void CreatingCsvParserWithNullStreamThrows()
{
    CsvParser sut;

    NUnit.Framework.Assert.Throws<ArgumentNullException>(() => {
        sut = new CsvParser(null);
    });
}
```

Astute readers will of course notice that while this does put the check for the exception within the body of the test, it really is more like arrange assert act when reading the code rather than arrange act assert.

Boundary Testing

Another type of functional blackbox testing is *boundary testing*. As the name suggests, boundary testing is a means of testing the extremes of input values. These extremes are typically minimum, maximum, and off-by-one from minimum/maximum. Sometimes known error values are included in boundary testing.

This type of testing is typically important for a couple of reasons. As the saying goes:

> *There are three hard problems in software: naming and off-by-one errors.*

Boundary testing makes an attempt to find off-by-one errors as soon as possible. But the other important part of boundary testing is really validation of an interface design or contract. For example, let's say I create a method like CreateArray that takes an int count of array elements to create. If each element is 30 bytes and the maximum value of an int is 2147483647, what this interface or contract is detailing is that it *will allow the creation of a 60 gigabyte block of memory*. At the time this book was written, that's not a common hardware configuration and barring lots of free space on the hard drive, not likely a successful operation to perform CreateArray(int.MaxValue).

Unit tests that test the maximum value (and maybe one more) are useful for validating that the interface is sound. If we know that a value above a certain value is almost certain to fail, we can modify the interface (see the section on parameter objects) or introduce some extra parameter checking to avoid the problem.

Acceptance Testing

As we say with given, when, then, another focus of testing is acceptance testing. To add a bit more detail, acceptance testing verifies that the requirements (the specification or contract) of a system are met.

What is deemed acceptable in a specification or contract may not always be functional quality attributes (or non-functional requirements) may also be included. Acceptance testing often involves verifying those quality attributes like performance, robustness, reliability, etc.

Loosely-Coupled Design

As you might be able to tell from reading about mocks (or experience using mocks), in order to use mocks on code that you would like to automatically test, you need a very thorough degree of loose coupling. In order to replace an object within a test with another one that acts as a double, spy, fake, or mock, it must already be loosely coupled to what we want to mock. This level of loose coupling is typically that the system that will be tested is not coupled to an object's constructor, nor coupled to the type being integrated with. Typically the system being tested is only coupled to an interface and the test system can have any implementation of that interface injected into it. It is this type of loosely-coupled design that offers a high degree of mocking and thus allows us to test our code with surgical precision. See the sections on dependency injection and SOLID.

Test-Driven Development

One way of performing unit tests is to write code, then write a bunch of tests to verify it. As we've seen with detail on doubles, stubs, mocks, spies, etc., isolating code to perform a unit test on it can sometimes be difficult. The ability of mocking an interface or even the ability to inject a dependency that might not be a mock can complicate writing *unit* tests.

Test Driven Development (or TDD) suggests that for new code, a unit test should first be written. Once written, code should be created/added to cause the test to compile but fail. Then the code should be updated so that the tests pass. One detail with TDD is that only the minimum work must be done to pass the test.

There are a few benefits to this. The most important part of this is that you're almost certainly going to write a test that injects dependencies before you design something that doesn't support dependency injection. So, rather than changing a design to support dependency injection, you end up writing most loosely-coupled classes from the start. This is partially semantics, but avoiding changes to code for whatever reason almost always results in more stable and reliable code.

We could use CsvParser as an example. Knowing that we need a CsvParser class to parse CSV data and that there may be a Parse method to parse a file, we could start a positive unit test like Listing 8-20 to help design the CsvParser class.

Listing 8-20. Positive CsvParser Test

```
[TestMethod]
public void ParsingCsvSucceeds()
{
    var sut = new CsvParser();
    var data = sut.Parse("filename.csv");
    Assert.IsTrue(
        data.SequenceEqual(
```

```
        new List<IEnumerable<string>> {new []{"1", "2", "3"},
            new []{"1", "2", "3"}}));
}
```

If we wrote this test first, we should quickly see that we need to do something with a file named filename.csv. In the context of a unit test, this is problematic. How do we get that file to a place the test can access it? What if another test does something with filename.csv? Seeing that we may quickly decide that we want an alternative way of getting data into the parser class, by stream for example. We may have to rewrite our test to be more similar to Listing 8-21.

Listing 8-21. Parsing Depending on Abstractions

```
[TestMethod]
public void ParsingCsvSucceeds()
{
    var stream = new MemoryStream(Encoding.Unicode.GetBytes("1,2,3\n4,5,6"));
    var sut = new CsvParser(stream);
    var data = sut.Parse(stream);
    Assert.IsTrue(
        data.SequenceEqual(
            new List<IEnumerable<string>> {new []{"1", "2", "3"},
                new []{"1", "2", "3"}}));
}
```

We now have effectively come up with a different design for CsvParser that is more maintainable (more things can use it; like things that can't create a file or don't yet have all the data). We haven't changed any code; you simply come up with a better design so we haven't risked breaking anything.

Integration Testing

While unit testing attempts to focus on testing units (methods) in isolation, what we're dealing with is really automated testing. The automated testing frameworks offer a great ability to also perform automated integration testing.

Integration testing is a form of blackbox functional testing that asserts that the interactions of components functions properly.

This type of testing is also isolated testing as it should be testing an isolated part of the system. There's nothing wrong with an automated end-to-end test (which could also be considered an integration test), those just tend to be performed in different ways.

For example, if we have a GUI application that interacts with the user to gather data and store it in a database, we may have unit tests that use mock or stub repository objects to verify the code that uses data from the database acts as expected (e.g., code that reads the database in a different way to verify the data in the database). But we may also have automated integration tests to verify repository objects act as expected with an instance of a database. These tests are still in isolation in that they only test the repository and the interaction with the database (or the code that uses the repository, the repository, and the interaction with a database), but not the user interface.

This type of testing is performed the same way as unit testing in that test classes are written with test methods that perform some style of test (arrange act assert, given when then, etc.), but assume a certain infrastructure exists to perform the integrated test. Where it differs is how we may need to differentiate integration tests from unit tests (or even some types of unit tests from other types of unit tests).

Typically with automated testing, we want to periodically perform these tests to make sure everything is okay (and we haven't broken anything or caused a regression). This could mean performing tests on commit/check-in, or performing them on a nightly build, or even when saving a file (continuous testing). Integration tests are typically time-consuming and could drastically increase the time it takes to commit/check-in or perform the nightly build. This is typically addressed by categorizing the tests and configuring the automated execution of these tests to ignore these integration tests. The Visual Studio test framework offers an easy way to categorize tests as integration tests. This is done with the `TestCategoryAttribute`. While the `TestCategoryAttribute` doesn't define specific test categories, you can categorize tests by textual name. For example, if we wanted to write test that was in fact an integration test, we could add `TestCategory("integration")` as an attribute of the test, as detailed in Listing 8-21.

Listing 8-21. Adding TestCategory("integration") as an Attribute of the Test

```
[TestMethod, TestCategory("integration")]
public void TestIntegrationWithDatabase()
{
    //...
}
```

The automated execution of tests can then be configured to ignore tests categorized as `"integration"`. You can group by these category in Test Explorer but, oddly, they're called "traits" there.

Integration tests could alternatively be placed into another project specific to integration tests and simply not be executed in these scenarios.

Summary

As you can see, testing is a diverse and complex task in software development. It's a vital part of producing software, one that performs some level of quality control to ensure (or assure) that the software being developed works as desired.

We can perform that verification in a variety of ways with testing frameworks, from unit tests to integration tests. These tests can be automatically run at various times to give us quick feedback on the quality of our system. This gives us the ability to fail fast and will hopefully inform us about problems while what we did is fresh in our minds.

This concludes *Practical Visual Studio 2015*. I hope you found it as useful as I found it enjoyable to write!

Index

© Peter Ritchie 2016
P. Ritchie, *Practical Microsoft Visual Studio 2015*, DOI 10.1007/978-1-4842-2313-0

■ W

■ X, Y, Z

Get the eBook for only $4.99!

Why limit yourself?

Now you can take the weightless companion with you wherever you go and access your content on your PC, phone, tablet, or reader.

Since you've purchased this print book, we are happy to offer you the eBook for just $4.99.

Convenient and fully searchable, the PDF version enables you to easily find and copy code—or perform examples by quickly toggling between instructions and applications.

To learn more, go to http://www.apress.com/us/shop/companion or contact support@apress.com.

09/18

CPSIA information can be obtained
at www.ICGtesting.com
Printed in the USA
FSOW03n1115160317
31990FS